This Awesome Challenge

THE HUNDRED DAYS OF LYNDON JOHNSON

BY MICHAEL AMRINE

This Awesome Challenge

THE HUNDRED DAYS OF LYNDON JOHNSON

By Michael Amrine

G. P. PUTNAM'S SONS
NEW YORK

Library of Congress Catalog
Card Number: 64-18001

MANUFACTURED IN THE UNITED STATES OF AMERICA

For Neil, Eric, and Douglas

Contents

PROLOGUE

"The President Is Dead,
Mr. President"

OH, NO.

Three shots in five seconds.

Then in forty minutes: "The President is dead, Mr. President."

After these words, four days. The instant death and the state funeral of a President took a Friday, a Saturday, a Sunday, and a Monday.

Cruel and incredible was the way our republic said the ancient words, "The king is dead, long live the king."

In our own homes, with our children and our friends, we saw it happen. We saw the plane land at Andrews Field. We saw the metal box containing the body of our President taken from the plane. We saw the shock in the brother and the widow. We could not turn off the television.

The camera—and our eyes—followed the metal box into an ambulance.

The camera went to another door of the same plane and we saw, alive, the new President of the United States. We heard those incredible words . . . President Johnson.

At twelve-thirty P.M. that day, Central Standard Time, the man himself had heard the shots and seen the garish nightmare in the Dallas streets. He had been thrown to the floor of his car and rudely guarded from attack by another human body. The

[9]

President now on our screen had seen the crowds, the police, the priests, the widow—and the blood. He had himself gone through terrible uncertainty. Then, ninety minutes after the shots he had been sworn to duty, with a wife and a new widow standing by his side, and aboard a jet plane he had flown at 700 miles an hour into the frame of responsibility. In five hours he was in the White House.

His transformation occurred because of an ancient cruel necessity: if the king dies, there is a new king. In a democracy, the oath of office is given as soon as possible. Coolidge received it from his father by kerosene lamplight in a kitchen. In 1945, Harry Truman was summoned to the White House to hear from Eleanor Roosevelt the words, "The President is dead." But the President was not dead in 1945; there was a new President as there was in 1963.

This November night we saw the ambulance carrying the body of John F. Kennedy, and we saw someone strange to us— our new leader—borne by helicopter from Andrews Field to the smooth lawn of the White House.

At that moment in the unnatural brightness of the television lights, the blades of the helicopter set up a small storm. The wind from the blades cut through the fountain like an invisible knife.

Then the President stepped out with his aides. The President, the strange President, the living President, disappeared through the door near Mr. Kennedy's office. The noise and whirl from the helicopter blades were gone. The fountains returned to their proper shape, and the man we all saw walk through that door picked up the papers another man had put down.

This book is some of the story of how he had to go to work, and how he chose to work. It cannot be all the story, nor have the perspective of time. But perhaps this story of history-in-the-making will save some facts which might otherwise be lost. Perhaps it may throw some light on the fountains of democracy, returning clear and strong after the winds of nightmare.

That Friday as the Senate adjourned, Chaplain Frederick Brown Harris prayed:

"Our Father, Thou knowest that this sudden almost unbelievable news has stunned our minds and hearts. We gaze at a vacant place against the sky as the President of the Republic goes down like a giant cedar green with boughs.

"In this hour we cry out words that were uttered in another hour of deep loss and bereavement: 'God lives and the Government at Washington still stands.'

"Hold us, we pray, and the people of America, calm and steady and full of faith for the Republic in this tragic hour of our history."

1

Dallas to Washington: The Man With the Football

"THE PRESIDENT IS DEAD, MR. PRESIDENT."

These were the words of Kenneth O'Donnell, John F. Kennedy's personal aide. He spoke to Lyndon B. Johnson. The time was ten minutes past one Central Standard Time on November 22, 1963. Mr. Johnson, his wife and various Secret Service agents were crowded into a small suite of medical treatment rooms at Parkland Hospital, Dallas, Texas.

Within minutes of that first word from Kenny O'Donnell, Malcolm Kilduff, Assistant White House Press Secretary in charge of the press on the November Presidential tour, came to Mr. Johnson and asked him about making an announcement of President Kennedy's death. It was then that the new President met and made his first decision.

Here is how it happened, in Mr. Kilduff's words:

> At 1:04 they were still trying to work on him. . . . It was only a few minutes later, however, that in talking to Kenny O'Donnell we knew the President was, in fact, dead. This was more or less a foregone conclusion by all of us at that point, because Mrs. Kennedy was sitting directly outside of the emergency room, just to the right, and just sitting there with her

hands in her lap, with the most helpless feeling that any human being can have on her face. . . .

. . . maybe 10 or 15 minutes after one I got hold of Kenny and I said, "Kenny, this is a terrible time to have to approach you on this," I said, "but the world has got to know that President Kennedy is dead." He said, "Well, don't they know it already?" And I said, "No, I haven't told them." He said, "Well . . . you are going to have to make the announcement. Go ahead. But you better check it with Mr. Johnson."

I walked through the hall, through the emergency room, and in the small cubicle where President Johnson was sitting with Mrs. Johnson and Rufus Youngblood, the Secret Service agent. When I looked at him, very frankly, I didn't know what to call him, and I just blurted out "Mr. President" and he turned around. I will never forget the look on his face, because I am fairly sure that this was the first time he had been called "Mr. President." *

I said, "I have to announce the death of President Kennedy. Is it all right with you?" And he reacted immediately. He said, "No, Mac, I think we had better wait for a few minutes." He said, "I think I had better get out of here and get back to the plane before you announce it." He said, "We don't know whether this is a worldwide conspiracy, whether they are after me as well as they were after President Kennedy, or whether they are after Speaker McCormack, or Senator Hayden. We just don't know."

To Kilduff, the President looked strained and shocked. He was nonetheless perfectly composed. Kilduff was enormously impressed with his presence of mind. He did not know that the Secret Service men, recalling the conspiracy which killed Lincoln, had already discussed the various possibilities with Johnson, and were anxious to get him out of the hospital and back to Washington.

Kilduff himself showed extraordinary presence of mind. Within the hour he was to make the announcement to reporters. Then he went to the President's plane, *Air Force One,* and saw to it that several reporters were placed aboard for the Washington flight.

* Kilduff did not know that O'Donnell had already used the phrase.

[14]

In Kilduff's own words, this is how he left the company of the new President and this is how the announcement was made:

> I went back and talked to one of the agents; in fact it was Roy Kellerman, the agent in charge for this trip, who was riding in the right front seat of President Kennedy's car when he was shot. He gathered a few agents together. By this time it was about 20 minutes after. I went back and talked to President Johnson, and I said, "Well, I am going to make the announcement as soon as you leave."
>
> So we got the agents together, we got the police together. We got the motorcycle escort lined up to get him back to the airport. Then the two of us, President Johnson and myself, walked out of the emergency entrance together, and everyone was screaming at me, "What can you tell us? What can you tell us?"
>
> It was a scene of absolute confusion. President Johnson had gotten into a car and left when I ran up the grass slope to the other entrance of the hospital and into the classroom.

Kilduff had a grim message on a piece of notepaper in his hands:

> President John F. Kennedy died at approximately 1 P.M. Central Standard Time here in Dallas. He died of a gunshot wound in the brain. I have no other details.

Kilduff recalls that although he and Mr. Johnson left the emergency entrance together, many of the reporters who saw him did not later remember seeing Mr. Johnson. They were after Kilduff for news of President Kennedy. As so frequently happens, the man who is Vice-President was invisible, or unnoticeable. It would be days or weeks before people would "see" Johnson when they heard his title.

His hands shaking, Malcolm Kilduff made his announcement in an improvised press room—a nurses' classroom.

> This was the first trip I had ever taken with President Kennedy just alone, and I got up there, and I thought, Well, this is really the first press conference on a road trip I have ever

had to hold. I started . . . and all I could say was "Excuse me, let me catch my breath," and I thought in my mind, All right, what am I going to say, and how am I going to say it? Because obviously there were certain facts that had to get out, and I had to get these facts out. I remember opening my mouth one time and I couldn't say it, and I think it must have been, it seems to me, like two or three minutes.

In retelling his version of the assassination on a radio broadcast, Malcolm Kilduff reported:

. . . We assumed that someone had been shot, someone had been hurt.

It occurred to us that perhaps it was the President, it probably wasn't, but it didn't occur to a single person in that car that, number one, the President of the United States really had been shot, or that he—or certainly that he was in the condition that he was in.

It was not until we pulled up at the Emergency entrance of Parkland Hospital and we all jumped out and ran over to the car. We saw President Kennedy lying on the seat. We saw Governor Connally spread on his back. Actually, Governor Connally looked at first glance to be in even worse shape than President Kennedy, because the bullet came out through his chest and he was just covered with blood on the front.

But then when you saw President Kennedy's head, you more or less assumed that this was a fatal wound. But, you know, you just don't think of this. I mean, you know, it just never occurs to you that this man is going to be killed. I mean, it is an inconceivable thought for that short period of time.

There had been a pause between the first and second shot. In that pause Agent Rufus Youngblood roughly pushed Vice-President Johnson to the floor of the car in which he was riding and threw himself on top of the Vice-President.

In the motorcade President Kennedy, Governor Connally and their wives had been in the second car. The Vice-President rode in the fourth car, in the back seat with Mrs. Johnson and U. S. Senator Ralph W. Yarborough of Texas. In the front seat with the driver, a Texas highway patrolman, was Secret Service Agent Youngblood.

[16]

In the first anxious moments, on the way to the hospital, the Secret Service radio in car number four received a message from Emory Roberts, the Assistant Agent in charge of the White House Secret Service detail: "Rufe, keep your man covered." Agent Youngblood said to Johnson, as he lay on top of the Vice-President, "I don't know how bad it is yet in the President's car but you had better prepare to be Acting President just as soon as we get to the hospital."

A little later Youngblood spoke into Johnson's ear. "When we get to the hospital, you follow me. We're going in fast." Johnson's voice was calm as he answered, "Okay, fine."

When they reached the hospital, Johnson for a moment massaged his chest and flexed his arms. He did so because he had been riding in a cramped position on the floor of the car with Youngblood on top of him, but his gesture of holding his arm started a rumor which traveled clear across the country. He had been wounded, the story said, or he had suffered a heart attack.

Seven Secret Service men escorted the Johnsons to the suite of minor-medicine-and-surgery rooms. A nurse hurried out with three patients who had been receiving treatment. The Vice-President and his wife went in. The inner room had one window overlooking the backyard and another looking out on the ambulance dock and the emergency entrance. Rufus Youngblood ordered the blinds pulled. The area became hushed as the Johnsons and the Secret Service agents spoke in lowered voices. Johnson leaned against the inner doorway, sniffing at a vapor inhaler which he often carries with him.

Outside the suite for minor-medicine-and-surgery an anonymous White House officer quietly moved into position. This officer, who is never photographed and never identified by name, had been riding in the motorcade in a car not far from President Kennedy. He is sometimes known as the man with "the football"—slang for the small bag which contains top secret codes and arrangements by which the President as Commander in Chief can give orders to meet attacks—perhaps even to unleash hydrogen bombs. The man with the football had been waiting to see where he should go next; waiting for official word that the power switch had been thrown, that a new man would now be giving the orders.

[17]

Agent Emory Roberts, in the room with the Johnsons, had started to think about hurrying back to Washington the moment that he realized President Kennedy was dead. Roberts said to Mr. Johnson: "We don't know all the ramifications of the shooting. We don't know, but maybe it's part of an overall plot. We need to get you back to the plane and to Washington as quickly as possible. We ought to leave at once."

Texas Congressman Homer Thornberry, an old friend of Johnson's who had been in the motorcade and who joined the Johnsons in their room, agreed with the agents, but Johnson wanted also to ask Kenneth O'Donnell and Lawrence O'Brien, aides to President Kennedy.

Agent Roberts went out, found Kenny O'Donnell and brought him back. He was close to a state of shock.

It was then that O'Donnell said, "The President is dead, Mr. President."

They asked him about leaving for Washington, and O'Donnell agreed with the Secret Service men that Johnson should return at once to the capital. Youngblood whispered to Agent Lem Johns to find an unmarked car for the ride to the airport.

Then Johnson asked Cliff Carter, one of his aides, to "get Valenti, Liz and Marie and get them to the plane." Jack Valenti was a Texas advertising man who had worked on the Texas tour, Liz was Mrs. Liz Carpenter, long-time friend of the Johnson family, and Marie Fehmer was a secretary to Johnson. They had all been riding in the same car in the motorcade.

From the minor-medicine suite a Signal Corps technician opened lines to the Situation Room, the military and emergency communications center of the White House, and also to *Air Force One,* the Presidential plane, which was on the ground a few miles away at Love Field.

Agent Roberts called his Washington headquarters, and found that his superiors agreed with him that the President should return to the capital at once. Roberts then called Colonel James Swindal, pilot of the plane, and asked him to be prepared for the flight. Swindal had only a light load of gasoline for the Boeing 707's planned hop to Austin, Texas. He quickly ordered more fuel.

While still in that minor-medicine suite in the hospital, the

President thought that some record should be made of some of the decisions being taken, and asked his wife, "Bird, why don't you make some notes on all this?" From time to time, then and on the plane trip home, Mrs. Johnson noted some impressions of events. Thornberry also began making notes and particularly noting time of various incidents.*

Later, the new President asked Kilduff to see if he could get a tape recorder to preserve some of the happenings for the record.

The President was then taken to the airport and the press conference was held. There was still, however, to be a delay in getting out of Parkland Hospital, a bureaucratic holdup because municipal regulations in Dallas forbid the removing of a body in a homicide case until certain procedures are followed by the coroner. A hospital functionary kept saying that the casket could not leave until these legal requirements were met.

Finally Kenny O'Donnell said, "We're getting out of here." The coffin was carried to the waiting hearse while Mrs. Kennedy walked beside it, her hand resting on it. Secret Service men and Dallas police cleared the way.

When O'Donnell, Larry O'Brien and the others reached *Air Force One,* several new people were already there with the new President.

One was Jack J. Valenti, who, from that day on, would spend as much time in the White House as the President. In the photograph of the swearing-in his face can be seen at the left— as shocked in its own way as Mrs. Kennedy—at the right—in the much-printed photograph. Valenti was soon to be in a hundred photographs, in the same position, always behind the President.

Another was Cliff Carter. Until 1 P.M. Dallas time Carter had been the manager of Johnson's political office in Austin, Texas. He had been a passenger in the motorcade. After the shooting he had helped carry the body of Governor Connally from the murder car into the hospital.

Then he had joined Mr. Johnson in the minor-medicine

* On the plane, later, Cliff Carter dictated some notes to Marie Fehmer, and Johnson also asked Secret Service agents to put down their own notes as to how they saw things happen.

[19]

suite, and the President had asked him to fly back to Washington with him. (That night the President asked him to close out the Austin office and come to Washington to be Johnson's No. 1 man for political contacts. Carter was to be a White House political captain for Johnson, working with O'Donnell and O'Brien.)

Also on the plane was Bill Don Moyers, a scholarly-looking twenty-nine-year-old who had formerly worked for Senator Johnson. Neither O'Donnell nor Moyers knew it in this hurried moment, but they were to share an office for months, and ultimately Moyers would succeed O'Donnell as Presidential appointments secretary.

Moyers at this moment, and for months to come, was officially a Deputy Director of the Peace Corps. As a Texan he had been asked to go from Washington to help Lyndon Johnson coordinate the campaign trip through Texas. Earlier that day, he had been having lunch in Austin, a scheduled tour stop which never took place, when a waiter handed him a telephone. Moyers' first reaction to the report was that it was a practical joke and said, "I don't have time for practical jokes, especially this kind." The voice on the telephone said, "But it's true. The President has been shot in Dallas. It's just come over the radio." Moyers hung up the phone, called the local TV station, and asked for the manager, an old friend. He confirmed the news that the President had been shot—perhaps fatally.

At that moment Moyers started thinking about the job ahead. He thought in a flash of the ten years he had known Lyndon Johnson. He had first been a summer "interne" or apprentice and student in his office in Washington, later a personal aide in the Majority Leader's office, then a constant traveling companion and assistant in the long campaign of 1960.

Moyers at the Los Angeles convention had slept for days in a large closet in the Johnson suite. As Moyers was to say in 1964, "At the end of a twenty-hour day [in 1960] we would sit alone and he would talk about what he wanted for this country. I came to understand something of the private man. What I saw I liked. For all the legends of his political magic, he was a warm, considerate human being."

Moyers' first instinct in Texas that day was to do all he could

[20]

to help Johnson in "these dark hours." Partly by luck he was able to get a chartered plane out of Austin and be in flight in fifteen minutes. It was an hour to Dallas. Thirty minutes out the CBS announcer on the plane's radio said, "The President is dead." Moyers' chartered plane landed him at Love Field. A few minutes later he was aboard *Air Force One.*

In his own description the first few minutes aboard that plane were blurred. He remembers General Ted Clifton, the White House Military Aide, asking the radio operator to get Washington. He saw Mrs. Lincoln, the secretary to President Kennedy, sobbing quietly. He saw Rear Admiral Berkley, the President's physician, sitting at the rear of the forward cabin, shocked and stunned.

A few minutes later Mrs. Kennedy and the casket were brought aboard and then, says Moyers, his disbelief began to fade, and he started to be convinced that John F. Kennedy was dead. Moyers spoke briefly to Larry O'Brien, seeking to express sympathy. O'Brien shook his head slowly and said, "It makes you wonder about public service." Moyers attended the swearing-in ceremony and he watched Mrs. Kennedy walk back with O'Brien and O'Donnell to the small compartment where she sat beside the casket all the way home. Moyers had an errand there and as he went by heard her say, almost inaudibly, "It's going to be so long and so lonely."

On the flight home from Dallas, Moyers gradually became aware that he was taking on another job, that of assistant to a new President. Soon after *Air Force One* was in flight the President, after a period of solitary and quiet thinking, picked up a memo pad and began to write with a yellow pencil the announcement he would make when he arrived at Washington. Later he asked Valenti and Moyers to look at it. He said, "I want it brief, this is not the time for words."

Moyers and Valenti and sometimes others aboard listened to him talk quietly and reflectively about what had to be done. The President was thinking about how intently the people would be watching him, looking for him to "show them leadership and purpose . . . compassion and understanding." He kept saying, "Now we have a really big job to do." Mr. Johnson also spoke of the way in which the Government and the Presi-

[21]

dency would be observed from the Kremlin. The Russian leaders would be watching to detect any weakness, any hesitancy, any sign of indecision. He emphasized that he would try to show that he was "a man of strength and conviction, but . . . also a man of peace." He emphasized above all that there must be continuity and continuity without confusion.

Continuity. This became the watchword of those first weeks.

Another "new person" aboard the plane was a woman still only half aware she was America's new "First Lady."

Earlier, riding in the procession alongside her husband, Mrs. Johnson had been thinking how they hoped to relax at the LBJ ranch that night. She thought about the row of pecan pies that were being baked and also of some fresh fruit for the dinner. Like everyone else, she observed that the crowds were giving President Kennedy a warm welcome.

At the hospital, when she and the President waited in the minor-medicine suite, she had asked a Secret Service man to take her to see Mrs. Kennedy. In her own words, Jacqueline Kennedy looked "like a helpless heap of pink, but totally composed." She put out her arms to Mrs. Kennedy and they just stood there, holding each other. She heard Mrs. Kennedy say, "We had ten years together." Then she went up a long corridor to see Nellie Connally, the wife of the Governor, who was at that time believed near death. After crying with Mrs. Connally for a few moments she went back to her husband and heard Malcolm Kilduff address him as "Mr. President." There was a catch in her throat as she realized what a responsibility had fallen upon him.

After *Air Force One* had been in flight for a time, Mrs. Johnson passed the Presidential compartment and her husband called to her and asked, "Where do you want to go when we get to Washington?" She recalls that this was the first she had thought of it. "I want to go home and begin organizing my thoughts." A little later, Press Secretary Liz Carpenter suggested that she have something ready to say to the reporters.

"I have no statement," said Mrs. Johnson. "The way I feel it has all been a dreadful nightmare and somehow we must find strength to go on."

"Just say that," Mrs. Carpenter said. "That can be your statement."

Kenny O'Donnell and Larry O'Brien had reached *Air Force One* while Mr. Johnson was waiting for Judge Sarah T. Hughes, an old friend of his family, to arrive to administer the Oath of Office. The President spoke to them and asked them to stay as long as they could. "I need your help . . . badly and not just now . . . but from now on in." Although it certainly was repugnant to him in a moment of sorrow, he must begin to act, he said; he must quickly show the nation and the world the basic continuity of the U. S. Government. He told them that he felt they were two chief symbols of Kennedy's authority and that they must remain with him for an orderly and united transition. He said: "You can't disrupt the institutions of this country with an assassin's bullet."

The Vice-President succeeds automatically to the Presidency when the President dies. The formal swearing-in, the taking of an oath, is a formality which is not legally necessary. Ordinarily, of course, the oath is given with formality in the Inauguration ceremony, on the steps of the Capitol. But the Presidency passes automatically when a President dies or is killed. That day at Dallas it was decided that the new President should be sworn in immediately, and under the circumstances no one could remember the precise words of the oath. The words could have been found in any American history text or encyclopedia, but no one was about to be sent out to a Dallas library to pick up a copy. Using the regular Presidential communications aboard the plane, a telephone call was placed to Attorney General Robert F. Kennedy and an assistant attorney general read the oath to President Johnson's secretary. It was then transcribed so that Federal Judge Sarah T. Hughes would have a copy.*

Once Mrs. Hughes, a kindly-faced woman of sixty-seven, arrived, there was a brief further wait for Mrs. Kennedy to compose herself and come up from the rear compartment. When she appeared she was dressed in the pink wool suit she had worn that morning when she had looked so radiant, shaking hands

* In the end, it turned out that Judge Hughes had brought a copy with her.

[23]

with airport crowds at the side of her husband. Hands reached out to her as she stumbled slightly entering the compartment. Johnson took her hands in his and motioned her to his left side. Mrs. Johnson stood at his right. Then Mr. Johnson nodded to Judge Hughes.

She said, "Hold up your right hand and repeat after me . . ." Merriman Smith of United Press International recalls that it was very quiet and outside you could hear a jet plane coming in for a landing.

The Judge held out the Bible she had brought and Johnson covered it with his left hand. She read:

> "I do solemnly swear that I will faithfully execute the office of President of the United States, and will, to the best of my ability, preserve, protect and defend the Constitution of the United States." *

The Judge added of her own accord the words "so help me God" and Mr. Johnson repeated them in a deep voice. Then he turned to Lady Bird and hugged her and kissed her, and then he turned to Mrs. Kennedy and put his left arm around her and kissed her, too.

The two-minute ceremony was over at 3:38 P.M.† Eastern

---

* In the absence of any other recording equipment when the President took the oath of office, Kilduff had resourcefully remembered that there was a dictating machine aboard which President Kennedy had used. As the President was given the oath by a Texas judge, Kilduff held up the microphone of the dictating machine and thus preserved for the historical record the sound of this impromptu and dramatic ceremony. The record albums of the assassination and of the take-over are able to carry the President's oath because of Kilduff's presence of mind.

† Johnson was not becoming President at this point; he was President the moment Mr. Kennedy died. Calvin Coolidge couldn't feel comfortable being sworn in by his father, so later in Washington he had himself *secretly* sworn in by a federal judge; but cautious Cal need never have worried about it; he would have been President just as legally if *neither* his father nor the judge had sworn him in. In Johnson's case the Treasury in a few days calculated his paycheck at a new rate, effective 1 P.M., November 22.

Standard Time. Seconds later the President said, "Now let's get airborne and get back to Washington." *

As many Americans will remember, on the flight home the President and Mrs. Johnson spoke by radio-telephone to the late President's mother, Mrs. Joseph P. Kennedy. They also spoke to the Governor's wife, Mrs. Connally, who was still anxiously waiting at Parkland Hospital. The President and others made additional phone calls from the plane.

Mr. Johnson suggested that he should be met by McGeorge Bundy, the White House Assistant for National Security; the Secretary of Defense, Robert S. McNamara; and the Acting Secretary of State, George W. Ball, Jr. When asked if the landing at Andrews Field should be closed to visitors and the press, the President gave orders that the authorities should make provision for "normal" press and television coverage. He had begun to think that the public would want a glimpse of their new President, for basic assurance that he was alive and functioning.

At first the President thought there should be a Cabinet meeting that night. It is the custom, when a President dies, for the Cabinet to gather at the White House. (Truman presided at a short meeting the night that FDR died.) Then, by radio from the Situation Room in Washington, Mr. Johnson was reminded that six members of the Cabinet were in a plane high over the Pacific, on their way to Tokyo.

To the White House that Friday afternoon the first dreadful news came when a United Press reporter called the press office and asked that he be cleared to come to the White House. Mrs. Helen Ganss, a secretary in the press office for many years, asked, "Why does he want to come? There's nothing happening."

She was told that President Kennedy had just been shot. It was 1:40 P.M. Eastern Standard Time. Within minutes members of the President's staff had gathered around television sets

* Several persons had to leave the plane after the swearing-in ceremony. There was room for only two reporters on the return flight, Charles Roberts of *Newsweek* and Merriman Smith.

[25]

in the press office. In Pierre Salinger's office, Lee White and Paul Southwick, White House aides, told reporters they knew nothing more than what was coming in by radio and television.

By three o'clock, some of Mr. Johnson's assistants had arrived. Walter Jenkins, his main administrative officer, appeared first, followed soon after by George Reedy, his press assistant, who had been at the Vice-President's "West Front office" at the Capitol. They set up temporary headquarters in the office of Jim McNally, a White House transportation officer.

As Reedy said later, no one felt like bothering Kennedy's staff, many of whom were completely overwhelmed with emotion. There were no large decisions to be made. Toward the end of the day someone had to decide how many helicopters should be sent to Andrews Field and whether there should be a greeting party there.

Many people that Friday afternoon worked on memos which were to go to the new President. Some were ceremonial but nonetheless enormously detailed, like the work prepared at the State Department and delivered to the White House that night. Some concerned the vital stuff of government, such as the preparation of the annual budget, which was already in process.

That Friday afternoon, when the first news flash was received at the Bureau of the Budget in the Executive Office Building just across from the White House, it happened that the Budget Director, Kermit Gordon, and his Deputy Director, Elmer Staats, were at the Pentagon. They were meeting with Defense Secretary McNamara with regard to the 1965 defense budget.

Just arrived at that meeting was McGeorge Bundy, who had had an early lunch at the State Department with George W. Ball, Acting Secretary of State. That budget meeting at the Pentagon broke up immediately, and Gordon and Staats returned to their offices.

At the Bureau, the information officer, Virginia de Pury, had raced into the office of William Carey, Assistant to the Director of the Budget, when she got the first news flash. The word spread immediately through the Bureau and through the Executive Office Building.

In a moment a large crowd of staff members had surrounded the ticker. They were in "an agony of tension as the fragmentary details came in," one of them wrote in his diary. Some staff members went off to their desks or into corners and prayed. Many burst suddenly into sobs and cried openly. For a time there was hope that the President would live; then came the rumor from press associations that the President was dead, followed quickly by the final confirmation.

Fifteen minutes later, Director Gordon gave the order to let staff members go home to their wives and families if they wished. The Director himself went to his home.

That afternoon, Mr. Staats and William Carey discussed the question of whether the work of budget review should be carried on through the weekend of mourning. For several reasons, it was decided to proceed. For one thing, the tragic death of the President had occurred at a crisis time in the budget process, and decisions could not be delayed. For another, the people working in the Budget Bureau, an integral part of the White House, wanted to be with their fellow workers anyway. It was a comfort that Saturday, Sunday and Monday to be with one's colleagues in the White House and the Executive Office Building.

For a time it was thought that the word from *Air Force One* was for everyone to wait at the White House and not to go to Andrews Field. No one at the White House liked that idea. The Majority Whip, Senator Hubert Humphrey, and others present decided in an informal consensus to meet the plane. As it turned out, the whole country was to watch the event on television, and everyone saw the Kennedy family, the Kennedy aides, and the new President as they appeared at Andrews Field. Then they saw the new President greeted by major officials of the Government. Mr. McNamara, Mr. Ball, and Mr. Bundy were there with their briefcases, the symbols of executive authority.

At the State Department, Chiefs of Mission had been told to go out to Andrews if they wished. The Chief of Protocol at State, Angier Biddle Duke, who was to be a principal person in managing the funeral and other state arrangements connected with the assassination, had gone to the White House early and then to Andrews Field with George Ball and Arthur Schlesinger,

Jr. Mr. Duke, White House Aide Ralph Dungan, and Sargent Shriver, brother-in-law of the President, were the men who would be responsible for the thousand details of the state funeral, which was already beginning to be organized.

Colonel Swindal hurried the flight of *Air Force One,* and the ground radar control stations gave top priority to the plane carrying the two Presidents, one alive and one dead. The plane reached the East ahead of schedule and the pilot slowed down in order to land at exactly 6 P.M., as planned.

The nation watched as the casket with the body of Mr. Kennedy was lowered from the plane and placed in a Navy ambulance to go to the Naval Hospital in Bethesda. The slain President's brother Robert joined Mrs. Kennedy for the drive to the hospital, and the gray Navy ambulance slowly moved away.

Then the television cameras moved to another sight—the new President and his wife coming from the plane and being greeted. The television audience could see Mr. Johnson step up, bareheaded, to speak before a battery of a dozen microphones. Marie Fehmer had typed the 57 words on a small white card:

> This is a sad time for all people. We have suffered a loss that cannot be weighed. For me, it is a deep personal tragedy. I know the world shares the sorrow that Mrs. Kennedy and her family bear. I will do my best. That is all I can do. I ask for your help—and God's.

Mr. Johnson was warmly greeted by several persons, among them Senators Mike Mansfield and Hubert Humphrey. Then he climbed into a helicopter with McNamara, Bundy and Ball. Mrs. Johnson and several aides also went in this first helicopter. Others followed them to the White House in two other machines. Then Mrs. Johnson, with Liz Carpenter, went by White House car toward the Johnsons' home, where her daughter Luci was waiting for her.

In the small cabin of the helicopter the new President went to work between Andrews Field and the White House. He had emphasized on the plane—even before he left Dallas—that he wanted the key Kennedy people to stay. Now he told Bundy and McNamara not only that he wanted them personally to stay, but that he wanted them to speak to others about remaining at their posts. He wanted also to make clear to the Cabinet and Ambassadors and other representatives of the State Department that the usual formal resignations would be unnecessary.

He also asked them if there was any action or decision that he had to take that night. He already knew of certain persons he would meet and things that he would have to do that night or the next morning. But his question was directed at finding if there were any major developments to come in the international situation. Was there anything they had expected to discuss by phone with President Kennedy that night? The President had been on a campaign trip. But the Presidency—and his communications—always go with him. Had there also been a hot hour-by-hour problem?

The answer was no.

There was no question, no emergency situation. (As it turned out, the several weeks after the President took office were relatively quiet, although there were many times when immediate action was required.) This had been a quiet day in global affairs—except for three bullets fired in madness.

When he landed at the White House, Mr. Johnson hesitated briefly for photographers and then entered the White House by walking around the Rose Garden and through the door by the Cabinet Room. He passed by the President's oval office but did not stop there.

During President Kennedy's absence, his office had been completely redecorated. Now it had new curtains and rugs that Kennedy never saw. By the time Mr. Johnson walked by the oval office, secretaries had already cleared Kennedy's desk of his personal mementos. These included the coconut shell in which he had carved a message of survival after his PT boat sank, a little silver calendar carrying the dates of the "eyeball-to-eyeball" confrontation with Russia over Cuba, and his personal photographs of Mrs. Kennedy, Caroline and John.

The new President continued through the White House and walked out the other side of the building to his old Vice-Presidential office in the old State Department building. Going through the White House this way is the shortest way to the

[29]

Executive Office Building, "Old State," * when one has landed by helicopter on the lawn. None but high-ranking persons would take this route, but those closest to the White House might sometimes walk through the President's suite of offices in his absence. Mr. Johnson—or Mr. Bundy, for that matter— had done it before.

Afterwards it was assumed erroneously by some that the President had gone in and sat down at Mr. Kennedy's desk. It was, indeed, suggested to him that he should begin work there the next day, but the new President would not hear of it. That night he merely walked through and, as the other helicopters landed, their passengers also walked through the White House. Many of them joined the new President and his assistants in Old State.

On arriving at his own office Mr. Johnson met first with Chairman William Fulbright of the Senate Foreign Relations Committee, and with Ambassador Averell Harriman, one of the State Department's senior advisers. Then he spoke on the phone with two former Presidents. Mr. Truman called and then Mr. Johnson called Mr. Eisenhower.

At 7:30 he conferred with Sargent Shriver, who had been selected by the Kennedy family as its representative to work on planning funeral arrangements. At 7:40 he met with Congressional leaders for nearly an hour. Shortly after 8 he ate a bowl of soup, his first food since breakfast. Then he phoned the late President's brother, Senator Edward Kennedy, at Hyannis Port, Massachusetts, and in other phone calls that night, he talked with Senator Richard Russell, Supreme Court Justice Arthur Goldberg, and (after the meeting) Speaker McCormack.

That same day, Mr. Johnson asked the White House to have some engraved official stationery brought to him in the EOB. Then he wrote in longhand his first Presidential notes—to two children, Caroline and John Kennedy.

* This is the gray old pile of a building next door to the White House which even President Grant thought was a strange mixture of architectural styles. For many years it housed the State Department. It is now nicknamed "Old State," or "The EOB," and it houses the executive offices of the White House, such as the Budget Bureau, Council of Economic Advisers, and Science Advisory Committee.

At 9 P.M., the President went home, taking Valenti, Moyers and Carter with him, and that night at The Elms, the Johnsons' home in the Spring Valley section of Washington, set a pattern. Each night during the first weeks, the President would get together with the same group, usually Cliff Carter, Valenti, Moyers, and Horace Busby—and often George Reedy and Walter Jenkins.* Mr. Busby, a former newspaperman, was a former Johnson staff man and later a steady consultant to the President, even prior to his April appointment to the White House staff.

Earlier, Mrs. Johnson and Liz Carpenter had been driven to The Elms, accompanied by a Secret Service man who had explained to Mrs. Johnson some of the changes which had already been taking place at their private home, among them the installation of the White House telephone numbers. As they came to the Johnsons' driveway, a crowd of people and reporters waited by the big iron gate. In the past the gates had always stood open, but now they clanged shut as the big car went up the drive.

That night Mrs. Johnson directed the kitchen to have plenty of fried chicken ready: "He'll probably have people with him, and he hasn't had anything to eat yet." When the President got home around 9:30, she told him they could eat right away, and he said, "I should have called you. . . ."

Mr. Johnson went to a private sitting room at the rear of his house. He asked for a non-caloric orange drink. As he drank it, he noticed a framed color photo of his old friend and mentor, Sam Rayburn, for so many years Speaker of the House. The President saluted and then half to himself said, "Well, Mr. Sam, I wish you were here tonight."

The new President is practically an addict of television newscasts, and in his crowded schedule he still likes to see the 11-o'clock news every night. He carries a wristwatch with an alarm

* The first night, Mrs. Busby was also present. So was the President's old friend and heart specialist, Dr. Willis Hurst of Emory University. But the men who were there have agreed that Dr. Hurst did not examine the President.

which he often sets to go off just before the time the TV news comes on.

That night when someone flipped on the TV, old films on the life of Kennedy were being shown. There were shots of Kennedy on vacation at Hyannis Port, frolicking with his children.

"Oh, God, no," said Mr. Johnson. "I don't think I could take that."

The set was turned to another channel, and that one had some pictures of Johnson's early life in Texas. The program gave him some amusement, as an old family album sometimes does. Then the set was turned off, and the group talked for a while.

After midnight, Mr. Johnson went up to bed.

Moyers, Valenti, and Carter were in their separate bedrooms getting ready for bed when each had a phone call.

"I want to talk some more," said the President, who had been unable to quiet down and get ready for sleep. When the men gathered in his room, he was sitting propped up by pillows, with official papers, including secret CIA reports, scattered over the bedspread.

"I want to talk some more," he repeated. "We've got a lot of work ahead. I want to think out my agenda."

So the four men stayed up, planning a schedule for the next day and going over the main themes which the President felt the national leadership must emphasize in the weeks ahead.

Bill Moyers has recalled that over and over in the first few days, the President stressed three major points:

1. There must be continuity. There should be no hesitancy, nothing to indicate that the U. S. Government had faltered.
2. The programs of President Kennedy would be pushed.
3. The country must be united to face the crisis and the transition of power.

Already, on the plane and in conversation at The Elms, the new President spoke of the Russians watching the United States. He felt the rest of the world, but primarily the Russians, must be wondering what to think about the assassination. A primary goal of a smooth transition must be to demonstrate the strength and stability of our government.

In the course of the evening, he had asked Carter to close the Austin office, and he had asked Valenti and Moyers to stay and "work for me a while."

"Good night, boys," he concluded finally." Get a lot of sleep fast. It's going to be a long day tomorrow."

Thus, the President said good night at nearly 3:30 A.M. to three men who that morning, like himself, had held different jobs. Now they were all working for the White House.

That night, the President later recalled, he fell asleep immediately after the three left. Moyers was awake a while longer. He knew that he would respond to Johnson's request and work in the White House for a time, but then he was determined to go back to his job as Deputy Director of the Peace Corps.

But as he opened the window that night Moyers saw Secret Service agents walking through the Johnson yard.

Time after time, both Kennedy and Johnson men would say in interviews, "I thought I had realized what happened—but then such-and-such happened—and I had to realize it all over again."

This was such a moment for Moyers. He was overwhelmed with a wave of realization.

The Secret Service men walking quietly through the shadows at 4 A.M. were guarding the President of the United States.

2

First Day as President: "I Need Your Help"

THE TWO BULLETS in Dallas had killed a young father. Millions of people that night thought of the assassination as the murder of a young man. Their emotions centered on the young widow and Caroline and John. The bullets had changed the future of what had seemed one of the most fortune-favored families in the world.

The two bullets had also destroyed a brain and with it a knowledge and a memory. The death, not of the young father, but of the President, had cut a thousand connections in Washington and had caused a pause in a hundred different affairs of state. There were many more broken threads than will ever be known. There were things which John Kennedy had intended to do the next day or the next year which he had told to no one. There were also of course many other plans known to many people. But who would ever hear all of them?

Then there were some events already in motion, or about to happen, which now would end differently because another man had taken over the President's desk.

An important diplomatic visit was one of the major affairs which had to be postponed. The German Chancellor, Ludwig Erhard, was to have arrived in Washington on Sunday, November 24, for a state visit. That diplomatic mission did not come to Washington at all. Erhard and his aides instead went to Texas after Christmas and held their conferences at the LBJ ranch.

Another diplomatic item, almost unnoticed at the time, concerned one of the tiniest countries on earth—the Republic of Panama. Since August that small country had not had an Ambassador from the United States. The previous Ambassador, Joseph S. Farland, had resigned after months of differing with the State Department. Just before his death, Mr. Kennedy had on his desk the final papers to appoint Frank M. Coffin, a former Representative from Maine, who was then deputy administrator of the foreign aid program. But the appointment of an ambassador to that small country did not seem a very large concern on November 23.

Foreign affairs were fairly quiet that week—but politics were already boiling. The Presidential campaign had started, and the tragic trip to Texas had been undertaken for political reasons. Mr. Kennedy had just met with his political chiefs—his brother, O'Donnell, O'Brien, and others—and another meeting was scheduled for the next week. That meeting of course would never be held.

The Bureau of Budget was engaged in the annual review of what money the U. S. ought to be spending. President Kennedy had already told the Bureau to cut the preliminary figures shown to him early in November. The Bureau had expected to work all the weekends in November and December, going over the figures with the various agencies, giving them a full hearing . . . and a tough argument. The President—whoever was President—had to look at that budget, as it changed from day to day, and he had to prepare a budget message.

There could be no postponement of some of these tasks. In January the new session of Congress would expect many messages from the White House—including the traditional annual message on the State of the Union.

A thousand hearings and committee meetings were being held that Thursday and Friday in Washington—in dozens of regulatory agencies—and before the committees and subcommittees of Congress. A vote important to the administration on the sale of wheat to Russia was scheduled for Monday—now it would be on Tuesday. And important to Lyndon B. Johnson was a pending decision from the Federal Communications Commission. The decision concerned his television station in Austin, Texas, and the outcome would mean a great deal to the growth of television in that city. The FCC had expected to hand down a decision on November 20th but had put it off for a few days so that it would not coincide with the Texas trip. There would now be much more delay, more heat, and more controversy about this conflict between the Johnson interests and a rival group.

And also important to the new President and his associates that weekend was the evolving story of an insurance man named Don Reynolds. On Friday afternoon, Mr. Reynolds had been on Capitol Hill in a secret session, telling how he had sold an insurance policy to Mr. Johnson. Then he told a story about a request from Walter Jenkins—but the details of that story were not to break until January.

Most of these considerations—like Reynolds and the FCC—were, however, far from the minds of most Americans on Saturday, November 23.

In the early morning a Navy ambulance brought the body of President Kennedy up the great curving drive to the White House as the Marine honor guard stood at attention.

The time was 4:22 A.M.

A small crowd of people had stood on Pennsylvania Avenue all night through.

In the hour just before dawn a sleepless Mrs. Kennedy went with the servicemen to see the casket placed in the East Room. There Mrs. Kennedy looked at her husband's face for the last time and then the casket was sealed.

A shocked Pierre Salinger, who had flown home with Cabinet members from the Pacific, had to go to work as best he could at 2 A.M. surrounded by reporters, photographers and the usual paraphernalia of television. A little after five o'clock Salinger went upstairs in the White House to talk with Larry O'Brien and Kenneth O'Donnell before the three men, all personal friends of JFK, were able to get two or three hours' sleep.

[36]

At nine o'clock that Saturday morning, movers entered the office of the President to take out all the furniture of John F. Kennedy. They took the desk, his paintings, and his rocking chair. By noon the office was barer than when he had entered it in January of 1961. The only pieces of furniture remaining were two white sofas by the fireplace.

As the late President's rocking chair trundled across the lawn on a mover's dolly, a photographer took the picture which brought tears to the eyes of thousands of Americans who saw it. To many the chair on the dolly symbolized President Kennedy's swift transition from vibrant life to tragic death. He had sat so many times in that famous chair talking to world leaders.

The first executive order issued by the new President concerned the funeral of President Kennedy and asked for the closing of "all executive departments, independent establishments and other governmental agencies . . . on Monday . . . as a mark of respect for President John Fitzgerald Kennedy." This order did not apply to special offices of the Department of State or Defense which were required to stay open for reasons of national security. And it could not apply to the small groups of men who had served Mr. Kennedy or Mr. Johnson. Nearly all of them had work to do.

Mr. Johnson's first day as President began at 8:41 A.M. when he and Jack Valenti and Bill Moyers left The Elms. A small crowd watched as D. C. Police and Secret Service men escorted him into his limousine and followed it to the White House where he met first with Attorney General Robert Kennedy. Then, accompanied by McGeorge Bundy, he went to the White House Situation Room, where he discussed matters of national security and foreign policy with Bundy and the head of the Central Intelligence Agency, John McCone.

The Situation Room is in the basement of the White House and is one of the most sheltered and well-guarded places in Washington. It is the nerve center of the command and control function of the President in his role as Commander in Chief of the armed services. To this room come secret intelligence reports and appraisals of the world situation in every part of the globe. From here the President and his top military advisers could "press the button" which would unleash a thermonuclear war.

Mr. Johnson was no stranger to this room as he had sometimes sat in on meetings when President Kennedy was away. At such times, however, he had not been really an acting President but the delegated authority whom the President would contact in an emergency. Mr. Johnson had been kept fully informed on the major crises in the world, and on all our major policies, the development of all our major weapons, the state of readiness of the services, and so on, in a way such as no other Vice-President before him. During the crisis with Cuba and Russia one year before, he had spent days in top-level meetings and many hours in this room.

The Situation-Room session was but a brief interlude in a day which involved a half-dozen different activities for the new President. He spent time with two former Presidents, presided at a Cabinet meeting, made dozens of phone calls—to government officials, to representatives of important citizens' groups, to personal friends, and to White House staff members. That day Mr. Johnson spent a good deal of time with Theodore Sorensen, President Kennedy's closest personal aide, urging him to stay. He worked on the budget. He heard some of the details of the early plans for measures against poverty in the United States.

And he and Mrs. Johnson went to the East Room to pay their respects to the memory of the man who had less than 24 hours before led their motorcade into Dallas.

One of the most significant phone calls Lyndon Johnson made that Saturday was a long-distance one to Robert B. Anderson, an old friend from Texas who had been Secretary of the Treasury from 1957 to 1960. Eisenhower had been President, but the Democrats had held the Senate, and Mr. Johnson was Senate Majority Leader. Anderson responded warmly to the President's invitation to come to Washington immediately, and for several hours on Sunday he talked with the new President in the Vice-Presidential office in the old State Department Building.

These men had been acquainted for more than 30 years. Washingtonians naturally wondered whether the new President would offer Anderson a high official post. Probably not, most observers thought, not only because of the Eisenhower connection, but because it was known that Mr. Anderson had no particular desire to return to Washington. But it was not impossible that it might happen sooner or later, because of the President's high regard for Anderson's judgment.

The President's conversations with Mr. Anderson have never been publicly discussed, but there seems little doubt that Mr. Johnson was already thinking of a drive for economy in government and concerned with the size of the federal budget and deficit. It is not unreasonable to assume that this unusual conversation, which continued over a period of two days after President Kennedy's death, had a great deal to do with solidifying Johnson's natural inclinations toward economy. And it later became known that at the same time, leaders of Congress—even over that weekend—were telling the President that federal expenses simply had to be reduced if Congress were to go along with such administration measures as the tax cut.

The President felt he should lose no time getting in touch with some of the key representatives of important national groups. Accordingly, he began talking on the phone to such people as Frederick Kappell, President of American Telephone and Telegraph Company, and chairman of the President's Business Council. In Labor he spoke to such men as David McDonald, head of the Steelworkers' Union, George Meany, President, and later to Walter Reuther, Vice-President of the AFL-CIO. Here are some notes from the White House log of that Saturday:

10:17 A.M., Call to Meany
12:35 P.M., Visit from former President Eisenhower
12:55 P.M., Call to Senator Humphrey, Party Whip, Senate
1:10 P.M., Call to House Democratic Leader Carl Albert
1:15 P.M., Call to Kappell
1:44 P.M., Call from Senator Yarborough (Dem., Tex.) expressing willingness to work for party unity in Texas
1:50 P.M., Call to Senate Republican Leader Everett Dirksen to make plans for the speech to Congress
1:55 P.M., Call to Robert Anderson
2:10 P.M., Call to Senator George Smathers about the tax cut bill

[39]

3:22 P.M., Call from Republican Governor George Romney of Michigan

3:32 P.M., Visit from Agriculture Secretary Orville Freeman

3:35 P.M., Call to Alex Rose, Chairman of the Liberal Party in New York State

3:53 P.M., Meeting with Justice Arthur Goldberg

3:54 P.M., Call to Speaker McCormack again, again on the subject of a Congressional appearance

4:15 P.M., Call to McDonald and then to Walter Reuther

4:30 P.M., Call from Democratic Governor John Reynolds of Wisconsin

4:57 P.M., Meeting with former President Truman

7:30 P.M., Meeting with the Secretary of Labor, W. Willard Wirtz

7:32 P.M., Call to David Dubinsky, head of the Garment Workers' Union

7:41 P.M., Meeting with Walter Heller, Chairman of the President's Council of Economic Advisers

9:11 P.M., Call to Mrs. Connally about progress of Governor Connally in Parkland Hospital

9:40 P.M., Call to McGeorge Bundy, to double-check on letters to heads of governments around the world, letters which assured them the policies of the U. S. would be continued much as they had been in the past.

Mr. Johnson also put in a flurry of other calls, some of them not completed for a day or two. For example, he talked that day or within a few days to all of the Negro civil rights leaders, and they later came to the White House: Martin Luther King, Roy Wilkins, leader of the NAACP, Whitney Young, head of the Urban League, and others. He made other calls that day, of course. He spoke to many staff members, and to members of his family. He talked to the FBI about the follow-up of the assassination. He also watched a news broadcast and saw Senator Eugene McCarthy.

Former President Eisenhower arrived from Gettysburg at 11 A.M. He waited in his limousine in the rain for several minutes near the executive offices of the West Wing until President

[40]

Johnson came over from room 274 in the EOB. The General said that he had come to pay his respects to the late President and to greet the new one.

That Saturday afternoon former President Eisenhower went to Johnson's Vice-Presidential offices. There he sat down at a board table and made many notes which he thought President Johnson might be interested in having. He used a legal-sized yellow tablet and wrote down with a lead pencil, said Mr. Johnson, "the things he thought I ought to know." Afterwards Mr. Eisenhower dictated his notes to a stenographer and Johnson later said that "some of the things I said to the joint session of Congress" came out of those suggestions.

At 2:50 P.M. the President met with the Cabinet and saw for the first time the six who at the time of the assassination had been aboard a plane on their way to an economics conference in Tokyo.

At the afternoon Cabinet meeting the six members—Secretary of State Dean Rusk, Secretary of the Treasury Douglas Dillon, Secretary of the Interior Steward L. Udall, Secretary of Labor W. Willard Wirtz, Secretary of Commerce Luther H. Hodges, and Secretary of Agriculture Orville Freeman—reported in and later two of them, Mr. Wirtz and Mr. Freeman, had separate conferences with the President. With the Cabinet members had been several other key officials: Pierre Salinger, Press Secretary to the President, Walter W. Heller, the Chairman of the President's Council of Economic Advisers, Myer Feldman, Deputy Special Counsel to the President, and Robert Manning, the Assistant Secretary of State for Public Affairs.

By a strange coincidence, this is the only time in American history that six Cabinet members had been out of the country in a group. The tragic assassination brought a realization that these circumstances should never be permitted again, and a few weeks later, President Johnson let it be known that no such trip was to be scheduled in the future.

At 1:30 P.M. (EST) on Friday the warning bells had begun to ring on the United Press teletype aboard the plane. The Presidential jet airliner on which the VIP's were traveling was 802 miles west of Hickam Field, Honolulu, at 35,000 feet above the Pacific Ocean. After the news service ticker gave the flash that the President had been shot, Secretary Rusk called the other members of the delegation to his forward compartment and told them the news, as received, that the President had been "seriously wounded."

Walter Heller kept a series of notes amounting to a brief diary of events on the plane. They received the news much as the nation got it, but in bulletins which were cruelly brief. They knew that the Governor had been shot, then a Secret Service man was quoted as saying that the President was dead, then there was the word that he was alive but critically wounded. The men on the plane discussed whether they should continue on the trip or fly back to Honolulu. In ten minutes Dean Rusk decided to turn back. Then there was some discussion as to whether they should go to Dallas or to Washington.

Secretary Rusk received a radiotelephone call from Undersecretary George Ball which said that the President was receiving blood transfusions and there was discussion as to whether this could be taken as a relatively hopeful sign. Then there came a message from the White House to Salinger signed STRANGER, the code name for the communications officer who was with the President's party in Texas. This order from STRANGER said that all Cabinet officers should return to the White House.

Secretary Rusk raised the question, "Who is the White House under these circumstances?"

As they flew back toward the U. S., nearly an hour of suspense and prayer went by. Before the news was final they began discussing some of the fateful complications of the problems of transfer and exercise of power, particularly of transfer of the power to order nuclear bombs used in war. They discussed the complications of disability if the President should live but be an invalid or suffer brain damage.

The men could hardly accept the possibility that the President was already dead. But the news on the ticker was so gloomy that they did discuss that final possibility. It was agreed that if the President should die, the Vice-President should be sworn in immediately and return to Washington as soon as possible.

[42]

After an hour of uncertainty, Pierre Salinger came back, from the news ticker, overcome with grief. He was able to say only two words, "He's dead." Then Secretary Rusk spoke to the other members of the flight over a public address system:

Ladies and Gentlemen: This is the Secretary of State speaking. We have received official confirmation that President Kennedy is dead. I am saddened to have to tell you this grievous news. We have a new President. May God bless our new President and our Nation.

There was no one aboard the plane who was dry-eyed. Men and women wept openly together.

In Honolulu, Navy personnel came aboard the plane and told the additional terrible details which the rest of the world already knew. The flight from Honolulu took eight hours and 19 minutes, and after landing in Washington, many of the men aboard went directly to the White House. Walter Heller went to his office and found all the senior staff members of the Council wide-awake and ready to work. They decided they should write a report on the economic outlook. Thus the new President could be briefed immediately on the basic economic factors believed to be influential for the immediate future. They finished at five that morning. Within fourteen hours Heller was discussing this—and other matters—with the President.

The President opened his first Cabinet meeting with a one-minute prayer. Present in addition to members of the Cabinet were: Theodore C. Sorensen, Special Counsel to the President; Bill Moyers, George Reedy, Jack Valenti, and Pierre Salinger, Press Secretary for the White House.

There was little business discussed at this meeting, not in the sense of the business of governing the country or of foreign relations. The meeting was entirely devoted to discussing the death of President Kennedy, the funeral, and a plea by Mr. Johnson asking the Cabinet members and other staff people to stay. To this plea there was a moving response by Adlai Stevenson. Stevenson's speech was impromptu and no copy was released, but it made a tremendous impression on its hearers. Mr. Stevenson recalled that he had been at the first Cabinet meeting that Mr. Kennedy had held and that he and his fellow members had pledged then to serve President Kennedy with devotion. Then he spoke for everyone, saying they all wanted to renew that pledge in this time of need. They would serve the new President as long as he had need of them.

On Saturday afternoon the Budget Bureau held a small top staff meeting after the Cabinet's meeting. The news was that the President would address a joint session of Congress in a few days and would deliver a brief address. His subjects would include the budget, taxes, foreign aid, foreign relations, and civil rights. The Bureau was asked to submit two pages. The preparation of material backing up these recommendations required that Bureau staff members work that Sunday.

That Saturday several people in the Bureau worked with Director Kermit Gordon on a historic one-page memorandum which was delivered to the President that same day. He read it immediately.

That memorandum has never been released, but this writer was permitted to copy some of the key passages from it. It helped start an "economy wave" which ultimately will affect the pocketbooks of nearly everyone in the United States.

In the opening lines it said "we stand at a critical stage in the 1965 budget process. . . ." Mr. Gordon told the new President, "Despite the fact that the time is late, I know that you will want to make this budget your budget. . . ." As it turned out, the President did indeed want to make the budget *his* budget. In the next few days he spent many hours working over the figures, and ultimately he and his aides came up with a final figure far lower than had been thought possible.

In the original memo Gordon explained that he had been expecting on the very next Wednesday to meet with President Kennedy and make another review of the budget proposals. The first budget proposed to President Kennedy had totaled well above one hundred billion dollars and had suggested a potential deficit several billion dollars larger than any the United

States had ever known. That preliminary budget had been pronounced unacceptable by top officials, and President Kennedy had ordered the Bureau to cut down the figures to be close to one hundred billion dollars. Kennedy did not see how it could be cut below a hundred billion—and said that if it did have to go over one hundred billion it was not to go more than a billion and a half over. That was to be the absolute limit. Accordingly the Budget Bureau officials and the budget people in all departments and agencies had already been engaged in a strenuous reexamination.

Mr. Gordon also gave to the President an arduous schedule dictated by the law and the calendar. The budget was to go to Congress on January 17, and December 26 was the final day for decisions on legislation. Even before that, in the period from December 2 to December 20, the final decisions would have to be made on various agency programs. Only ten days remained before really crucial decisions were made.

While the new President worked mainly on the business of government and politics, others in the White House were making plans for the funeral of John Kennedy.

Along with Sargent Shriver, Ralph Dungan, one of JFK's presidential assistants, was in charge of a kind of command and control center for the complicated arrangements for the late President's funeral. All this was done in close cooperation with the State Department.

The representatives of great and small nations were already arriving in Washington. On Friday afternoon the Japanese chargé d'affaires had called at the White House to present his condolences, and a book was provided for visiting dignitaries to sign. That Friday night a representative of Spain was already flying across the Atlantic.

For a time it was planned to hold the funeral in the huge Shrine of the Immaculate Conception, which is some distance from downtown Washington. On Saturday it was decided that it should be held closer to the White House, at the Cathedral. Because the Cathedral was so small, and the crowd of dignitaries one of the largest ever assembled, available space had to be measured foot by foot. A massive column at the corner of St. Joseph's Chapel blocked the view of half of the Diplomatic Corps and although they were in the Cathedral, many diplomats had to watch the proceedings on television. A television set was taken from the Secretary of State's office at the State Department and installed in the Cathedral for this purpose.

Two chairs had to be provided for the Emperor Haile Selassie because his sword used up a second precious place. The servicemen who were to carry the President's casket and the other persons who were to participate in the state funeral on Monday were already rehearsing some of the ceremonies and procedures they would follow. Early in the morning that Sunday, before the capital was awake, some servicemen went to the steps outside the great rotunda of the U. S. Capitol and practiced the form and ritual they would follow when later that same day they carried the casket from the caisson into the Capitol rotunda.

There is an ironic Viennese saying: "When someone dies you mourn for three days and then you fight over who gets their big leather chairs."

In the case of the more peaceful conflicts of politics, it was shocking to many people how swiftly Washington began talking politics after the tragic news from Dallas, how quickly people began to think of what different persons would be sitting in the big leather chairs of power.

Most newspapers that weekend carried stories about the changed political picture. *The New York Times,* the same day as it carried the news of the assassination, i.e., Saturday morning, carried an article on the political outlook for 1964. Warren Weaver, Jr., wrote in the *Times:* "The shock of the President's death stilled the official voices of politics in the capital. But so profound was the potential effect on the government and leadership that private consideration could not be silenced."

Mr. Weaver's story raised many of the questions which persons interested in politics could not help from asking themselves, even on that Friday afternoon. Could Mr. Johnson win support in the North, in view of his Southern background and his Southern accent? Could he win support in the South despite

[46]

his many forthright statements on the civil rights cause? Would people turn against left-wing or right-wing extremists—or both? Would not this assassination give new life to Republican hopes?

On the day after the assassination, although they were all still stunned, most political leaders and political commentators turned in part to their ordinary business of politics. As Joseph Alsop wrote, "Whatever else happens, politics goes on as usual." There was even a man who got word to Johnson that weekend that he was ready and eager to be the Vice-Presidential candidate in the summer.

There was general agreement among the commentators on several points. Unanimously it was agreed that the campaign chances of Senator Barry Goldwater had been seriously damaged, whereas those of Richard Nixon had improved, and that Johnson's voting support would be weakest in the industrial North.

Most commentators in the early days thought Mr. Johnson would be a far weaker candidate than Kennedy would have been. It wasn't until weeks later that they began to write that Johnson would be something of a new face and not inherit the enemies—as in the South—whom Kennedy had made. Thus in the end he might prove a stronger candidate than Kennedy.

In this century three Vice-Presidents have become President before Johnson. They were all subsequently nominated by their party and all elected—Theodore Roosevelt, Calvin Coolidge, and Harry Truman.

Douglas Kiker of the New York *Herald Tribune* on that Saturday wrote a story which was published under the heading DEATH TAKES A LEADER—BUT POLITICS GOES ON. In this article he wrote that "President Johnson would seem to be assured of nomination, virtually by acclamation."

Kiker, like others, thought that President Johnson was assuming the high office "with more insight, knowledge, and preparation than any man ever had." And he concluded that the new President would not be the same "Lyndon Johnson of 1960, the wheeling-dealing Texan who whiplashed the Senate into doing his bidding during the Eisenhower administration."

Another change was more certain: the Lyndon Johnson of

1965 would not be the same man who led us into 1964. Of all the things which are clear and unclear about the Presidency, one is humanly and politically most impressive: the White House changes the man who lives there.

3

A Time for Action

LYNDON BAINES JOHNSON is not a man who is regularly troubled by insomnia, but by nature he does not have an easy-sleeping temperament. In this respect he differs from Kennedy, Eisenhower, and Truman, all men who made their decisions as they came along and then went to bed at night and slept well.

That first Friday night, the President said good night twice. When he made the second good night, around three o'clock in the morning, he slept the sleep of the exhausted.

The next night, after the tremendous Saturday of meetings and telephone calls, he had a similar group visit at his house, again including Horace Busby, who in April would join the staff of the White House.

The President went home fairly early—for him—at about 9:30. Then he had a relaxing massage in his bedroom while his former staff member, Busby, sat in a chair by the bed.

About 10 o'clock the lights went out, but the President asked Busby to stay in the room for a while. Busby obediently stayed in his chair until he thought he detected sounds of sleep from the President's bed. Then he tiptoed quietly toward the door. He had just reached it when he heard the President's voice: "Buz . . . Buz . . . are you still there?" Busby went back to his chair. Twice more he tried to tiptoe out only to be stopped by the President's "Buz . . . Buz. . . ." He finally got away at two o'clock in the morning.*

On a few other nights in the first weeks, the President was unable to sleep. One day he told Isabelle Shelton of the Washington *Star* that he had lain awake for hours the previous night worrying about a pending Congressional vote. Generally speaking, however, the President's nerves held steady, and he seemed to have "the constitution of a horse."

In his first three weeks Mr. Johnson visited with three thousand people. Here is Bill Moyers' summary of the visitors with the President in the first thirty days:

> He talked to the top policy officials of the State Department. He talked to the top policy leaders of the Defense Department. He met and talked to 95 heads of state and other world leaders who had come to the funeral of President Kennedy. He talked to the Ambassadors of the OAS countries and assured them of our continuing interest in pursuing the Alliance for Progress. He talked to all the Ambassadors stationed in Washington and assured them of the desire of the United States Government to meet its commitments around the world. He talked to farm leaders. He talked to 80 of the nation's leading businessmen. He talked to the Executive Council of the AFL-CIO. He talked to the United Nations. He addressed the nation in a speech to Congress and two days later in a special Thanksgiving Day message.
>
> He began intensive work on the national budget and he began to work on the State of the Union message.
>
> He arranged for and held his first meeting with a head of state—a meeting hailed in both the United States and Europe as highly successful. He arranged to meet four other heads of state.

That first Sunday was, of course, a day of sorrow, and it was quite a long working day for the President. At ten o'clock McGeorge Bundy and John A. McCone, the Director of the Central Intelligence Agency, went to the President's Spring Valley

* According to a story told by Stewart Alsop in the *Saturday Evening Post,* February 15, 1964, p. 21.

home. They were, of course, discussing foreign policy matters with him which he would have to take up at a special meeting with his advisers that afternoon. He also needed to be well-prepared to meet some of the representatives of foreign countries who were coming into the city for the funeral on Monday.

As far as most Americans were concerned, this was the day on which the body of President Kennedy, which had been lying in state in the East Room of the White House, was placed upon a horse-drawn caisson and taken on a slow and mournful march from the White House up Pennsylvania Avenue to the Capitol. As the procession moved up the avenue, with shocked Washingtonians listening to the muffled drums, many were also listening to their transistor radios. At that hour they got the news that Lee Harvey Oswald had been shot by Jack Ruby in Dallas, Texas.

The President that day was occupied with many other matters, but he too was shocked again when he heard of the additional violence in Dallas. He had already been thinking about the many rumors and counter-rumors flying through the country. And that first week he was to set in motion the beginnings of the "Warren Commission" to investigate the assassination and the circumstances surrounding it.

When Chief Justice Earl Warren responded to a request from the President to discuss this subject, he expected to tell Mr. Johnson he could not do it. Members of the Supreme Court shun such outside assignments. But Mr. Johnson insisted and persuaded him to accept—one of the first major victories for the LBJ persuasive "treatment" in the White House.

To return to that Sunday morning, Mr. Johnson, his wife, their daughter Lucy* and the family friend, Representative Homer Thornberry, went to St. Mark's Episcopal Church. They heard the Rev. William Baxter say, "To be sure, we have continuity, and how swiftly it was emphasized, but I can imagine it was not done so easily but with a travail of soul." Mr. Johnson is a member of the Christian Church, but he occasionally went to St. Mark's while he was in the Senate. Mrs. Johnson, who is Episcopalian, has attended the church regularly. The new Presi-

* Later she changed the spelling to "Luci."

[51]

dent was solemn and quiet and did not join in the hymns except to sing "America" with the congregation.

The presence of the President and the sermon moved those in attendance. When the congregation reached the verse of "America" which says "and crown thy good with brotherhood," there were few in the church whose emotions did not reach the point of tears. The President, an emotional person, was himself touched, and that moment gave him the idea of using the last verse of "America, the Beautiful," to conclude his Wednesday message to Congress.

On this morning, their first Sunday and their second church service as President and First Lady, they sat entirely surrounded by Secret Service men. After the service the President and his wife surprised the congregation by taking part in the customary coffee hour. They remained about half an hour and spoke warmly to everyone. When they did leave, the crowd burst into applause. Members of the congregation and the minister expressed appreciation of the fact that on this extraordinary day Mr. Johnson would come, as he had done in times past, to meet and shake hands with the congregation.

A friend told the writer how he approached the President as he was getting into his car. The guardians had already closed in, and the friend was held back. Mr. Johnson started toward him, but then apparently realized that to do so would only mean disrupting the Secret Service men's line and a further round of handshaking—and no private word with his friend, anyway. "He gave me a sort of helpless look and shrugged his shoulders, and we seemed to realize at the same moment that certain casual gestures had now become impossible."

After the church service, the Johnsons returned to the White House. Twenty minutes later they had joined Mrs. Kennedy and her children in the limousine which drove slowly to the Capitol behind the caisson bearing President Kennedy's casket.

After the eulogies in the Capitol rotunda, Mr. Johnson placed a wreath of flowers at the end of the casket. His head bowed, he fingered a few of the flowers and then turned away. He clasped Mrs. Kennedy's hand for a long moment at the foot of the Capitol steps after the ceremony. Then he was taken alone by motorcycle escort to a foreign policy meeting.

This was a forty-five minute meeting with Henry Cabot Lodge and top national security advisers (in Room 274 in the Executive Office Building). At this meeting also were the Secretary of State, the Secretary of Defense, and the Undersecretary of State, George W. Ball. The main discussion concerned Southeast Asia, and a few hours later the word was given out that President Johnson had pledged the United States to continue aid to Vietnam.

At five-thirty this Sunday afternoon, the President met with some of the various representatives of foreign countries who had come to Washington for the funeral.

It was also on this Sunday that the President spent two hours with Robert V. Anderson, a session which turned out to be of prime importance in relation to the economy drive. The old Texan friend of Mr. Johnson called it "just a social visit," and when asked if there were any talk of his returning to Washington, said, "That hasn't been thought of."

Various political officials, such as Democratic Governor Otto Kerner of Illinois, and Mayor Richard Daley of Chicago, visited the President. And that night a Negro social worker in New York City was seated in his living room with his wife watching television when he received a telephone call from President Johnson. The social worker was Whitney Young, the National Director of the Urban League. The President had been calling all the outstanding leaders of the civil rights movement. He was already acquainted with Mr. Young, having worked with him on various occasions in years past, including the President's Committee on Equal Employment Opportunity. The President was determined, of course, that civil rights leaders know he intended to carry forward the fight for legislation. He wanted Mr. Young to visit him in Washington soon, as soon as a visit could be worked out, and he inquired whether he could come down for the funeral of Mr. Kennedy, which would be held the next day.

Mr. Young said that he had expected to come down and that he had been told that he would receive an invitation. But, he said, there had probably been some organizational mix-up because he had not received one. The President said, "I will ask Bill Moyers to check into that right away, and I am sure it is just a slip-up and you better make plans to come down anyway."

The Youngs went back to watching television, along with millions of other Americans. Their telephone rang again about twenty minutes after the first call. They assumed that it might be Moyers or a White House secretary, but it wasn't. It was the President. "I checked into that matter and there has been a slip-up. You come down tomorrow. There is a plane they tell me you really ought to take. It will get you in at 10:20 and you will be met by a White House car and the chauffeur will have your invitation."

Mr. Young followed the instructions and he was met with precision. The car was just for him and he was driven to St. Matthews. Always Mr. Johnson is a perfectionist in this kind of operation. He will know things like exactly what plane to take, what hour it will arrive, and just what the running time by car is from the airport to the Cathedral. He can also be a perfectionist when it comes to keeping in touch with human beings, and this story is but one of dozens which exemplify this trait. For that first week, the President was seeing everybody, talking to everybody, and writing notes, it sometimes seemed, to everybody else.

That Sunday night President Johnson called Senator Hubert Humphrey, Party Whip, at his Chevy Chase home. First of all, the President wanted to know why "the Mundt bill" * was being brought up now. He thought it was a poor time. The Senator reminded him there was a unanimous consent agreement that had been arrived at two weeks before. Humphrey said that he personally wasn't in favor of bringing it up now but that he couldn't alter an agreement.

Then the President said, "How many votes do you have?" Humphrey replied, "Well, I am not sure."

The President then teased him about it, and said, "That's

* This vote was important to the Democratic administration. The Mundt bill was aimed at preventing the sale of American products behind the Iron Curtain. The legislation would have prohibited the Export-Import Bank or any other federal agency from guaranteeing loans to finance trade with the Soviet Union or other Communist countries. Such guarantees are a normal part of international trade.

the trouble up there now. You fellows just don't have the votes counted."

This half-serious remark was a way of reminding the Party Whip that when LBJ as Majority Leader had operated the Senate, he had always been sure of the roll call before a highly controversial bill came up for a vote. Senator Humphrey assured him that they would have a good tabulation on the vote before the bill was called up for final passage.

Even on the day of the funeral, Monday, Lawrence O'Brien went from the White House to Capitol Hill and, with Senator Mansfield and Senator Humphrey, went to work checking out Senators as to how they were going to vote. Larry has described how he had a weird moment in the office of Senator Mansfield during this period, when it suddenly came over him in a wave that "the President" really was dead, and here he was still working over the count in the Senate in a sort of a nightmare. He shook off the feeling as best he could and went on with his work.

Tuesday morning, before the Senate met (it ordinarily meets at noon), Senator Humphrey worked with the same group, adding the Secretary of Agriculture, Orville Freeman, and others to help check out every Democrat.

That Tuesday he was able to tell the President that it looked as if the vote would be about 56 to 37 to defeat the Mundt bill.

After the debate was over and the vote was taken that night, Humphrey called the President around 9:15 P.M. "I want to report to you your first victory. We have defeated the Mundt bill by a vote of 57 to 35." The President was pleased with the result, and invited Senator Humphrey to come over for dinner.

These first days, in which Mr. Johnson worked fairly quietly but busily while the funeral pageantry was carried by television to millions of Americans, were not typical of the new President's days as they would go by a few weeks later. But the opening days, though shadowed by tragedy, gave solid clues as to what his methods would be.

In retrospect, it could be seen that they clearly demonstrated some of the major Johnson characteristics.

It was thought at first that he would not stay so extraordinarily busy and work such long hours, but in the end he kept on at about the same rate. He continued to use the telephone all day and all through the evening. Congressmen and others learned they might expect a call at midnight or before seven in the morning.

In between engagements and appointments, he would often telephone or write little notes to be sent to people. His notes are not as famous as his telephone calls, but he is forever sending a handwritten note of sympathy to someone in the hospital, or to someone who he thinks deserves congratulations.

These early days also highlighted some of the President's problems. To experienced political figures in Washington, the new President had two big jobs. It might be thought that the two new jobs were 1) to take over the domestic affairs of the country, and 2) to work on foreign affairs. Someone else might divide them into the work which comes to a civilian President and the responsibilities of a Commander in Chief. To experienced national political figures, however, the two big jobs were always the same: *One* was being President, and *Two* was taking over the direction of the election campaign.

The 1964 campaign had already started. The trip on which President Kennedy was killed was essentially a political trip.

Some persons fleetingly thought there remained time enough for the Democratic Party to reconsider its Presidential nominee, but this idea never occurred to the professional politicians. A Presidential campaign starts quite early. This one had started. There was no thought in high Democratic circles that there could be opposition to the nomination of Mr. Johnson. He was the President. He was the party leader. He would be the nominee.

Being sure of the nomination by no means meant that Mr. Johnson's hands were not full of political problems. On the contrary, it was up to him to make a good record as President *and* to start instantly at full speed to manage a campaign which was already started.

Mr. Johnson was the eighth man to become President of the United States through the death from illness or assassination of the President. Of all the eight, Mr. Johnson had the least time to serve in office before election.* In fact, he was really the only man who ever had to take over the Presidency and run full speed for the Presidency at the same time.

Not in decades had a new President been so well known in Washington. But in the rest of the country it could reasonably be said that he was neither known nor unknown. Millions of voters were essentially unfamiliar with his personality and record. Yet he was not viewed, as some new Presidents have been, as a nobody.

Harry Truman was known to a slight degree in Washington, but was a great unknown when he entered the White House. General Eisenhower was a world figure, but few in top governmental circles in Washington knew what to expect from him in 1952. Franklin D. Roosevelt was not well known to the country nor to Washington when he took over. As a matter of fact his character was changing so much that he was, in the words of Sam Rosenman, "hardly recognizable" as the "playboy" of his previous political life. And even though John F. Kennedy was a well-publicized figure, particularly in the last two years before he came into office, his personality and character were but dimly perceived for what we later learned them to be. Few Presidents have ever been so well known in the Capital City as Mr. Johnson.†

* There has been only one change-over in Presidential history which was even close to being as late in the term as the Johnson-Kennedy transition.

That was when Coolidge followed Harding after Harding had been in office two years and five months. It may be noted that Harding's death was sudden and Coolidge was thrust into office without notice and in a great hurry. But the times were quite placid compared to the pressing problems of the H-bomb era.

President Truman, of course, had three years of the term left, Theodore Roosevelt had three years, and the first President Johnson had three and a half years after succeeding Lincoln.

To some observers, coming in so late in the term meant that for the time being, in the words of Professor Henry F. Graff of Columbia University, "President Johnson is wedded to the Kennedy image."

† To go through our century, there was Theodore Roosevelt coming to power through an assassination, William Howard Taft somewhat known but not as an administrator, Woodrow Wilson relatively unknown, Warren Harding a complete dark horse, and Calvin Coolidge a minor, shadowy

It may seem unbelievable to those outside Washington, as it often seems simple-minded to those inside Washington, but it is very important simply to know a lot of people in our capital if you want to get things done. In other words, it was an undeniable asset to the new President that he knew on a first-name basis, and often on a personal basis, innumerable key people—many of them already obligated to him—in all sorts of government functions. It also held the possibility of trouble, at least in the adjustment period, for many men tend to respect an office more if they have not known the incumbent before, and sometimes in those early weeks a man would be thinking, It isn't really a President, it is only Old Lyndon trying to be a President. Sometimes, this writer suspects, that man would be LBJ, not believing that he, himself, was President Johnson.

So the President and the men around him went to work to make the country feel it had a real President. And it was of crucial importance that his first appearance before the people (not counting the brief speech at the airport and another brief one concerning the day of mourning) be well-prepared.

One of the main considerations for the President and his advisers on Saturday was the question of the time and place for that first speech. Gradually it was decided—within about 48 hours—that the occasion should be an address to a joint session of Congress. The beginnings of that speech had been discussed on Saturday with the Bureau of the Budget. Strong opinions about the speech and about the budget were expressed by people on Capitol Hill, and some felt it should not be a Congressional speech, but should come from the President's desk in the White House.

Other advisers, including Senator Humphrey, had felt that the President would do a much better job in the environment of Congress "which is really Lyndon's home . . . he feels natural there and at ease." The President decided this was the only alternative. He recalled that Harry Truman had made his

figure, coming to the White House through the accident of death. All were far less known in Washington than the man who came into office that November afternoon in 1963. Half the town referred to him as "Lyndon" and it seemed that he knew half the town on the same basis.

[58]

entrance as President through a Congressional speech, and he thought he should do the same.

As it turned out, many individuals were to work on this document. The man in charge of the speech-writing operation was Theodore Sorensen and his first draft had been to a great extent an eloquent eulogy of John Kennedy.

There had been various suggestions from the Cabinet. The former Ambassador to India, John Kenneth Galbraith, had produced a draft, and Adlai Stevenson and Horace Busby had also produced drafts or at least a great portion of a complete speech.

On the Tuesday night before the speech, Senator Hubert Humphrey, Abe Fortas and others were at President Johnson's home for dinner and he read aloud to them from different drafts. Others present were Jack Valenti, Mrs. Johnson and Cliff Carter. After dinner the President asked Humphrey to work on the speech. "Hubert, you and Abe go ahead and redraft these speeches and get me one that will be suitable for tomorrow."

Fortas and Humphrey went to work at about 10:15 and finished at 2 in the morning. While Humphrey and Fortas worked on this, Lyndon's nineteen-year-old daughter, Lynda Bird, was pressed into service as a typist. There had been secretaries there that evening but after midnight Lynda was asked to help.

The next morning there were still a few minor changes to be made. The President and others worked on them almost until the time of delivery. Going up to the Capitol, Johnson took the same men with him whom Kennedy frequently took; namely, O'Brien, Sorensen and Salinger. Sorensen was not pleased, according to some accounts, with what had happened to his work.

The speech was an enormous success. Millions of Americans were impressed by and would always remember the President's opening sentence—"All I have I would have given gladly not to be standing here today."

Then he continued, "The greatest leader of our time has been struck down by the foulest deed of our time. Now the ideas and ideals which he so nobly represented must and will be translated into effective action."

The President appeared serious and dignified, speaking more slowly than is his custom. He emphasized continuity and unity and the fact that "this nation will keep its commitments . . . from South Vietnam to West Berlin." He pledged that he would follow through on the Kennedy program, and he emphasized that we would maintain our military strength and that we would continue foreign aid to Asia and Africa and Latin America.

He was particularly eloquent on civil rights:

> We have talked long enough in this country about equal rights. We have talked for 100 years or more. It is time now to write the next chapter, and to write it in the books of law. I urge you again, as I did in 1957 and again in 1960, to enact a civil rights law so that we can move forward to eliminate from this nation every trace of discrimination and oppression that is based upon race or color. There could be no greater source of strength to this nation both at home and abroad.

He also spoke out strongly for the Kennedy administration's tax-cut bill.

> No act of ours could more fittingly continue the work of President Kennedy than the earliest passage of the tax bill for which he fought all this long year. This is a bill designed to increase our national income and our federal revenues, and to provide insurance against recession. That bill, if passed without delay, means more security for those now working and more jobs for those now without them, and more incentive for our economy.

This has been one of the earliest decisions of the President, to make specific recommendations for legislation in his first appearance before the Congress. Some advisers had first thought that this speech should be almost entirely about Kennedy and about the need for unity and be somewhat limited to generalities. On Saturday, the day after President Kennedy's death, Mr. Johnson discussed this matter with the White House Congressional Adviser, Lawrence O'Brien. The President thought the speech should have some specific legislative items in it, and

O'Brien agreed. The President felt that it should have a real going-back-to-work atmosphere, and his manner and words on Wednesday emphasized that this was "a time for action." (This phrase later became the title of his own book of speeches.) Another key phrase of this speech referred to President Kennedy's inauguration address in which he said, "Let us begin," and President Johnson said, "Let us continue." This phrase, too, became a theme for the transition.

The President's speech was interrupted several times by applause, and he received a very emotional response near the end when he said, "Let us unite."

> Let us put an end to the teaching and preaching of hate and evil and violence. Let us turn away from the fanatics of the far left and the far right, from the apostles of bitterness and bigotry, from those defiant of law, and those who pour venom into our nation's bloodstream.

As he spoke, the country was also impressed and disturbed by the sight of two aging men behind him, the House Speaker and the Senate President pro tem, Mr. McCormack and Senator Carl Hayden, seventy-one and eighty-six respectively, who would in turn be the successors to Mr. Johnson should there be further deaths at the top of the American Government. Millions thought of the fact that "one more bullet" could have made Mr. McCormack President.

In general, the response of the nation and of the editorial writers seemed to be excellent. Many made it clear, almost in so many words, that they had not expected Mr. Johnson to "look so much like a President." Others commented on his poise and presence. It was recalled that Harry Truman, on a similar occasion, was so nervous that he began his speech and had to be stopped by the Speaker of the House, Sam Rayburn, who said, "Wait a minute, Harry, let me introduce you."

Mr. Johnson appeared to be perfectly controlled and in calm command. Before he went out to make the speech, he was met by Congressional leaders in a hushed and self-conscious gathering. One of the men there told the writer that they were absolutely "sunk in gloom." When he had finished, they felt neither "normal" nor exhilarated, but they felt America had a new leader, and one who would be equal to the job before him.

That week many leaders voiced the hope that the aftermath of the assassination would be increased unity and not increased disunity in America.

It began to appear that this was the case, during the month of official mourning. Leader after leader counseled moderation. Civil rights leaders said there was no official moratorium—but they called no major demonstrations. Extreme conservatives were silent and even the foreign affairs field was quiet. The Communists and the John Birchers did not completely disappear from view, but they were greatly subdued.

Meanwhile, as the President worked on his domestic program he was perfectly visible as President. The Republicans may have been silenced by the period of mourning, but Mr. Johnson was not. His face and voice were becoming familiar and they were becoming popular. Democratic leaders began to have the first presentiments that this man might be as strong as or—was it possible?—a stronger candidate than Mr. Kennedy.

Of course it was foreseen that there would be a great wave of sympathy for this man who had been thrust instantaneously into awesome responsibility. It was also foreseen that unless he or his program offended them, millions of Americans would want "to give him a real chance to see what he can do." And some few began to realize that *voters would not want to change Presidents twice, so soon.* Only a very few, however, began early to realize that the country might retain a feeling of sympathy for Mr. Johnson in a very real way for much longer than thirty days.

One astute historian, Dr. Henry F. Graff, of Columbia University, thought there would be "a vast crystallization of sympathy" around the Presidency and what Johnson "now seeks to do." He thought that, in a way, any man looking at the "unaccomplished work of Kennedy" would find it "both a glorious opportunity and, curiously, a straitjacket." Professor Graff thought "the room for maneuver he will enjoy is probably very very narrow for the immediate future."

Dr. Graff did see the possibility of a historic parallel to 1850 when Zachary Taylor died and President Fillmore became President. It was then, said Graff, that "the Compromise of 1850 which had seemed impossible of achievement was passed with far less friction than anyone had conceived of if Taylor had lived." Professor Graff emphasized, however, that the issues of that period were not in any way comparable to issues today.

As the period of mourning ended and politicians once again felt free to be as bitter and sharp as they liked, the New York *Daily News* urged Republicans to "make up for lost time." The *News* thought the first thing to be done was "an all-out attack on Chief Justice Earl Warren's commission to investigate the Kennedy murder, plus a drive to persuade Congress to give Warren & Co. the heave."

But it took Republicans a while to get their voices back, and they had seldom had more contenders on the platform or in primaries. Commentators seemed to agree that the chances of Barry Goldwater for the Republican nomination had been hurt by the new political alignment. The other Republican names most prominently mentioned were Pennsylvania's Governor William Scranton, New York's Governor Nelson Rockefeller, the former nominee Richard Nixon, and, just beginning to be mentioned more frequently, Henry Cabot Lodge.

On the Democratic side, the names most commonly mentioned for the Vice-Presidential nomination, which of course would be decided by the vote of one man, President Johnson, were Hubert Humphrey, Eugene McCarthy, Robert Wagner, Adlai Stevenson, Pat Brown and Sargent Shriver. The name of Robert Kennedy was not much mentioned in the early days because of the uncertainty, including his own uncertainty, about his plans.

4

The Men Around the President

IF YOU HAD SAT DOWN at the President's desk in January, these are the names you would have seen on his telephone box, the people you could call directly in the offices closest to you:

> Jenkins
> O'Donnell
> Moyers
> Valenti
> Vicki
> Juan
> Marie
> Gerry
> Sorenson
> Salinger

The three men closest to the President in the early weeks were of course on the little green box: Walter Jenkins, Bill Moyers, and Jack Valenti. The name "Juan" is for Juanita Roberts, Mr. Johnson's personal secretary, and Marie is for Marie Fehmer, another secretary who has worked for him for years. Gerri Whittington is a new secretary who arrived in December, and she is the first Negro secretary to work in the White House. (Whoever typed out the cards for President Johnson's box misspelled her name as they did the name of Sorensen—*not* Sorenson.) Vicki McCammon is another secretary.

O'Donnell is Kenny O'Donnell, of course, who was appointments secretary and political lieutenant to John Kennedy and worked in both of these capacities through the early months under Johnson. Pierre Salinger was Press Secretary. In January, George Reedy, who was to succeed Salinger, was still working in the old State Building. He was a member of the inner circle and was on the White House switchboard, but he was not yet on the main box.

Aside from "hot" secret lines there are other extra phones in the oval office. This little green box sits on the President's desk and another one like it is over on the coffee table. From either point or from the *"think-tank,"* the little room where the President sometimes naps or thinks, telephone calls may be made. Since January the green box has already seen some changes. As this book goes to press, Salinger's and Sorensen's names are gone. George Reedy's name is added. O'Donnell's is the last of the JFK names there, and it has been nominated as the next departure. Otherwise, it is expected that the other names listed will remain, barring accident and fate, as long as their Chief remains in the White House.

Who are the assistants and advisers to a President? As Bill Moyers describes it, they come in approximately four classes:

Personal: A President has need of several secretaries, for his correspondence is probably the country's largest. He also needs one or more personal assistants who are as close to him as a secretary, and just as much a part of the inner office. These assistants are vaguely described as "staff people," or as "administrative assistants." They are extra eyes and ears and hands for the President. For the new President these men are Moyers, Valenti and Jenkins. Their equivalents for Kennedy were O'Donnell, O'Brien, Sorensen and Dave Powers. The latter, however, was mainly a companion and not involved with affairs of state.*

---

* Powers was a frequent companion of Kennedy in his hours of relaxation. His title at the White House was "Doorkeeper." His status was almost that of a member of the family and for weeks after the assassination he

Professional: The Presidency today also requires the constant presence of certain professional or technical aides. For Science Adviser, Mr. Kennedy had Dr. Jerome Wiesner (who resigned just before the assassination, to be replaced by Dr. Donald Hornig). There are legal advisers with the title of Special Counsel, and there may be deputies. Theodore Sorensen and Ralph Dungan were Special Counsels, and Myer Feldman as Deputy Counsel often worked with Sorensen. They were very much of a team and it was something of a surprise that Feldman did not leave when Sorensen did.*

Then there is the press information post, which is also technical to a degree. It requires a special background.

Government Advisers: There are many persons in government with a special responsibility for service or counsel to the President. There are the Cabinet members and other members of the National Security Council, the heads of various independent agencies and most particularly the Bureau of the Budget, which before and after November was headed by Kermit Gordon.

Outside Advisers: Outside the Government there are many persons who constantly advise the President. Some of them send advice whether or not it is solicited. (For example, the President hears or asks to hear from the key people in business, in labor, in education, in veterans' organizations, churches, and the like.)

But each President also has certain outside persons who are advisers. Usually, but not always, they are also close friends. In the early weeks it was generally thought that President Johnson, as might well be expected under the circumstances, turned more often than most Presidents do to outside advisers. Naturally there was speculation as to how many of these persons—Abe Fortas, Dean Acheson, Clark Clifford, Horace Busby and others —would eventually be brought into the White House or some other part of the Government.

---

went over to Georgetown nearly every day, to be company for John. "His mother thinks he eats more if I am there," Powers said in February. Even later, Mr. Powers remained at the White House, working in part as a receptionist. His official title is "Special Assistant in the White House Office."

* Feldman had worked on a Senate Sub-Committee Staff on Preparedness when Lyndon Johnson was chairman of the Sub-Committee.

[66]

These are the people who help the man and the institution which is the President and the Presidency. In Mr. Johnson's early weeks in the White House there was great strain upon the "old people," some of whom were going, and the "new people" coming in. But there was also a third group which always works silently, whose story is seldom told and will not be told here. Many of this third group were there before Kennedy and will be there after Johnson.

The three groups were the Kennedy aides, the Johnson aides, and the permanent band of virtually anonymous civil servants.

In this third group are the White House ushers under the direction of Chief Usher Bernard West. There are, of course, the uniformed White House police and the Secret Service men in their plain suits. Then there are the usual housekeeping servants, mail-room employees, transportation people and others. There is the Executive Secretary, William Hopkins, who has worked for several Presidents, and has had nothing to say about any of them.*

In addition to ushers, security agents, and business management people, housekeepers, transportation, and the like, there are in the executive offices many other long-time government officials. The Bureau of the Budget is not a part of the Treasury, but of the White House offices. The skills of all these people were essential to the transition just as they are essential to the day-to-day operation of the government. Their knowledge, their loyalty, and their courageous ability to work in emergency and under pressure of great events were seldom more needed than in the crowded weeks after November 22.

In addition to the old Kennedy people and the *old Johnson* people, and the civil servants, there were two men—Moyers and Valenti—who arrived at the White House that Friday night in November with Mr. Johnson. Yet neither had been (on that fateful Friday morning) working as members of the Johnson organization. Bill Moyers had *formerly* worked for Johnson and could be considered "a Johnson man," but Jack Valenti

* When this writer asked about the possibility of interviewing Mr. Hopkins, the answer was, "He wouldn't do it of his own accord and no one has the authority to direct him to give an interview."

had never been on Johnson's staff, and had never had any job in Washington.

Moyers said he was on temporary duty and many believed that. He seemed to believe it. Jack Valenti also assumed he might soon be going home. Walter Jenkins and Reedy were moving their offices, and Washington wondered who would be next to move in or out.

On the day after the assassination most people assumed that several members of the Kennedy staff would resign immediately. As to who would first pull out and who would be pushed out, Washington buzzed with rumors—nearly all of them wrong.

In the first place, those who were very close to Kennedy personally, such as David Powers, Kenneth O'Donnell, Ted Sorensen, Arthur Schlesinger, were expected to leave, if only for reasons of grief and heartbreak. Then there were questions of personal ways of working. It had been years since most of these people had worked in any way but the way John Kennedy wished. It is just not possible to switch swiftly from one political leader to another if you have been through so many battles in so many years. Besides that, some of the men in the White House had fought hard battles against the very man now taking over the White House.

Douglas Kiker wrote in the *Herald Tribune* the Sunday after the assassination:

> It is known that President Johnson often strongly disagreed with Congressional liaison chief Lawrence O'Brien's approach to Congress . . . he was not especially close to Presidential assistants Kenneth O'Donnell, Timothy Reardon, Ralph Dungan. . . . How could he be? These were the New England political lieutenants who beat him in 1960 and had run the Democratic Party since then.

So in the early days it was expected there would be an exodus of Kennedy people, particularly his most "political" people. They would be the first to go, it was thought. (In the course of events it developed that the political men were the last to leave.)

Even in stories written by Washington's most able commenta-

[68]

tors there were frequent errors of fact in the early days, not to mention much speculation which later seemed completely wide of the mark. Everyone was trying to establish that he knew who was who among "the Johnson people," but the Johnson people for the moment were inaccessible—working nearly around the clock.

Many of the early stories described Bill Moyers as not only the closest confidant but as the first assistant to Mr. Johnson. Early accounts greatly underestimated the role of Walter Jenkins. He is not the all-purpose deputy that Sherman Adams was to Eisenhower. But he *is* the oldest and most experienced of Johnson's staff. And he did move physically into "the other corner office" of the White House—the office similar in size (but not shape) to the oval office. It is the physical spot once occupied by Sherman Adams.

It was commonly assumed that Pierre Salinger would depart at the first opportunity and many newspapers printed that Carl T. Rowan, the man who was later made head of the USIA to replace Murrow, was to be Press Secretary for the White House. Others said this was incorrect, that George Reedy was certain to become Press Secretary at any moment. No one—not to the knowledge of this writer—predicted that a public relations man already *in* the Johnson White House would come to play an important role in White House press relations. No one foresaw that within a few weeks the head of the table at *The New York Times* luncheon for a White House party would seat these persons in this order: Arthur Ochs Sulzberger, L. B. Johnson, Arthur Hays Sulzberger and Jack Valenti. In the early days Jack Valenti was there all the time, a shadow to the President, but like a shadow he was completely unremarked.

Two months after Mr. Johnson entered the White House there had still been few departures and there had been no major additions after the first few days, when Jenkins, Reedy, Moyers, and company settled in.

By the middle of January things had settled down, but the chain of command and the nature of the job of each person was by no means clear.

One day the Secretary of Commerce, Mr. Hodges, brought a

report over to the White House and he gave one copy to the President's secretary, Juanita Roberts. He gave another copy to Walter Jenkins, he left one for Theodore Sorensen and he sent one to Myer Feldman, Sorensen's deputy. The President gave the report—it was on textiles—to Feldman, saying: "You really know all about this, you take care of it and write me something on it." That was the original copy. Jenkins and Sorensen did the same so that Feldman ended up with all four copies.

Similar things sometimes happened to many other reports coming in from the outside, or the inside. Under JFK, people ordinarily sent an original of any document addressed to the President and perhaps one copy to a staff member who would be the action man on the matter. People never sent more than one copy, but weeks after November people were still thinking that they ought to send at least three extra copies. They would aim one to work on what might be called the Johnson side of things and the other on the Kennedy staff side of things. People seemed not quite sure about what to do even after they were told the old channels were still in effect. A Cabinet officer in January told the writer he just couldn't be sure who were the main assistants anymore. A top government official told the writer in late April that he still didn't know who was the real "man to see." He said that JFK had two main men, Sorensen and Bundy; Johnson had a half-dozen, all on the same level.

When the new President moved to the White House, Valenti, Moyers, and Jenkins went with him. A Kennedy aide, Ralph Dungan, insisted on moving out of his large office so that Jenkins could have it. Jenkins thus got a large ground-floor office, which he filled with assistants. Dungan moved upstairs. Moyers doubled up with O'Donnell. Valenti literally "hung around," using whatever place he could find, until a tiny office was found for him.

Two men "left behind" in the EOB were George Reedy and Cliff Carter, but they were hardly out of touch. This writer, going around the cavernous corridors of the EOB in those early days, found Valenti, Moyers, and Jenkins on the phone or dashing physically here and there to keep the team humming. (And, of course, the President called Reedy and Carter half a dozen times a day.) Organizationally, the President used all these men as his personal staff, and they all "went with him" to the White House to help him in his Executive duties.

Washington—and perhaps a lot of the rest of the country— was keenly interested in knowing who were the men closest to the President. But even when their names became clear to official circles and to the White House press corps, these assistants remained too busy to emerge in the light of day and become known.

All that could be seen, for the time being, was a very busy man at the top, who had taken over with great presence and command. He had a crew with him—but they were hardly visible. Men like Sorensen and Schlesinger, whose names were household words in the capital, were on their way out, and in their places, it was thought, were some shadowy unknowns. Here are some of the main facts about the men behind the scenes.

For months after the assassination, Jack Valenti* remained the man closest to the President. He and Bill Moyers frequently had dinner with the President and stayed on into the night talking with him. For weeks he had breakfast daily with the President and then remained at his side or near it through the rest of the day.

It was and is his job and his mission to assist the President, to carry out the President's own decisions and own policies. He is not at all comparable to a Harry Hopkins or a Theodore Sorensen, who were men expected to come in with specific programs and ideas. Except perhaps in the political area, Valenti does not have any special background which could lead him to urge the President to take a particular course of action.

Valenti's official biography is quite short. He says that his father, now seventy, "spends part time puttering in the real estate business . . . they live modestly." Mr. Valenti had to work his way through high school, working after school as an usher in a movie theatre, distributing movie posters, etc. Yet he finished high school very early—he was the youngest graduate in Houston at the age of fifteen. He began going to the

---

* Since this was written, Mr. Valenti has continued to gain in influence. He now has one of the largest offices in the building and has begun to handle appointments for the President.

[71]

University of Houston at night and got a job as an office boy for the Humble Oil Company.

From 1942 to 1945, Valenti was a pilot with the Air Force, then a part of the Army. He served mainly in Italy and flew 51 combat missions. He was awarded the Distinguished Flying Cross, the Air Medal with five clusters, the European Theatre ribbon with three battle stars, and one of the rarest decorations of all for his outstanding unit—a Distinguished Unit citation with one cluster. This unit was the 321st Bombardment Group of the 27th Bomber Wing.

Of his military career Mr. Valenti said, "I had a meteoric rise in the Air Force. I went from second lieutenant to first lieutenant without any pull whatsoever."

Valenti was graduated from Houston University in 1946 when he came back from the service. Then he went on to the Harvard Business School for two years. Going back to Texas, he entered the advertising department at Humble Oil Company and then in 1952 started his own advertising agency.

The Weekley and Valenti Advertising Agency started with 3 employees and when Mr. Valenti severed his ties with it in November it had 12 employees and billed about $3,000,000 a year. Mr. Valenti says, "By New York standards, it is a small agency." This agency did not do much public relations work—as distinguished from advertising. However, it did handle a political campaign account for Lyndon Johnson, and also did such work for other candidates, as well as taking an active interest in politics as citizens.

In 1954 he began to write a weekly essay column for the Houston *Post*. As he tells it, he had gone to Mexico to watch the Pan-American Road Race. He was so excited by it that he wrote out his impressions. When he got back to Texas, an editor of the Houston *Post* asked him to send along what he had written. It was printed and it led to Valenti's writing a weekly column.

In 1957 some of the Saturday morning sketches were published as a book by the Premiere Printing Company of Houston. The book includes much of the day-to-day essay material which many columnists work with, such as the Cocktail Party and the Traffic Problem. But many of the essays are short biographical sketches, and the book is called *Ten Heroes and Two Heroines,* the twelve being: Winston Churchill, Audie Murphy, Abraham Lincoln, Alexander Hamilton, Joe Louis, Beethoven, Kay Starr, Zsa Zsa Gabor, Thoreau, Andrew Jackson, Bing Crosby, and Ernest Hemingway.

The sketch on Lincoln describes a personal visit by Valenti to the Lincoln Memorial in Washington. In it he wrote:

> This ugly, gangling, awkward man, with no formal education, no hint of immortality in his forebears, no promise of anything except integrity in his growth, beaten in everything he tried, torn apart in love, vanquished in politics, a failure, an utter, defeated failure, became President of the United States.
>
> Stand close to this man sitting in the great chair. Stand close to him in the clear night and say softly, "Mr. President." The words are strangely sturdy with dignity. "Mr. President," say again softly.
>
> If the air is still enough—and it probably will be; if the sky is clear enough—and no doubt it will be; if you stand close enough—and I suspect you will; there will come to you a throbbing, eerie, warming, weirdly satisfying sensation. You will feel lifted. You will feel alive. You will feel courage.

In another section of the book there are two brief sketches side by side. One is called "The Most Powerful Man in the World" and is about the Presidency. It concludes, "We are probably one of the last peoples on earth who have a free choice in selecting an ordinary mortal and making him the world's most powerful man." The other sketch is called "The Great Persuader," and was written after Valenti had met Lyndon Johnson for the first time. Here is some of the description from "The Great Persuader."

> He's a tall man, tall in the cord-lean frame of a man used to being fit. He is brown with the imprint of the Texas sun etched in his face and around his eyes. His laugh comes easily and he rears back to give the laugh hearty support. His voice is clear and strong and garmented in the unmistakable accents of the ranch Texan.

[73]

There is a gentleness in his manner, but there is no disguising the taut, crackling energies that spill out of him even when he's standing still. And no mistaking either the feel of strength, unbending as a mountain crag, tough as a jungle fighter.

If the senator had a heart attack, then coronaries are good for you. He looked like he could do a quarter-mile and four rounds with a Russian delegation without even being winded.

Then Valenti wrote that if Henry Clay would be called the Great Compromiser and Oliver Wendell Holmes the Great Dissenter, "then Lyndon Johnson is the Great Persuader." He concluded:

> This was the personal force and the soft yet remorseless voice that cajoled, argued, suggested, exhorted, persuaded and patched up the rents of sectional senatorial fury. The senator freely admits his creed is to the prophet Isaiah: "Come, let us reason together." *

The column no doubt helped, but Valenti's real introduction to the Johnson group came when Valenti met Mary Margaret Wiley, the pretty secretary of Vice-President Johnson. He was married to her in June, 1962, at a wedding in Houston, and Mr. Johnson himself gave away the bride.

It was in 1961 and 1962 that Valenti was courting Mary Margaret and making frequent trips to Washington to see her. In the course of these days he often saw the Vice-President and a real friendship grew up between them.

In November, at the time of the assassination, the Valentis had just had their first child, whom they had named Lynda. Mrs. Valenti was asked by the President to come back to work but she replied that she could not leave her infant daughter for such a demanding job.

Month after month, all day every day, often until 1 A.M., Valenti remained the man who was physically closest to the President. He had an office close to the President, and for weeks

*After the section on "Politics and Presidents" there is an essay on Harvard stoutly defending it—and one on Texas, also stoutly defending it.

[74]

he lived in the White House.* At first, no one knew him and no one—except the President—knew what he did or what he could do. Completely unobtrusive on most of his errands, he came and went softly and swiftly. Kennedy staff people nicknamed him "The Spook."

Just what did he do for the President? For a time no one outside the White House knew. For weeks even other White House aides were not sure as to the nature of his job. One White House reporter said, "I thought for days that he was a new Secret Service man—it seemed logical that there might be a new man put on. And you never saw him leave at night. He was just a quiet man who was there."

Of Jack Valenti's ability to work, the President recently said:

> The first man I appointed to my staff when I became President was Jack Valenti, whose grandfather came from Italy and who incidentally is about the best fellow with me. He gets up with me every morning. He stays up with me until I go to bed at night, around midnight, and he is the only one who can really take it. The rest of these fellows are sissies.

Mr. Valenti was known to do some writing, but that at first was considered quite incidental. He was also known to do typing—he could make his electric typewriter sing like a bird; but no one ever thought he was there as a typist. Then he and Moyers began to be noticed at major policy sessions such as those on the budget or on the State of the Union message. Valenti was described as "something between a valet and an ambassador." In official ranking in the Government an Ambassador is about the highest position on the protocol list. In his assigned country an Ambassador outranks the Secretary of State; an Ambassador is the personal representative of the President and the official voice of his government. It did indeed develop

* This is something very few men, except Presidents, have ever done. The first President Johnson brought in numerous relatives and in-laws. FDR liked to have Louis Howe or Harry Hopkins in the same house with him. But neither Truman nor Eisenhower nor Kennedy had staff or advisers live in the White House.

that like an Ambassador, Valenti would represent the President —informally. And—like a valet—he performed all manner of personal services—bringing in coffee, taking the tray away, putting in phone calls, finding anything or anybody the President needed. Actually, it could be said that most Presidential assistants could be vaguely described by the phrase "something between a valet and an ambassador."

It was true the President would ask Valenti or Moyers to do things such as he would never ask of the older experienced assistants, the men who had worked for JFK. He was heard to say to Valenti, "I thought I told you to get that door handle fixed." But that did not make Valenti an exception in the Johnson entourage, for the President had always mixed up business and personal errands and political and social matters. His attitude toward "the help" and the office in general is that it is all one family, and he is the head of it. And like a father he will help out if you are sick, but if you are well he may ask you to do almost anything around the house. Also, like a father who gets angry, he feels he has a right to raise his voice when he doesn't like something you have done.

It is often said Valenti's photos make him resemble a movie gangster, and he does have heavy eyebrows, dark coloring, and a certain way of wearing a trench coat. People who met him personally, however, did not get a "heavy" impression—quite the opposite. He is a small man, with a birdlike delicacy and alertness, and like a bird he is quick to see and quick to respond.

He is really quite short—a British correspondent called him "pint-sized." When he is alongside the President, who is unusually tall, they make a striking Mutt-and-Jeff combination.

Although he has a Texas accent and uses words like "podner," Mr. Valenti will never be mistaken for a Ranger. He is not Mack the Knife, either, although he may well be a Machiavelli. Most people in the White House have some ability to maneuver and manipulate. Those who survive at the top usually have a lot of ability to maneuver—or to understand the maneuvers of the Chief. Valenti's role is the latter. He is an expediter. He works very quietly. He walks softly and speaks softly. He greets people very cordially. His greeting is more like advertising or show business than like politics—more likely to be

Hello-sugar-how-are-you? than the hail-fellow greetings of the campaign trail.

Mr. Valenti dresses as a Texas version of Madison Avenue. He is fond of stripes, and they are not dainty Ivy League stripes. Along with many other Texans, he wears large cuff links—one pair features large shiny coral stones set within a gold fringe. He likes to pin his shirt collar with a gold pin. His clothes have a certain rakishness, or at least they seem to have against the White House background.

In contrast to his clothes and his Texas vocabulary, his speech is exceptionally quiet and not at all flamboyant in intonation. His prose style, however, might be judged flamboyant and emotional.

He is genuinely surprised to find himself where he is, and to this observer, in the early days he seemed genuinely humble about his story and his new life.

Valenti seemed to be infinitely patient and durable in the early days. Everyone who saw him wondered how long he could keep up his schedule. His basic attitude was to work any kind of hours if that would help the President. "Any time I can save him fifteen minutes of time I feel I have accomplished something."

It was the middle of January before he really had an office to himself, and it was certainly a very small one. But it was just a few steps from the President. (The intervening offices were occupied by O'Donnell and Moyers, and by the office manager of the White House.) The Valenti office was barely large enough for a small desk, one chair for Valenti and one chair for a visitor. On a bookcase there were the standard tools of the speechwriter's trade; that is, books of quotations, *Roget's Thesaurus,* a book of great speeches, as well as a paperback book, *Facts About the Presidents.**

On his desk on a typical day would be a dozen folders containing papers, or drafts of speeches, each marked in block letters with a "magic marker" felt pen. They would bear such titles as "Miami Speech," "Queen of Greece," "Action," "Busi-

* Somewhat out of place on this shelf, it seemed, was the book, *The Age of Louis XIV* by Will and Ariel Durant, but that book was one of Valenti's favorites.

ness Council," or "Health Message." As he described his job, it was clear that one of his main duties was to keep track of and follow up on certain papers or projects. But from his own account and from other evidence, it was clear he might work on almost any stage of one of these projects. By the end of the 100 days he was frequently working on speeches and other papers.

All major speeches and speech requests were referred to his office, and Mr. Valenti consulted with the President and with the people who might be working on the drafts. For example, a foreign policy speech might start with material from the State Department. Then the President would discuss it with Valenti and suggest people to work on it. At the next stage, Valenti might work with the writers—that might be McGeorge Bundy and Bill Moyers. Valenti might well do some work on the actual text himself. But mainly he was a kind of superintendent of the speech-making process, in direct touch with the President and with other writers in the White House, as well as the people with the basic informational material from other government departments.

Jack Valenti was like the unknown soldier; he was surrounded by pomp and marble, and nobody knew him.

But the most invisible man in the White House was not Valenti, nor the President, nor any Secret Service man. The invisible man was Walter Jenkins.

Yet it was generally concluded, and it was flatly stated by William S. White, the newspaperman considered to be closest to the President, that Walter Jenkins was the Number 1 assistant. White said that he was closest to the new President just as Harry Hopkins had been closest to Roosevelt, Sherman Adams to Eisenhower, and Sorensen to Kennedy.

Sometimes in official pictures of the Security Council or at an important budget meeting, one would see the face of Walter Jenkins. Often when in another office of the White House, one would hear the message that Mr. Jenkins was calling, and one would see the electric response which resulted. Mr. Jenkins, like the President, was in constant motion, and he was often on the phone.

[78]

A plain, somewhat red-faced man, Mr. Jenkins is unimpressive in appearance, but outstanding for the friendliness and courtesy he maintains in his hectic workday.

A veteran White House visitor said it was really comical to think of the difference between the corner office when Sherman Adams had it and the situation now:

"Mr. Jenkins hops around like the young assistant whom you find in every Senator's office. He's writing with one hand, holding the phone with the other. And in there with him seems to be a crowd of people—two secretaries—and *his* young assistant (Dick Nelson). He doesn't seem to think a working place should be anything but crowded and bustling. And, of course, the West Wing *is* crowded. Why shouldn't his place be?

"In Eisenhower's day, Sherman Adams sat there in lonely and icy grandeur. On the front of his desk was a great medallion—the seal of the President of the United States.* And you felt a Presidential aura in the office—and you knew this man wielded great power with great gravity. You spoke in quiet tones and generally you waited for him to speak."

As a matter of fact, Mr. Jenkins is known to wield great power, but he is *never* suspected of using power in his own right. He executes missions for the President. Making decisions and policy is not part of the job as he sees it.†

Mr. Jenkins generally avoids public occasions, and he does not receive much personal publicity. He is personally quiet and shy, and doesn't like pictures and publicity. There are only one or two photographs—both showing him on the telephone—which were printed over and over in those articles in which newspapers or magazines attempted to portray "the men around the President." With knowing smiles and cynical winks, Washington cocktail chatter implied various reasons for this unobtrusiveness. The simplest view, to the cynics, was that Mr.

---

* The White House at one time in Mr. Eisenhower's day found itself with two desks carrying the "great seal." Mr. Eisenhower gave one to Mr. Adams, and he used it.

† Eisenhower clearly used Adams as a Chief of Staff; there is no real parallel between these two in terms of the jobs their Presidents asked them to do.

Jenkins was taking shelter from the political sniping in the Bobby Baker case.

As a matter of fact, however, everyone who had known Walter Jenkins before November, 1963, said that he had always worked very quietly, and that he had never cared for publicity, preferring by personal choice to remain in the background. In previous administrations, one seldom saw Sorensen on a public platform, and the same was true of the assistants close to Mr. Eisenhower. Mr. Jenkins' unobtrusiveness was, in fact, in the White House tradition of anonymity.

Washingtonians were keen to know more of what Jenkins was like and what he did.

What was he like? Here is a sketch by William S. White on Jenkins as White saw him after November:

> He is simply the kind of man who is—and in memory seems always to have been—*there*. He is as quiet as Mr. Sorensen. He is as executive-minded as was Sherman Adams but never gives the impression he is running things or trying to.
>
> He works at a furious pace which, because of his down-played personality, paradoxically seems almost hesitant. He is casually gentle; but very far from lamb-like. He can be very "tough," if he must, though nobody not knowing him well would sense it.
>
> He is a compact, slightly florid-faced man of 47, with heavy, dark and slightly graying hair. He is a deeply conscientious man whose worries settle in his stomach rather than show on his face.

Then Mr. White seemed almost to go overboard as a friend of Walter Jenkins':

> He is, drawing no long bow at all about it, one of the ablest, most devoted, most truly moral but totally unself-righteous public men this country has known in a long time. And in a profession where most men use sharp elbows on the way up, Walter Jenkins has never learned that those joints have any other use than to swing as he walks along.

Mr. Jenkins is a native of Wichita Falls, Texas, the youngest of six children of a farm family. He went to high school and a junior college in Wichita Falls and then went to the University of Texas. He has worked for LBJ for 19 years, beginning when Mr. Johnson was a member of the House of Representatives, except for two interruptions. One was his World War II service in Africa, Corsica, and Italy. He left the service with the rank of major. In 1951 he left Washington to run for Congress from the 13th District of Texas, but was defeated and returned to Mr. Johnson's office.

He has often been assigned to look after the business affairs of the Johnson family, and he was also often the man to see about political matters, particularly concerning Texas.

The Jenkins and Johnson families have been close personal friends for years, and in the early days of his administration, the Johnsons would sometimes go out to the Jenkins home for dinner.

The Jenkins have six children, one of them a boy named Lyndon.

George E. Reedy, President Johnson's Press Secretary as of the 120th day of the administration, is often described as "huge" or "hulking," just as Pierre Salinger before him was always tagged as "portly" and "cigar smoking." Reedy is not that large. He is 6'2" and today is more of a big man than a fat man. He weighed over 250 pounds before he entered the hospital for a gall bladder ailment and went on a diet, but while in the hospital, he lost twenty-five or more pounds. His blood pressure also became normal for the first time in five years.

He lived in a hospital room with two telephones, one a direct line into the White House. He was visited twice a day by his secretary, and he was frequently on the telephone to Mr. Johnson. The President also visited him in the hospital and ordered him to stay there until he lost weight. He lost quite a bit. Then one day a White House aide called Reedy in the hospital and urged him to come in immediately. Only when he reached the office did he learn Salinger suddenly had resigned. In a few moments Reedy was Press Secretary, saying, "It all happened very rapidly."

But George Reedy never gives the impression, as some large men often do, that he is throwing his weight around. He has a deep voice and usually uses it very gently. Sometimes, as during the long days of the railroad negotiations, his voice shows some irritation in answer to rude questions. Ordinarily, he is a model of patience—and needs to be. With his shock of prematurely white hair and his black-rimmed spectacles he looks older than his real age of forty-six, and his style is generally that of an amiable professor. Unlike many of the men around Johnson, he has read widely, and he has an almost scholarly approach to the problems of government. He can remember not merely how the House and Senate, or their committees, voted on civil rights in 1957 or some other key year, but he is likely to refer to Henry Clay or Woodrow Wilson to illustrate a point.

An assistant to Mr. Johnson in his days as Senator and Vice-President, Reedy often served as Press Secretary. But he also worked on speeches, or on correspondence, and was a fact-gatherer, a research man on policy matters. He was the kind of man to whom Mr. Johnson could say, "Please go through this report and also get me what the other side is saying. . . ." The subject matter might be civil rights, automation, housing, urban renewal, or any of the other complicated questions which might be the topic of legislation or political action.

Like other men around Johnson, Reedy always gave his chief absolute loyalty. Although he gave many "background interviews" to reporters, they sometimes had the feeling he was not giving out enough, and they criticized him for it. This criticism is made of many people who stay in press relations. Usually it does not mean they are not good press relations men for their employers; it means the opposite.

Mr. Reedy is the only non-Texan in the Johnson group. He was born in East Chicago, Indiana, and was graduated from the University of Chicago. His father was a newspaperman who once worked for a Washington newspaper, the old *Herald*. Mr. Reedy worked for the Philadelphia *Inquirer* and then for the United Press. He covered the Senate for the UP from 1939 until 1951 when he joined Johnson's Senatorial staff.

In World War II he served in the Pacific with the Air Force and was a captain when he left the service. He is a pipe smoker, a gourmet, and a man with an interest in many different things, from fishing to chess. His wife, the former Lillian Greenwald of New York City, has a law degree from Fordham University. She is also famous as a cook, but Mr. Reedy is now on a 1000-calorie-a-day diet—and many nights is at the White House and not home for dinner.

His personal speaking style at briefings was completely different from Salinger's. In his early days on the job, it was the subject of satirical columns. He was accused (by Mary McGrory of the *Star*) of having "the gravity of a judge about to pronounce sentence." Miss McGrory expressed sympathy for him, since he had to get and give out information on "one of the most unpredictable men in the Republic," but she did not like sentences like this: "I certainly would not anticipate what the President would do in the likelihood of an eventuality that has not taken place."

Newsmen generally respected him for being a man with a good "news sense" who did not play favorites, but they gave him many sharp questions as he began to make clear the news policies of the President.

Bill Moyers is often called "the only real intellectual" in the Johnson inner circle. He has the complete confidence of the Johnson group, and is considered a dedicated idealist who wants to serve a cause. As an assistant to Sargent Shriver in the Peace Corps, Moyers also became well-known and well-liked by many of the New Frontier. Thus he has been invaluable in the transition months as "a man who could speak the language of both the Kennedy people and the new people." * A tall, pale, thin-lipped young man, Moyers looks like a scholarly divinity student, and that is what he used to be.

Moyers came to Johnson's attention in the summer of 1954 when he spent his vacation from the University of Texas working in the Senator's office. He was not yet twenty. After returning to Austin, Moyers got a job as Assistant News Editor of Station KTBC, owned by Mrs. Johnson. He kept up a full schedule of classes while he worked full time and still he won

* Mr. Moyers' early description of his job: "I'm just a pipe fitter . . . whenever there is a couple of things that aren't quite fitting together he may send me in to link them up. I just do whatever comes up for me to do."

one of the highest academic averages in the history of the University. (Since Valenti did much the same, it appears that working and studying day and night is a good background for working for Mr. Johnson.) After Texas, Bill Don Moyers, as he was and is known in Texas, went to the University of Edinburgh in Scotland under a fellowship sponsored by Rotary International. A year later he entered the Southwestern Baptist Theological Seminary in Fort Worth and was ordained a minister in 1959. He never, however, planned a career as a minister. He said his choice of subjects as a student—Journalism, Government, History, Theology and Ethics—was made "in deliberate preparation for a career in public service."

After divinity school, Moyers went back to work for Johnson and during the 1960 electoral campaign he was Johnson's right-hand man. He and the then Majority Leader were inseparable and to many people Moyers became "the person to see" before one saw Johnson. (Walter Jenkins was and is also "the man to see," and there seems to be no one doorkeeper; Moyers now has the main responsibility for appointments.)

When the Peace Corps was being established, Moyers became intensely interested, and the Vice-President reluctantly consented to let him leave to work in the Peace Corps headquarters. He did a job of lobbying on Capitol Hill for the bill setting up the Peace Corps, and he helped Sargent Shriver work out his method of making calls on Capitol Hill, going from one Congressional door to another so that no one was overlooked. To this day Shriver and the Peace Corps enjoy unusual Congressional approval.

At first Moyers took a relatively minor post as Chief of Public Affairs for the Peace Corps but about a year ago he was promoted to Deputy Director immediately under Sargent Shriver. This gave him experience with the development of a successful agency and an international organization. It also made him well-known among dozens of young people with special talents. Very often these people have ambition for a political career, so Mr. Moyers is well acquainted with some of the brightest rising stars in the Democratic Party, as well as with the established figures. When Mr. Johnson was Vice-President, the young Texan had his desk right outside the door of the Vice-President's office and he served more or less as an appointments secretary, in addition to other duties.

In the early White House days, Mr. Moyers for some time shared an office with Kenny O'Donnell, who had been Kennedy's appointments secretary. In late February, as Johnson's emergency team seemed to settle into permanent status—or at least until after election—it did not appear likely that Moyers would be going back to the Peace Corps.

Moyers is praised not only for his intelligence and wide range of interests, his quick action and initiative, but for his ability to remain calm under pressure. This particular quality undoubtedly was of great service to Johnson and the country in the early weeks. The only *odd* thing about him, politicians say, is that he doesn't smoke or drink. The same is true of Sorensen. And it is said of both of them that they are serious to the point of being grim, and perhaps a little deficient in sense of humor. Their responsibilities and working schedules, however, do not leave much time for fun and games.

Moyers has given a few speeches since he joined the White House staff and he writes and speaks well. With his background and talents, it is assumed that one day he will be interested in running for office himself.

A "White House man" who is not actually in the White House is Clifton C. Carter, President Johnson's political liaison man, currently assigned to the Democratic National Committee. It is expected that someone else, a well-known Democrat, will be publicly named as the President's campaign manager,* but behind the scenes will be Cliff Carter.

It is expected that Carter and Lawrence O'Brien and Kenneth O'Donnell will be the basic team of the Johnson campaign organization.

In 1937, Mr. Carter, as a teen-ager, campaigned for Lyndon Johnson. In 1948 he managed Johnson's Senate campaign in one Congressional district, and by 1954 was heading the state-wide Johnson organization. He was prominent in the Kennedy-Johnson campaign in 1960 and on November 22, 1963, was managing the Johnson office in Austin, Texas. When Johnson first became

* This appointment had not been made when this book went to press.

President, Carter was one of the small inner circle which met nearly every night, first at The Elms and then in the White House.

In March the White House was said still to be interested in securing a speechwriter.

On April 4 the President announced the appointment of his old associate, Horace Busby, as a special assistant at the White House. Busby, forty, is a former Texas newspaperman who has recently been editing a successful business newsletter in Washington. Busby had worked for the International News Service. In 1948 he had helped Mr. Johnson in his Senatorial campaign and he later served on the staff of the Senate Preparedness Committee. The announcement of his appointment said he would work on a variety of matters, including appointments, national security, and preparedness. The announcement did not mention speechwriting, but Mr. Busby for years had helped Mr. Johnson with speeches and he continued to do so in his new position. This appointment may not mean an end to Mr. Johnson's speech production troubles. Soon after Busby's arrival, however, Mr. Johnson scored some smash hits with speeches—to the Associated Press editors and to businessmen at the U. S. Chamber of Commerce, both in April.

When Mr. Johnson moved into the oval office two long-time secretaries of the Johnson entourage went with him.

One was (Mary) Juanita Roberts from Texas, his personal secretary and practically a first assistant, and another was Marie Fehmer. Their office is in the room next door to the President, between the President's office and the Cabinet Room. In the first hectic days, Jack Valenti also worked in that office, or he sat outside it and used an adjacent chair as his "office."

Bill Moyers brought over from the Peace Corps a secretary who had worked for him, Carol Welch. Soon Carol and Ann McCamley were both working—perhaps ten hours a day—on the Presidential papers handled by Moyers.

Working with Walter Jenkins in his office was Mildred Stegall, and another quiet assistant seldom mentioned in the newspapers, Richard Nelson, age twenty-four, who had been an assistant to Vice-President Mr. Johnson since the summer of 1963.

Mrs. Evelyn Lincoln, personal secretary to the late President Kennedy, remained on the White House staff but was moved to an office in the Executive Office Building. She is working on the melancholy but important historical task of putting President Kennedy's papers in order for the Kennedy Library. At the special request of Mrs. Kennedy, the President's personal flag which had stood beside his desk throughout his time in office was given to Mrs. Lincoln. She never set foot in her old office after that sorrowful weekend. And out of respect for her feelings, Mr. Johnson's secretary, Juanita Roberts, never called her for guidance.

Regular visitors to the White House quickly noticed that not only was there a great difference between the old and new personal staffers but there was a tremendous difference in their secretaries. The new ones, whether from Texas or not, were likely to be more breezy, and remarkably quick to call people by their first names.

The new contingent seemed to be just as good at handling complicated tasks. However, as might be expected, they took a while to pick up that extraordinary tight-lip which belongs to the White House. The old JFK secretaries would never say, as a new one might, "Well, we're all confused here today. Number One got in at nine instead of ten as he promised—everybody's running around like mad. And X is like a man putting a drunk octopus into a half-gallon jar."

Outsiders were betting, moreover, that a good deal of the breeziness and folksiness would remain as long as Mr. Johnson was in office. Practically everyone short of Cabinet rank went on a first-name basis after his second or third appearance in the White House inner offices. One British visitor found this astounding, and he felt somewhat stunned. When the numbness departed, he liked it—"Not really unpleasant—after the third time round there you are—a first-name family member at the White House."

Some of the secretaries were quite young, too, considering their responsibilities. To see Moyers, twenty-nine, and Nelson, twenty-four, racing down the hallways, with secretaries who seemed to be just out of high school, made one realize youth had not left the White House when the Kennedys departed. Mr. Johnson told a visitor in December, "I like to get my advice from the old and my action from the young."

In the early months of action his staff was mainly young and he got advice—from everyone—and from an outside group.

Men close to the President insisted that Mr. Johnson did not use outside advisers any more than did President Kennedy or President Eisenhower. But close observers of the White House thought otherwise. The consensus was that no recent President had gone so regularly to a group of steady advisers on an almost daily basis. Moreover, they were men of great capacity, and some of them had been Cabinet members or outstanding staff men in the White House. These Johnson advisers had all at some time had experience with Government. The way in which Mr. Johnson went to them and the way in which the Eric Goldman appointment was announced may indicate there is some strong feeling in Johnson's mind or temperament about outside advice. He is strongly inclined to get a steady stream of advice from persons who are not on any government agency payroll.

Among these outside advisers, the top three were probably Abe Fortas of the law firm of Arnold, Fortas and Porter; Dean Acheson, for many years in the State Department and former Secretary of State for President Truman; and Robert Anderson, the well-known Texas banker who was Secretary of the Treasury as a Republican under President Eisenhower. Another frequent consultant is Benjamin Cohen, the famous lawyer who, with Thomas Corcoran, wrote and helped to carry through most of the New Deal legislation of Franklin Roosevelt's first term.

Another important adviser is Clark Clifford, who in President Truman's day was legal counsel at the White House. Clark Clifford also played a key role for President Kennedy in planning the orderly transition from the Eisenhower to the Kennedy regime. Mr. Clifford by now must be the country's chief practical authority on Presidential transitions.

Another close adviser, but not so active because of recent illness, is James Rowe, who worked with Johnson on his campaign for the Presidency and who is also a close friend of Senator Hubert Humphrey's. Rowe, a Harvard man and former law clerk to Oliver Wendell Holmes, has been close to Johnson for years. He worked for Johnson on the Democratic Policy Committee in the early days of Johnson's Senate leadership, also worked on campaign plans for Senator Hubert Humphrey and later helped in Johnson's 1960 campaign.

Other close advisers are Gerald Siegel, vice-president and counsel of the Washington *Post,* and Warren Woodward, vice-president of American Air Lines. Gerry Siegel served as chief counsel of the Senate Democratic Policy Committee from 1953 to 1958 when Johnson was Chairman. Siegel is credited with helping Johnson draft the 1957 Right-to-Vote bill in such a way that it could pass the Senate. Siegel was born in Iowa and received his law degree from Yale in 1947. He left the Senate Committee in 1957 to become lecturer and member of the faculty at the Harvard Business School. In 1960 Siegel came back to help Mr. Johnson put another Voting Rights bill through Congress in an election year.

High on the list of "outside" advisers would also be certain Senators, for few Presidents have ever consulted Senators the way Mr. Johnson has. They are numbered among his best friends. And they are the men whose judgment he knows and respects. The President often consulted, in the early weeks, on a day-to-day basis with Senators Mike Mansfield, Hubert Humphrey, William Fulbright, and with certain Congressmen such as Representatives Hale Boggs of Louisiana, Jack Brooks of Texas, Albert Thomas of Texas, and other favorites in the Texas delegation. Other favorite Senatorial advisers or friends include Eugene McCarthy of Minnesota, Warren Magnuson of Washington, Thomas Dodd of Connecticut, Lister Hill of Alabama and John Pastore of Rhode Island.

In past years Senator Johnson had a particular fondness for Senator Richard Russell of Georgia who is, of course, the leader of the attack on the Civil Rights movement. The friendship between Mr. Johnson and Senator Russell is not as close as it once was, but nonetheless Senator Russell went to the White House for a long conversation early in the Johnson regime and there is no doubt that the President has the highest respect for him.

No discussion of Mr. Johnson's staff and his advisers would be complete without a mention of a resource available to him which not many Presidents have had: an extraordinary acquaintanceship in the top levels of government. There can have been very few men in the White House who had as many friends scattered through the Government—at all levels—as has Mr. Johnson, and his experience as Majority Leader brought him into contact with most of official Washington.

In Washington if you want to know something about an agency or get something done, it is a great help to know anyone —even the stock clerk—in that agency. Knowing people is the basic job of most lobbyists and most politicians. It is often said that Johnson has been a long time in Washington and is experienced in the ways of our government. Perhaps that is just another way of saying that he knows the people.

There are former protégés or friends of his in every major department, of course not all at the top. Some of them are quite close friends who may be given higher posts if Mr. Johnson is reelected. Perhaps the highest ranking is Cyrus Robert Vance, now Secretary of the Army, who was formerly special counsel of Mr. Johnson's Preparedness Subcommittee. In the Navy there is Assistant Secretary of the Navy Kenneth D. BeLieu, who once served as Staff Director of the Preparedness Subcommittee. Another Defense figure is Solis Horwitz, who also formerly helped Mr. Johnson on party policy and Preparedness matters and who today is Chairman of the Pentagon Office of Organizational and Management Planning. Others are O. B. (Bill) Boyd, Public Affairs Director in the National Aeronautics and Space Administration, who formerly worked directly for Johnson; Edward C. Welch, Executive Secretary of the National Aeronautics and Space Council which Mr. Johnson headed while he was Vice-President; and Charles C. Boatner, formerly a press officer for the Vice-President and now Public Affairs Director for the Secretary of the Interior.

In his second week in office the President began to organize still another way of getting advice and information from the outside.

At Princeton University there was a very rare bird, namely a well-known professor who had never worked for the United States Government. Since most famous experts eventually do some kind of work—or get some kind of contract—with the Government, his colleagues sometimes thought that sooner or later Eric F. Goldman, a historian of our times, would work for the Government. They never dreamed, however, that he would start out at the top.

Yet on December 5, less than two weeks after the assassination, Professor Goldman in Princeton received a phone call from that well-known telephoner, Lyndon B. Johnson. The call was an invitation to come to Washington to meet with the President and "talk things over."

Eric Goldman had known two or three members of the President's staff and in particular was well-known and much admired by a young staff man, Richard Nelson, only 24 years old. Goldman has often been voted "best lecturer" by the senior class at Princeton and is known for his work in public affairs programs in television. Since 1959 he has been the regular moderator for the NBC intellectual discussion program, *The Open Mind*.

Professor Goldman went into the oval office in the White House with Richard Nelson, who stayed with him for a time. He also remembers that Bill Moyers came in and joined the discussion and that Jack Valenti came in and out. Goldman was with the President, as it turned out, for about an hour or more.

The President explained that he had a specific idea in mind and Dick Nelson had thought that Goldman might be just the man to do it. Mr. Johnson was searching for a way to get the Federal Government in touch with America's brains in many specialties—particularly with those who were working independently, and not in touch with any government project. The President also wanted to set up an office to which scholars, thinkers, writers, teachers and various specialists could send in suggestions when they thought they had an idea or some information to contribute to the better management of the Government.

Professor Goldman was somewhat dazed by this proposal. He agreed to take it on as an experiment if he could continue to occupy his chair at Princeton. So he remains Rollins Professor of History at Princeton with an arrangement to be on part-time loan from the University. It was clear from the beginning that his appointment was not at all to be as a "replacement" for Arthur Schlesinger.

This post for Goldman was the first new White House job created by Lyndon B. Johnson, and through the early weeks it gradually became clear to Goldman that there were several things which such an office might do. The first thing that happened to the Professor was a flood of mail from all over the country, much of it from ordinary citizens. He and the Princeton University post office were swamped by it. But Professor Goldman did not foresee that when the job was announced it would be greeted not only with enthusiasm, but also with hostile comments and even with laughter and derision. The White House itself prepared a press release which began:

> President Johnson today called on the Nation's top scholars, thinkers, writers, teachers and specialists in all fields to generate fresh, new and imaginative ideas for the benefit of the Government.

The announcement also said:

> The President wants to insure a "wide-open window for ideas" in the White House. Dr. Goldman will help keep a continuous flow of specific proposals, general approaches, and opinions from a wide range of experts outside the Government.

The blunt way in which this announcement said the administration wanted ideas struck certain intellectuals as too simple for words. Some of the newspaper stories made Dr. Goldman out to be some kind of animated Suggestion Box. Or it appeared he was a post office address for ideas.

As Dr. Goldman sees his job, it is to maintain an open door

and a welcome for people outside the Government to contribute ideas. But more importantly, he will take the initiative to locate people. He began to build up and maintain a kind of list of persons who are authorities in different areas. By early spring he had begun to get in touch with various leaders in different fields, such as education, rural life, medicine, etc. He built up an advisory council of experts in various fields.

A little tired and a little harassed by the hurly-burly of the White House after the quiet of Princeton, Dr. Goldman at the end of the first hundred days still felt that his was a very interesting experiment and one that he was going to follow through.

How well did the President delegate work to others?

In the early months, the men the President brought into the White House were all personal assistants. They were "expediters." None were specialists. They were all part of a personal entourage. They wrote, listened, phoned, fetched and carried. They looked things up, they located people, they assembled papers, and assembled people in meetings. They made appointments, and they stalled off other appointments. These personal assistants helped the President get things done. Perhaps most of the day-to-day work of the White House depends upon such things—getting the people and the papers together.

The President likes to do a lot of different things in a single day and seems to enjoy going from one meeting to another. He likes to see a couple of dozen people a day. He may take more than a hundred phone calls. As he gets news in the course of the day, his schedule is constantly being revised. It is commonly expected that on most any day he will call for a "surprise" or instant visit from someone inside or outside government. The President is physically restless and likes to keep things moving and schedules changing. This busyness means that his assistants have to move fast to keep up with the day as it is planned—and then they must scurry even faster to keep up with each day as it actually happens.

One official working on the economy and budget program found that he had to discuss his topic with the President in at least ten different places. Once was in a helicopter, once was while being driven around the President's ranch, and once was around the edges of a funeral which the President was attending in Texas.

Considering the circumstances of the change-over, it was not surprising that the new President wanted to know about everything and did not wish staff people to take too much responsibility. Yet the conviction began to grow that Mr. Johnson must eventually learn to delegate more. People thought that it would be easier if he were elected in his own right and had his own team to rely on, not only in the White House, but in the various Cabinet departments.

The old Johnson group, people from his Senatorial office and from his Vice-Presidential office, always kept a meticulous log of what went on at their desks each day. When one visited one of Johnson's key deputies one might see on his desk blotter a kind of logbook, not dissimilar to those kept by the White House guards at the gates. The staff aides kept notes so that at the end of the day there would be a record of all visitors and of all subjects covered. The practice goes back many years. Johnson used to like to feel that on an average day his office would handle 70 callers, 650 letters and 500 phone calls. Each staff member had to fill out a box score to show what he was contributing. Like many other executives, Johnson likes statistics, and tends to believe that the heart of almost any matter can be put into a few figures.

His senior staff members, of course, had to furnish some analysis and interpretation with their logs. Some of them say that they are asked first to bring up the critical items or the negative reactions they have heard in the day or the week. Mr. Johnson, as President (or when Senator), knows that he is not too often going to hear criticism directly from people. So he expects his assistants to listen for it.

The President even as Senator drove his staff hard. He works them late and for one month after he became President at least one of his assistants—George Reedy—did not even have time to get a haircut. If Mr. Reedy ever got the time away from the telephone and the desk it was always at a time when barbershops were closed.

Once when he was a Senator, Johnson decided that his office

had so much to do and so many early and late calls that it should operate on a twenty-four-hour shift. It didn't work out but, to a person of Johnson's temperament, it is still a logical idea, and it would not surprise his old acquaintances if Johnson eventually put in some kind of round-the-clock office service in the White House. Of course, even in the Senate days there were occasions for big mailings of letters to constituents, when the staff members worked through the night. Since he now has a job where he "lives in," there have been some times when he and staff members went home after working for nearly twenty-four hours.

Johnson works early and late and expects his secretaries and assistants to do likewise. In Johnson's own secretarial office it was finally decided in February to stagger the hours. After that the girls did not have to work as long hours as the main boss— and the other key staff members.

Johnson, like many active men, is an early riser. He wakes at 6:30 or sometimes even at 5:30 A.M. Even though his working day is a long one, he likes to get organized and have his staff at work quite early. So, in a phrase, they expect to come early and leave late. When the President said at his first press conference that he expected "to be at his desk pretty much straight through" no one understood him. He was just stating how he expected to work—days, nights, and weekends.

To many, it didn't seem humanly possible that the White House working hours would continue to be from 8:30 A.M. to 8:30 P.M. But that was often the case for key personnel. Often, of course, White House aides work far into the night. That was not new. But it *was* new to have so much work done on Saturdays and Sundays, and to maintain such long hours day after day.

Is there any "no man" on the Johnson staff? Washington wondered.

Is everyone in the Johnson entourage mainly an assistant? Is anyone around him a mentor or a political partner—even a junior partner? Men outside the staff, but close to the White House, thought there was not yet anyone there who would really "stand up" to Johnson. Experienced government people believe that most Presidents are not likely very often to have close to them a man who may seriously disagree. Presidents do not seem to care for men who talk back to them, or who give a firm "no" when asked if they think the boss is right about a certain pet program. However, Harry Hopkins, Sherman Adams, and Sorensen were more in a position to advise the President than is anyone now on the staff.

It was obvious from the way Mr. Johnson demanded unquestioning loyalty and the driving way in which he worked that there was little opportunity for his advisers to raise searching questions. Washington often wondered—as people looked at the men closest to him—who was there who could develop into an original idea man or take the role of being a "no man." Walter Jenkins is mature and experienced, but he is not an idea man. He is not an originator of programs. He has never worked for anyone but Mr. Johnson and completely identifies with him. Bill Moyers was known to have initiative and creative talent but he is a very young man. Jack Valenti is new to Washington and in any case is a completely subordinate and dedicated assistant.

In the past, George Reedy had been one staff man who reportedly sometimes "said no" to the President. At least that was the belief in the capital. And it had often been his job to get the facts—to look into a topic and defend a point of view based on the facts. But when Salinger left, George Reedy became almost completely occupied with the duties of Press Secretary.

In general it was thought that critical comments and guidance came to the President in the early period from his outside advisers—such as Abe Fortas, Clark Clifford, and others.

In view of the importance to the White House of speeches and statements, it is remarkable that no one man emerged as *the* speechwriter in the first hundred days. It was also remarkable how many different persons would work on the main papers of the new President. It is common for several hands to work on a Presidential paper, but it is not common for three different people to supervise three different drafts, and for more than a dozen to be involved with a single speech. That is precisely what happened in the early days with the new President.

[96]

The State of the Union message was one of the shortest in American history. It took only 40 minutes to deliver. But it took six weeks to write. Some two dozen persons worked on ten to sixteen revisions, and the last draft alone was discussed or "cleared" by some 123 people. The number included the six leaders of the House and Senate, the large group from the Executive Council of the AFL-CIO and some 80 members of the Business Advisory Council.

Theodore Sorensen and the President did most of the writing but many others were involved, including Cabinet members Rusk, McNamara and Wirtz. Walter Heller of the Economic Advisers, McGeorge Bundy, John A. McCone, Director of the CIA, and David E. Bell, Administrator of the Agency for International Development, also had important parts in the production.

Furthermore, Mrs. Johnson also went over revisions with the President, and Washington began to realize that not even Eleanor Roosevelt had been so directly involved in government business as was this new First Lady.

In the case of the State of the Union message, the President kept the latest text on his bedside table at the White House each night in case he should get new ideas on it late in the evening or early in the morning.

There was a persistent rumor in the early days that Sidney Hyman, a political scientist and author of several books and numerous magazine articles on the Presidency, would be coming in to fill the writing part of Sorensen's role. However, Hyman had not been seen going and coming at the White House and was not known to have worked on any of the major speeches. As mentioned elsewhere, Mr. Sorensen, Mr. Busby and any and all members of the Johnson entourage—except Jenkins—had some part in speeches. Outsiders were frequently asked to help. It was known that Adlai Stevenson, the economists J. K. Galbraith and Walter Heller, and many others had contributed. Johnson even tried out Richard Goodwin, formerly an aide to Kennedy, to work on a civil rights speech. That was a time when Horace Busby, who had been mainly responsible for Mr. Johnson's famous Gettysburg speech on civil rights, was in the hospital.* Of course, numerous persons within the Government had worked on areas of their known competence. Senators had sometimes worked on them and frequently had been consulted.

By April it was believed that Mr. Johnson had come to rely —for foreign affairs speeches—primarily on a three-man team: Bundy, Moyers and Jack Valenti. These are respectively an ex-Harvard dean, an ex-Baptist minister and a Democratic politician-businessman, to some a very strange trio. A few months before, one might have thought that it would be impossible to imagine the florid style of Valenti and the ice-cold style of Bundy ever meeting anywhere.

But it appeared the President was still not satisfied with his speechwriting machinery, and that the addition of Horace Busby to the staff in April might still not be a complete answer.

The fact was that Mr. Johnson attached extraordinary importance to the written word and to the style and salesmanship of the written or spoken word. Here, as elsewhere, he was a hard man to please.

Mr. Johnson's press and speech problems raise questions about his fundamental ability to delegate. It was frequently Mr. Johnson's concern to edit the copy of newspapermen. He does this by explaining things precisely and persuasively to them beforehand or by criticizing them after. It was easy then to picture how he might edit his subordinates' copy—with rapier and bludgeon, with honey and with hell-raising. Could this concern with the press—and his troubles with his own speeches— be related to something more basic, to an inability to let others go ahead and do their jobs even when the work might not seem done to perfection?

Around the new names, Valenti, Moyers, Jenkins, a new network of power began to be apparent at the top of Washington.

* Many persons think that "the Gettysburg address," given by Johnson at Gettysburg on May 30, 1963, and largely prepared by Busby, is the best single speech that Johnson had ever given up to the time of his speech to the joint Congressional houses immediately after Kennedy's death.

Top officials quickly began to know the names of the staff, the outside advisers, the key friends—and the newsmen who were "in" with the new group.

Meanwhile some of the JFK people were leaving one by one. Other JFK men were settling into the new machinery, perhaps a step below and perhaps a step above their previous level. Some, like McGeorge Bundy, seemed to be as busy as ever, but their work was so secret few outsiders knew whether their position was the same or changed.

The last time a Vice-President had suddenly become President (Truman after Roosevelt) many administration people had departed—and sometimes with a public uproar. (Two Cabinet members left with strong statements—Henry A. Wallace and Harold L. Ickes.) This time the story was entirely different, although inevitably some persons left.

The departure of Theodore G. Sorensen, a brilliant young Nebraskan who had been John Kennedy's alter ego, was announced on January 15th. His actual departure in late February,* although it had been anticipated from the first, came as a distinct shock in the capital. Although he was almost unknown to the country at large, he was recognized in the capital as one of the key architects of the New Frontier. No one, except Robert Kennedy, had been closer to JFK.

Mr. Sorensen resigned, he said, mainly to write a book about Mr. Kennedy and Kennedy's public career. It was a book that John F. Kennedy had expected some day to write himself (with Sorensen's assistance). For eleven years he had worked with Mr. Kennedy, essentially as a speechwriter. In that time he had made major contributions to Mr. Kennedy's maiden speech in the Senate and many other speeches, such as the Inaugural address and most of Kennedy's important Presidential speeches. He had also worked on the Kennedy book, *Profiles in Courage,* which won the Pulitzer prize in 1957.

But throughout the inner world of the top officials of Washington, Mr. Sorensen was also known as the intellectual equal and political twin brother of John Kennedy. With such a personal relationship with the deceased President, it was not con-

* His departure was announced January 15, to be effective February 29.

[99]

sidered likely that Sorensen would stay on with Mr. Johnson.

It was known that President Johnson had made a particular appeal on his first day in office and several times after that to keep Mr. Sorensen on the staff. There could be no doubt that the President wanted him to stay. The first Congressional speech —not all Sorensen's but his main responsibility*—won Mr. Johnson the highest praise of his entire career. Staying might not have been too unlikely if Mr. Sorensen had not had a strong desire to write a book and an analysis of the career of Mr. Kennedy. He was still stunned and grief-stricken at the time he made his announcement to depart. To some observers he seemed like a man walking in his sleep.

As he left, there was little or no speculation about dissension between the Sorensen viewpoint and the prevailing views at the White House. For once Washington tended to believe the comments in the exchange of letters between Sorensen and the President. Mr. Johnson said the resignation was accepted "reluctantly and regretfully" and he added "while many men may have received the benefit of your work only one man—the President—can fully appreciate its impact on the office itself."

Mr. Sorensen said that he was flattered by the President's desire that he stay on and "my admiration for you and for your progressive leadership makes your request very difficult to resist. . . ."

Before Mr. Sorensen left the White House, he was given a testimonial dinner which was remarkable even by top Washington standards. He was privileged to hear many laudatory speeches and greetings from Army chiefs, Cabinet members, Senators, and members of the Supreme Court. This was a grand occasion and a touching one.

Nearly everyone with any knowledge of Sorensen's contribution regarded him as an exceptional example of the quiet public servant. He had not sought or received public recognition, but with his outstanding ability he had become one of the key men of his generation. Washington looked forward to his book and

* Sorensen had main responsibility for three main speeches of the new President: the first address to Congress, the speech to the UN and the State of the Union message.

expected that although he was not likely to be a candidate for office he was likely to appear again in public office.*

On January 28 after rumors and even news stories saying that he would go and some saying flatly that he would stay, Arthur Schlesinger, Jr., the famous historian who had served John Kennedy, resigned, to become effective March 1. Like Mr. Sorensen, Mr. Schlesinger said that he intended to write a book about his years with President Kennedy.

Mr. Johnson wrote him a warm letter saying "I know the academic world will be the richer for your return but the White House will not be quite the same without you." Mr. Schlesinger, in fact, planned to remain in Washington, and he did not intend to return to Harvard for some time. He pledged to the President that "you may count on me for any assistance I can render in the forthcoming Presidential campaign."

There was no surface evidence of differences between Arthur Schlesinger and Mr. Johnson, but there was no authoritative source to claim that those two temperaments had worked well together. In the transition period, Mr. Schlesinger had worked almost entirely on personal matters for the Kennedy family.

After Arthur Schlesinger had retired from the White House, he took a small office in Washington to begin his book. His office was jokingly called "CASH," the initials standing for the "Center for the Advanced Study of History." He told people that he was "forgotten, but not gone." Shortly after his departure, a gala party was held in a Georgetown rathskeller which was described as a "gay, dancing, comical, celebrity-filled party . . . like a flashback to the Kennedy administration." It was attended by the French and British Ambassadors and various Cabinet members. Late in the evening, the party was honored with the presence of Mrs. Jacqueline Kennedy and her sister, Lee Radziwill.

An impromptu show was presented, with a reading of excerpts from "the Schlesinger history of the Kennedy administration," which, of course, was yet to be written. Even more fanciful was

* A brother, Thomas C. Sorensen, remained in the U. S. Information Agency as Deputy Director of Policy and Plans.

the reading of an imaginary personal letter which President Johnson might have written to Mr. Schlesinger. The columnist Art Buchwald explained to the party that "everyone knows when you leave the White House, the President writes two letters, one for publication and one for the person being fired." Buchwald read passages from the fictitious letter: "My dear Arthur . . . as you recall, when I first became President I said I needed you very badly. Mr. Valenti advises me that we need the space more. . . . For one thing we plan on appointing a woman to your position. . . . I've always been impressed with your modesty and your dedication, it's your dancing I don't approve of . . ."

The satirical shafts at this party had sharp points, and showed that there had, after all, been friction in the transition.

But in general everyone commented on how smoothly the arrivals and departures had actually gone.

A Kennedy aide who seemed to be doing the same kind of work as before was Myer Feldman.

In early April (April 4) it was announced by the President that Mr. Feldman was appointed top-ranking legal officer at the White House. Mr. Johnson referred to him in the new assignment as "my general counsel." Actually, there is no such title, and the announcement did not change Mr. Feldman's job in any way.

It was explained later that Feldman would retain his present title of Deputy Special Counsel, but that he would be the top-ranking legal official at the White House. Apparently this meant that the job Theodore Sorensen had held was still vacant, but there was no indication that it was going to be filled. Another implication of the announcement was that Mr. Feldman had decided to stay indefinitely.

Mr. Feldman was born in Philadelphia and attended Girard College. He later attended the Wharton School of Finance and the University of Pennsylvania Law School. He was graduated from both with honors. After serving in the U. S. Air Force, from 1942 to 1946, he was appointed as attorney for the Securities and Exchange Commission. In 1952 he had the highest staff position in the agency, that of Executive Assistant to the Chairman.

In 1953 he had a "transition job," in a change-over between Presidents. He was assigned as liaison between the Truman administration and the Eisenhower administration to help arrange a proper change-over in the SEC. In 1955 he was appointed counsel to the Senate Banking and Currency Committee and acted in that capacity in the stock market investigations.

In 1958 he joined the staff of Senator Kennedy as legislative assistant. He handled correspondence, helped draft bills, and worked on speeches and public statements. He was director of research for the Kennedy-Johnson campaign.

On the day of the Feldman announcement, the main purpose was to say that Hobart Taylor, Jr., Negro attorney from Detroit, was appointed Associate Special Counsel at the White House. Lee White, a Kennedy aide since 1961, was promoted from Assistant Special Counsel to Associate. Thus, Taylor and White had equal ranks just below Feldman's. Taylor had become well-known to the President when Johnson was Chairman and Vice-Chairman of the President's Committee on Equal Employment Opportunities.

Of all the early departures only that of Pierre Salinger caused sharp political comment in top Washington circles. In the first place it was—somewhat erroneously—thought that Mr. Salinger had gotten along exceptionally well with the new administration. While it was true that for a time he had more influence on policy matters than he had had with Mr. Kennedy, reporters in and out of the White House every day saw numerous slight indications that he was not really as happy with the new regime as he said he was and as he appeared to be publicly.

Toward the end of his stay Mr. Salinger seemed—perhaps for the first time—to show real irritation with some of the stories in the press. The amateur psychologists of the White House press room deduced that he was *really* irritated with having to keep up a smiling front while his advice was being disregarded. In any case, he finally became so irritated that he himself gave an interview. Ordinarily press relations people regard it as an unwritten law that they themselves do not give out their own opinions. His interview was, however, on the subject of his specialty—press relations.

Dickson Preston wrote the story under the double headline:

"SOREHEADS" * GIVE WHITE HOUSE A HEADACHE
PIERRE PANS PRESS CRITICS

According to Preston, Mr. Salinger at that time was "hopping mad over criticism by newsmen of President Johnson's relations with the press." Mr. Preston said that Salinger had implied that most of the critics were soreheads "seeking special treatment." Preston quoted Salinger as saying, "The reporters who wrote those stories are the same guys who have been around asking for private interviews with the President."

Mr. Salinger well knows the old rule that press relations people should avoid, like the plague, speaking out, particularly against the press. The word in the press office was that he was indeed "hopping mad," as Preston described him. That in itself was a new development for a man justly famous for keeping a good temper under difficult circumstances.

In any case, he left in a hurry on March 19. It was characteristic of some of the early arrivals in the Johnson administration that they were appointed in a great hurry, but Salinger and Roger Hilsman, Assistant Secretary of State for Far Eastern affairs, were the only ones who took off in what seemed to be haste.

Salinger, the subject of many jokes because of his size and his refusal to go along on the fifty-mile hikes, set new speed records when he walked out of the White House. He told the President that he was going just a few hours before he departed. He left with not even twenty-four hours remaining for him to file his candidacy for the U. S. Senate in California.†

* Mr. Salinger told this writer he never used the expression "soreheads."

† As it turned out, the status of his legal residence—Virginia or California—was in such doubt that it was thought he could only be the subject of a write-in campaign in California. Thus Salinger left in such a hurry he was not even sure he could be an official candidate for the job that he wanted.

[104]

Of course this speed was not just related to what he was leaving but to what he was going to—a political race. Salinger obviously was divided in his mind about entering this election contest. But reporters had observed a few intimations from others of the staff, not Salinger, and they had seen some things with their own eyes that made them feel that Salinger was not temperamentally suited to remaining in the Johnson regime. One man told this writer he first began to think about it when he saw the President with his press aide in Texas. He saw Mr. Johnson and Salinger riding along on horses and there was something about it that seemed quite incongruous with the temperament of the sophisticated and sensitive Salinger. For all his striped shirts and big cigars, Salinger is a literate and subtle man, and not disposed toward cornball humor and the folksy approach. This reporter said, "When I saw Lyndon having fun with Salinger and putting ten-gallon hats on him and so on, I just had a feeling Salinger wasn't going to wear that hat very long."

A plausible chain of reasoning assumed that Mr. Salinger could never have counseled the President to say what he said about the famous stereo hi-fi and about the kickback in advertising on the Johnson television station. Correspondents knew that many of Johnson's staff had been opposed to the general line of statements that the President had made. There is not much satisfaction in being an adviser whose advice is not taken, and perhaps that had something to do with Salinger's departure.

Some thought the departure of Pierre Salinger was so abrupt as to be rude. Some thought it was indicative of the fact that the new President had made the White House a difficult place in which to work. But the fact was that not a single person leaving indicated any resentment, and the staff which stayed on did an extraordinary job of welcoming newcomers and absorbing them into the organization. This process went off to the great credit of everyone, and the main credit surely goes to Mr. Johnson.

A staff member—from the "old" Kennedy side—told the writer, "Don't believe the portraits which make him into an ogre to work for. He is not an ogre. He's very demanding, he asks everything of you, and he gets irritated at what he thinks

[105]

is poor work. But he's an emotional person—he gives more blame *and* more praise than most employers. And the main thing is he is working just the same way you are. You may be working late but you know he is in there as late and very likely later, so you don't feel so sorry for yourself."

At the end of the early period, the man who had been an instant President had held together an excellent staff and administration. Very few cracks had appeared in the structure that others had labored so long to build. Very shortly people took this for granted. But it should not be forgotten that holding the structure together was difficult and was a genuine achievement of the Johnson administration.

5

At Home: From Closet Lights
to Civil Rights

THE WHITE HOUSE is a tremendously busy place. This may seem childishly obvious, but newcomers coming in from the outside are impressed over and over again with just that, its busyness. Under Johnson it became not only bustling and noisy, but at times confused. Yet in all the first months, there was no real blooper of confusion. There was no telegram sent wrong, no memo released by mistake, no real error of crossed wires. Yet there were a dozen chances a day—it sometimes seemed—for the stepped-up emergency machinery to break down in some important way.

The main business of the White House, as of every large command center, is communications. That means paper. On any day in the White House there are a dozen formal papers —statements, speeches, proclamations, bills, reports—to which something important *must* be done, and of which something public *may* be made. There are a hundred other documents not yet in the crisis or in the action stage.

The White House, then, is a busy, rushing publishing house. People are bringing in boxes of books and reports printed somewhere else, or people are putting together 8o-page statements. Or they are working on speeches which will all have to be mimeographed or multilithed, collated, stapled, and sent out to a waiting world.

When there is a major speech like the State of the Union Message, there are people working on it in clusters and all alone. There are people reworking it before and after the President has seen it. And it goes through a dozen drafts. There are people doing a section of it that has to be stitched into the middle of it at the appropriate place at the appropriate time. Meanwhile the middle of it is being changed into the end, but only one man knows that! The executives and the assistants are busy. They sit with dictating machines, notepaper, great yellow pads of ruled paper, and three or four telephones. And even the important assistants often have a typewriter at hand so that they can turn around and dash off a memo with their bare hands. Neatness does not always count at the White House. Speed nearly always counts. Accuracy is only vital.

Generally, when you call someone in the White House, you go through his secretary, and some of the White House secretaries must be among the best in the world. They can handle all sorts of things, take all sorts of messages, explain, "Oh, you are calling about clearance on Joint Defense Meeting. That has been taken care of and you are to go to the four-o'clock meeting."

These secretaries, and their bosses, will speak, many of them, in a quite brisk, staccato way. They almost talk in Morse code. In their speed will be the White House high tension, the crackling transmission lines of power.

"Get State to go over this thing entirely and mix in more of what the report said."

"Call in photographers and get the wire services."

"No, the Inter-Departmental has been shoved behind the Ambassador—it is now at 4 P.M."

"Well, keep trying Seattle. And report again on London."

Neither in the Kennedy nor Johnson administration has there ever been a White House staff meeting. There just isn't time to gather the crew together and plan a program. The program is happening.

The White House is a place where it is always today. The White House is a place where the reporters sometimes move so fast that they bump into people—the writer saw a reporter break an arm rushing out of the President's office one day—literally break an arm.

When a conference is held, there may be three stenographers, and what is being said will be typed up or mimeographed almost simultaneously while the conference goes on. Within minutes after a Presidential press conference is over, for example, a few pages of the transcript will be brought fluttering, and damp with fresh ink, into the press lobby. Then the other pages drift in and the stenographer may have put on a heading, "Conference on Panama and Related Subjects." But down the pages it will turn out that a question from a reporter had caused the President to make a statement about a present from Bobby Baker under the heading, "Panama and Related Subjects."

The White House is a thousand pieces of paper in motion, a few of which may change history for millions of people, some of which are fascinating and many of which are completely unmemorable and dull. And every one is important, for it represents action taken in the name of the man who in America has the unique responsibility of representing the entire country.

One week after he took office the President sent a memo to all government agencies urging thrift and frugality. He asked that they reexamine all their requests for funds for next year. In his first Congressional speech he had also referred to economy. The word began to spread through government offices. How much of this was going to be just talk?

Every senior government official who thought about politics at all—and that is 99.5 percent—was able to understand the message, or so he thought. It was a campaign year, so in order to get Congress to pass the tax cut bill the President was going to reduce government expenditures and give his administration *the reputation for economy*. The critics and the cynics surmised that the White House might not be too interested in economy but was all-out interested in the reputation.

People who had known Mr. Johnson a long time, however, knew that thrift to the point of frugality and stinginess was an inbred personal characteristic. Within a few weeks the Washington *Post* was to criticize the President severely for turning off lights in the White House. All over the country military bases had been closed or shrunk in size, and government spending was headed downwards for the first time in years. In the first two weeks the reaction of government employees was that the economy drive was a political gesture. They thought it was logical but purely political for the President to come into power talking about getting a dollar's worth for every dollar spent. Even Franklin Roosevelt, old-timers recalled, had run on a cut-the-budget platform, and in his first weeks in office had actually cut some expenditures.

Then it began to appear that the new President was quite serious about this program. Within ten days, Budget Director Kermit Gordon laid down a strong line to a meeting of executive officers of federal agencies. William D. Carey, Executive Assistant to the Budget Director, spoke perhaps even more strongly in a speech to Internal Revenue men and officials from other agencies.

Carey said that the belief that "the stress on manpower reductions and frugality is election-year politics and will blow over . . . is a fatal misreading of the signs."

No one had been quite so explicit about the President's intentions as Mr. Carey, and his speech was given extended newspaper coverage. Government employees began to believe this was "the word." Carey said, "We have been with the President often enough and long enough to know that his convictions on these matters run very deep. Other Presidents, including Mr. Kennedy, had strong feelings about government efficiency, but the force of President Johnson's attitude simply has no match. It is part of the man and his outlook, and it is here to stay."

Mr. Carey also warned his audience not to look on this as a sort of "numbers game, a sort of statistical run-around" and not to believe that "the smart operators know ways to beat it, as by contracting for work that would otherwise be done within the government agency." In a direct warning, Mr. Carey said, "No agency head with any respect for his commission is going to try to play tricks on the President."

Even at that early date the remarks and intimations from the

White House that some government workers were not really working very hard or that there were too many people clogging the corridors in some places had somewhat affected government workers' morale. It did not take much in the dark days after the assassination to make government workers feel even more depressed.

So Carey felt that he should say that it was just a myth or a rumor "that the era of the 'proud and lively' career service is ending, to be replaced by a sort of Dark Age in which we are to feel guilty about working for the Government . . . this is the kind of gripe mentality that can get started and do a lot of harm. All it takes is the ever-present office troublemaker to dish out this sort of poison, and we can depend on them to do their usual thorough job." Carey emphasized that the President was "proud of meritorious public service, just as he is angry at signs of laxity and featherbedding."

Speeches like Carey's and the stories in the paper sometimes made Mr. Johnson appear like a rather strict father. It seemed that Dad was determined that the place should be run with more work and less play—Heaven help you if he found the porch light burning after everybody was home. One government worker said, "You could feel a little as if a handsome and gay young father had died and a grandfather was taking over. The older man meant well and wanted to see you get the proper food and that you did what you should. But he couldn't make life seem as much fun anymore."

Economy is always a live subject in Washington. Everyone—even those in government—knows how to cut the budget in other agencies than his own. Everyone knows there are too many employees. The only trouble is deciding who should go.

The economy program was the subject of many jokes, much sweat, and probably a few tears. Next to the assassination and civil rights, it was probably the main topic of conversation in the capital through the early weeks.

By March 1 all government departments and agencies had issued their own memoranda about turning out lights when not needed. One agency even mentioned *closing Venetian blinds sometimes when lights were needed.*

The Treasury, in a circular to its employees, said:

In addition to the practical aspect of economy, there is a psychological factor . . . the public takes a critical view of buildings which are brilliantly lit at such times as it would be quite evident they are not being occupied by the working tenants. . . . Where it is necessary that certain lights be burned at night . . . it would be helpful if the Venetian blinds were lowered and then the slats tilted to close them.*

An Associated Press writer thought that perhaps Treasury officials realized Mr. Johnson could see their headquarters building from White House windows.

On Friday the thirteenth of December, Budget Director Kermit Gordon and his assistants stayed late in their offices. From time to time harried men with briefcases dismounted from taxicabs in front of Old State and ran up the stairs bringing in to Gordon their revised budget figures. Sometimes their final budget statement had merely been written out in pencil on a yellow pad of paper.

Gordon and his chief lieutenant stayed close to midnight, until the last man had reported in and they had gone over a preliminary total. Friday the thirteenth was the deadline for final budget figures.

As Mr. Gordon was just struggling into his trousers the next morning at seven o'clock, the telephone rang. No reader of this book has to be told who was on the other end of the line.

President Johnson had waked up wanting to know just what could be cut off the budget at that point. Director Gordon's answer was five hundred million dollars and ten thousand jobs. It was at this time that one official said that if the Budget Bureau had been asked to pass on the number of the Apostles, it would have reduced their number from twelve to ten. When a budget official heard this story he replied that Mr. Johnson would have cut the number to eight.

Gradually the story began to be clear. On June 30 there would be a net reduction of some five hundred to one thousand

* The Treasury also asked its employees to be careful to use all old paper clips and rubber bands and not throw them away. The directive said, "This kind of waste is certainly unnecessary. . . . Although the cost of paper clips and rubber bands is small for each individual office, the total cost to government is significant."

employees *instead of the seventy-five thousand more govern-ment workers* which the departments and agencies originally had requested. A Democratic President was trying to stem the tide of government spending. He was also trying to reverse the public picture of Democrats as "spenders" and Republicans as "savers."

The President never relaxed the pressure he was putting on the Budget Bureau and all government agencies—he had made some kind of resolve with himself not to bring in a budget over one hundred billion dollars.

That first Saturday he had met Mr. Gordon all the way in his determination to make this budget his budget. The very next day—the Sunday detailed in Chapter 3—he went over the basic figures with Gordon. Mr. Gordon said it would be a tough, tight schedule, but he could make it if he were determined to do so.

The President gave orders to his staff that the budget was to have top priority. He told Moyers and O'Donnell that in mak-ing up his schedule, they were always to see that Mr. Gordon had time to get in to see him. He gave Gordon virtually an open door so that in ensuing weeks the President and all his budget officials could wrestle over and over again with the figures.

One assistant to Gordon said in late December that Mr. Johnson seemed to have been in the White House for a year instead of only four weeks. He thought his grasp of the figures "seemed incredible" and there was no doubt that the President was making the decisions "pretty much by himself." When the President left for his Christmas visit to Texas, the budget was pretty well closed out so far as total figures were concerned.

As Cecil Holland wrote in the Washington *Star,* "Mr. Gordon prepared to relax for the first time in weeks. As he was about to leave his office [on Christmas Eve] the telephone rang. It was the President calling from his plane en route to Texas. He wanted a memorandum on manpower."

Working upon the budget concerns every activity of our huge government, in tiny detail and on the grandest scale imaginable. No one can imagine very clearly what it is like to spend one hundred billion dollars. But top officials of the Government try to work with such sums by breaking them down into smaller parts, and specific programs, and by comparing today's figures with those of the past. The men of the Budget Bureau, and of the Defense Department and the other large agencies, and most particularly in the White House, try to manage expenditures by judging the past and attempting to predict the future. So every budget involves a consideration of much of our foreign and domestic policies—and a judgment on where we are going.

Making decisions at one end of the budget may unsettle the other end. To cut the budget at any place requires a program and plan and some sense of all the wires (and red tape) which hold our government together. How much is our economy dependent upon military expenditures? How much can we afford to spend on space? Shouldn't we be starting more work in certain areas where the American dream is falling down? How much can be cut out of defense before we risk a chance of being unprepared?

When a family or a business plans a budget, it has to make some decisions about the life it wants to lead, and it has to make a lot of decisions about what will happen in the future. The same is true of the Government. One of the biggest controversies in Washington in Kennedy's administration concerned how much money we should put into missiles and how much we should put into manned bombers. Then when we were in the missile confrontation with Castro and Khrushchev, and Russian supply ships were steaming toward Cuba, we ordered a naval blockade, and we were very glad at that time that we had some "old-fashioned" naval ships to send in there. How much money should be put into planes or ships, or missiles or the State Department, or the Department of Agriculture?

When the President plunged into preparing the budget, he rolled up his sleeves literally and figuratively to work with matters that did not just involve money, but related directly to blood, sweat, and tears.

The President first mentioned lights in the White House in his random off-the-cuff remarks to the Internal Revenue Service tax collectors on February 11.

He began by saying, "I wouldn't want to be held to this, but

[114]

the light bill at the White House a few months ago was $5,000 a month. This month it is $3,000."

He explained further that "a lot of closets that had lights burning in them all day long and a lot of stairways that people didn't use, that had lights burning, a lot of rooms in here where the chandeliers were going full time when no one was in here were all used. . . ." This sentence did not seem to have any beginning or end, but his point was, "When people get economy conscious and just start watching things like we used to on the REA line* when we had a minimum bill of $250 a month and we never wanted to go over the minimum . . . things can be reduced."

The President, in his first mention of the White House lights bill, said, "It has not all been due to our efforts . . . some of it came about for other reasons . . . but we hope next month it will come down another $500 a month." The President said, "The people of the country, I think, will really appreciate when they realize you are saving $2,500 a month on electricity in the House in which you live."

He further sternly admonished the tax collectors to "go back home and see how much electricity you can save in the building in which you work. See how many lights you leave on when you go out at night."

The President constantly returned to this point. He directed White House electricians to change the doorframe switches in the mansion's closets. Now they don't snap on automatically when the closet door is opened, and, therefore, they are not burning up current when they are standing ajar.

When he had Budget Bureau officials in to witness the signing of his first federal budget, he said, "Someone told me that the light bill in the White House ran several thousand dollars a month. I challenged Mr. Valenti, and our maid this morning when I left . . . to turn off all those chandeliers when there is no one in the house. Mrs. Johnson had gone to New York, and I was the only one there, and I didn't require that much light."

On this occasion also he said, "I don't know how much we

* A reference to the Rural Electrification Authority in Texas.

saved. I want a bill for the last three months to see if we are making any headway. And see that that goes down to every government building. A stitch in time saves nine. You don't accumulate anything unless you save the small amounts."

He was also quite pleased to let it be known that Mrs. Johnson had gone to New York on a commercial airline flight—the "shuttle"—which is the equivalent of going tourist class or coach.

Once again, in his 100 days telecast, he said, "I don't believe that we are going to make the Treasury over by cutting out a few automobiles or turning out a few lights." But he added that it "is a good example when you walk through the corridor, and you see the closets where the lights burn all day and all night just because someone didn't turn them off."

A man who had worked with Johnson as Senator told this writer that when he left his office and then came back to find all the lights on the desk had been turned off, he would merely ask a secretary, "What time did he drop by?"

In the absence of cost documentation, there were those who refused to accept the President's estimation of the saving on electricity.

Representative Bob Wilson, Republican of California, doubted that the President could save two thousand dollars a month in the electric current bill of the White House. He made a speech discussing the calculation he had made—that the President would have to turn off "about two million one-hundred-watt bulbs for an hour" to save that kind of money.

The Republican National Committee spread far and wide Mr. Wilson's calculations: "Even if the President switched off the lights for a 14-hour period each night, he would have to turn off at least five thousand bulbs to effect the savings he claims. I doubt if there are that many light bulbs in the White House."

Representative Wilson considered the White House lights story to be "a tall Texas tale" and he went on unkindly to say, "If the President's estimates of the national economy are as far off as his estimates of savings effected by turning off the White House lights, the country is in for a pretty rough time."

[116]

Wilson figured the Capitol power rate averages about 1.2¢ per kilowatt hour.

Press Secretary Pierre Salinger, when asked about this at a briefing, cut off discussion by saying they were not going to discuss the White House light bill or phone bill, they never had and they never would. The Potomac Electric Power Company, which might ordinarily be interested in publicity stories about supplying electric current to the White House, was as secretive as the FBI on this matter.

Later it developed that the lights the President had turned out in the White House were all on the inside and that people who had complained about the outside being dim were mistaken. The outside of the White House, George Reedy insisted at one press briefing, was precisely the same as it had been for many years. He thought that all the hubbub, including quite a bit of mail which had come to the White House from tourists, made this a striking example of how people see what they want to see. Mr. Reedy, like Mr. Salinger before him, did not make any move to release the actual light bill or phone bill of the White House.

It appeared there would never be any more light on the light bill and it was seldom recalled that when the President first mentioned it he said, "I wouldn't want to be held to this . . ."

He had managed—perhaps with luck and perhaps with pluck and certainly with prestidigitation—to take credit and not to take credit for saving money in the dark. And apparently he had accomplished two purposes:

He had convinced government workers he meant it—save money!

He had convinced the voters he was a real penny pincher. They seemed to like it.

In late February the Louis Harris public opinion poll showed a handsome political result of the President's budget-cutting measures. The Harris poll found that, by an 81 to 19 percent vote, Americans gave the new President a favorable rating on his ability to keep spending under control. This was a sharp turn from the previous unfavorable score on spending-by-Democrats, which ran the other way, 35 to 65 percent, just before President Kennedy's death in November.

Mr. Johnson's economy measures, moreover, impressed Republican voters far more than Democrats, according to this poll. Thus the Louis Harris poll concluded that Mr. Johnson was accomplishing something which Presidents Truman and Kennedy never achieved. He was convincing "large numbers of Republican voters that a Democrat in the White House is not necessarily unfriendly toward business, nor economy."

Professional politicians believe that Louis Harris has no superior when it comes to political polling. The results of polls that he made were influential in determining President Kennedy's actions on a number of occasions. These polls were read all over Washington in the spring of 1964 in the belief that they showed the President was reaching the grass roots and getting some really new results.

What is the secret of Mr. Johnson's popularity with the public? To many observers the word *secret* is well-chosen. There is certain solid evidence that the public, with some tangible reasons, liked the tax cut and liked what they had heard about the budget cut. Obviously people believed that the Vice-President as he took over was doing quite a good job. Obviously, too, the public did not want to have three Presidents in the space of a year. So the natural inclination of the voter would be to vote for the man who was in there.

When all this was said, however, it did not seem to explain the great popularity of the new President. One view had it that while Mr. Johnson did not fire the imagination or really startle people with new ideas and programs, he did correctly understand the mood of the country. This view said the American psyche was searching for some peace and quiet and steady progress without alarms and crusades, and it was well epitomized by Vermont Royster who, after Mr. Johnson's television "conversation," wrote a widely read piece called "The Comfortable Man."

Royster, who is the editor of the *Wall Street Journal,* said that the television hour with the President "might well have been written by the same writer who does Dr. Kildare." He said the topics all dealt with *ailments,* such as poverty, com-

[118]

munism, death, and taxes. "All the symptoms were discussed with proper clinical gravity by young men seeking the answers." But, Mr. Royster wrote, "if there were any answers they escaped us, but just like Dr. Gillespie, the man in the black rocking chair listened gravely, nodded in occasional agreement and now and then pointed out a consideration overlooked by the questioner. He never showed impatience but always gave the feeling that he had thought about the matter beforehand and was patiently awaiting a few more X-rays or the pathologist's report from Saigon before making any momentous decision." Thus, said Royster, it was nothing like President Kennedy. It had "none of the young doctor's flashes of wit; rarely a smile, and even then a rather sad one." Thus, said Royster, it could be easily faulted, or even ridiculed by those who think "that Presidents, like doctors, should know all the answers for what ails us." Mr. Royster and many others wrote that the country was in the mood for a comfortable man.

The economy program was the main way in which President Johnson grasped the reins of the executive side of government.

In most other areas he had to deal with Congress—and in fact, the budget of course is submitted to Congress.

This book cannot cover the whole range of the Kennedy-Johnson program, but it can look at some of the record. The civil rights bill was not voted on in the Senate at the time this book went to press, but was on the front page every day. Another principal program of the President was the war on poverty.

Civil rights will probably remain the hottest domestic issue of the day, whether the bill itself is passed by the Senate or not. As the new President took office many Negro newspapers printed at length an interview that he had given in July, 1960, as a Vice-Presidential candidate:

> I think I have had to go through the same kind of struggles as the colored people. My family was poor and I was poor. My father worked for $150 a month. For two years, I had a job working for $1 a day.
>
> When time came for us kids to go to college, the money wasn't there. We couldn't go to the university. Because of all

that I had to suffer. I can appreciate the economic lot of the colored people.

I know what employment discrimination means to him. I know what educational discrimination means. I know what discrimination means.

At the time he took over, the Negro leaders generally expressed support of the President and joined in the chorus of voices which were calling for an end to extremism. Martin Luther King, however, did say that there could not really be a ban on protest demonstrations. Roy Wilkins of the NAACP said the nation should not expect a moratorium. He said that the subject of demonstrations was not brought up during this forty-five-minute session with the President, but meeting reporters afterward he said:

"If Congress continues to postpone action as though a man had not been murdered in Jackson, Mississippi, and as though four girls had not been killed in a church in Birmingham and as though the President of the United States had not been assassinated in this climate, there is nothing for Negroes to do but demonstrate."

By December 1, however, James Farmer, the National Director of the Congress for Racial Equality, had advised regional CORE leaders to give up any active demonstrations during the 30-day period of mourning. In a telegram sent to leaders, he said, "Our CORE chapters feel it inappropriate to engage in direct action projects immediately in the wake of the President's death. I concur in that feeling." Nonetheless, Mr. Farmer said that he thought each local chapter would have to decide "on the basis of the situation in its own locale" whether there might be an action program.

Despite the President's Congressional speech it also appeared an open question as to how many rank-and-file members of the Negro movement believed, as the leadership apparently believed, that Mr. Johnson was devoted wholeheartedly, personally as well as politically, to the cause of civil rights. And to counteract any such doubts, the President went immediately to work for passage of the civil rights bill.

Several times Mr. Johnson has described his position on civil rights with a parable from another Texan, the former Vice-President, John Nance Garner:

> He was a great poker player, and he told me once that there came a time in every game when a man had to put in all his stack. Well, I'm shoving in all my stack on this civil rights bill.

The bill went through the House by a good margin—290 to 130—on February 10, but everyone knew the real battle would be in the Senate. As Mr. Johnson went over the subject countless times with visitors, and in many speeches to delegations and special audiences, it became clear that he was doing all he could to push for this legislation.

"I am hopeful and I am an optimist," he said, "and I believe they can pass it, and I believe they will pass it, and I believe it is their duty to pass it, and I am going to do everything I can to get it passed."

It wasn't great prose—but it carried the message to the Senate and to the citizens who wanted to see their rights defended.

Many people believe that the acid test of any President is how well he can get his program through Congress, and this Congress facing this President promised to be one of the most interesting legislative-executive confrontations in years. A Congress already under severe criticism for being slow and unwieldy was going to be confronted for months and perhaps for years with a President who was considered to be one of the greatest Congressional leaders of American history. One of the main American challenges of our time is whether Congress can move fast enough in this fast-moving and complicated age. One of the greatest challenges to Mr. Johnson, in his beginnings or at any time, would be whether he could do better with Congress than his predecessors in office.

Within two weeks of taking office, the President had demonstrated that he was hoping to keep in constant touch with Congress through dozens of personal contacts, by telephone, by personal visits, and by unusual social affairs in the White House.

As Vice-President, Mr. Johnson had been out of things. Now it seemed almost that he was going to be President *and* Majority Leader, too.

In the first few days, the President not only went up to Capitol Hill to lunch with the Texas delegation, but he also made an unheralded visit to the Capitol office of Speaker McCormack. He conferred with House leaders in the "Board of Education" room, a traditional after-hours gathering place of the House hierarchy ever since John Nance Garner was Speaker.

In the White House, a team of staff people under Lawrence O'Brien maintained constant communication with Congressmen and mapped out a program of regular legislative visits to the White House. Neither Mr. Kennedy nor Mr. Johnson ever depended entirely on such things as their White House "leadership breakfasts" with Democratic leaders. Mr. Johnson took care to have private meetings with the Senate Republican leader, Everett Dirksen, of Illinois, and the next day he ate "thick bacon" with House Republican leader Charles A. Halleck (R., Ind.). He also had private talks with Senator Harry Flood Byrd (D., Va.) and Richard D. Russell (D., Ga.), the two men who had been the most opposed to a tax cut bill and to a civil rights bill. According to Washington stories, Senator Byrd had made it clear to him in his first week in office that there would have to be budget cuts before there could be a tax cut bill approved by the Congress. Neither party has ever spoken out explicitly on this matter, but in Washington legend, this is said to have been one of the key visits of the transition.

White House staffers say that the President shortly learned that he could not go on meeting everyone pell-mell, and a regular Congressional schedule was worked out. After all, there are 535 persons "up there," and the President could not very often do what he did on that December day, inviting hundreds of them to come on short notice for a party.

No one, however, should underestimate the effects of the unprecedented cordiality at the White House. The Congressmen's wives, even Republican ones, certainly remember when they have danced with the President, and were then taken on a tour of the White House by the First Lady and made to feel at home.

But Mr. Johnson was doing something else, however, more important than seeing Congressmen, more important than telephoning them and remembering to send them thank-you notes and handing out dozens of pens in exchange for a minor part in getting a bill passed. The President was seeking to bring Congress closer to the center of power.

The Congressmen were not only getting regular briefings by Secretary McNamara and Secretary Rusk, they were being asked at various foreign policy meetings what they thought the Government ought to do. They were almost given power of decision on important policy matters concerning Panama. On the Panama occasion, the President even asked for an informal vote, but he really did not receive any crisp answers. The President found that Congressmen might wish to make many many speeches about just what ought to be done, but they proved reluctant to speak out at a solemn session where their words might actually have counted.

So far as Congress was concerned, another major step of leadership from the President came at the first "Presidential Leadership Breakfast," a traditional periodic meeting at which the President has Congressional leaders to the White House to discuss proposed legislation. The breakfasts are one of the main avenues of communication between Congress and the White House. They are ordinarily held in the Executive Mansion and the men from Congress are Senate Majority Leader Mansfield, Senate Whip Humphrey, and Senator George Smathers; from the House the leaders are Speaker McCormack, Carl Albert, and Hale Boggs. Ordinarily those from the White House include Walter Jenkins, Lawrence O'Brien, Kenneth O'Donnell, and Valenti and Moyers.

The first Leadership Breakfast with President Johnson was held in the Cabinet Room. For the first time at these meetings Senator Carl Hayden appeared, and since then he has met regularly with the group (being No. 3 in the line of succession if something should happen to President Johnson and Speaker McCormack). At that first meeting President Johnson informally brought in George Meany, head of the AFL-CIO, to say "hello." He had been visiting the President at his home (LBJ was still in The Elms).

At that first breakfast, the President made it crystal clear that he wanted all of the appropriation bills promptly passed. There were men at the meeting who said it couldn't be done. The President asked, with some irritation, "How in the world could the Congress justify not being able to provide money for the Departments of Government and indeed not even being able to provide money for its own operations?"

The President in the latter case was referring to the legislative appropriation, which at that time was dormant and apparently dead for the session.

At that time there were many appropriations still to be acted upon, such as foreign aid, agriculture, public works, and the money for Congress itself. Following this legislative meeting, the President called Party Whip Humphrey into his office and made it clear that he wanted the Senator to go to work to see that those bills passed. Senator Humphrey, on his return to the Capitol, held a press conference and announced, "We are going to pass every appropriation bill before this first session of the 88th Congress adjourns."

The reporters seemed rather skeptical but Humphrey said that the President had insisted upon it and "I am going to follow his orders."

At that first breakfast, the men from Capitol Hill had no doubt that the new President was going to take a constant and direct hand in the affairs of Congress. At that meeting he went over every major bill that was pending. He bore down particularly upon the tax bill, the civil rights bill and the foreign aid appropriations.

In comparing Presidents Kennedy and Johnson at these meetings it is said that the main difference lies in their different personalities, and, paradoxically, a greater willingness by Johnson to be open with them—and at the same time an occasional growling comment to indicate that if matters came to a conflict it would be a rousing one. For despite all that is written about the "new closeness" of the President and the Congress, it should not be overlooked that some of the closeness might also add

[124]

warmth to an open conflict if that should come. As one Senator told the writer, "Jack Kennedy did not want any fight with Congress—but Lyndon makes it clear he would fight if he had to. And he knows where all the bodies are buried up here."

In mid-December, before the President had been in office a month, he decided that there would have to be even at this early date a historic showdown with Congress—with the House —over the issue of foreign aid, and specifically related to the shipment of wheat to Russia.* The Republicans were out to cut down drastically on foreign aid and to pass the Mundt amendment, which would hold back on the sale of wheat to Russia.

The question was whether that vote should be put off until later and whether the President should risk his prestige by asking for a vote in a matter in which he might well lose. It was considered that the world might feel that there was a weak President in the White House if he pressed this for a vote and lost the vote.

The President decided that the gauntlet was down and he had to meet the challenge. It appeared to him that if there were no vote he might be thought of abroad as a weak President. Before the great push was over on this foreign aid bill, some extraordinary measures had been taken. Many of the Congressmen had headed for their homes when this decision was made over the weekend of December 21.

The President and his aides got on the telephone and the first "Congressional air-lift" in history was arranged to pick up some of the members at their homes and fly them back to Washington in time for the vote.

To speed along an atmosphere of goodwill, on December 23 on two hours' notice the President decided to have a reception at the White House for members of Congress. This turned out to be a smashing success and it was here that the President stood on a chair to make a brief peroration.

The next morning, December 24, the House of Representatives met—perhaps for the first time in history—at 7 A.M. to make its decision on whether to put a wheat deal into Premier

* This was the same amendment and bill on which the Senate had voted the day after President Kennedy's funeral.

Khrushchev's Christmas stocking and a vote of confidence into Mr. Johnson's.

The quality of debate on that winter morning was not epochal, although the meeting hour was. No one could remember that Congress had ever met at that hour before. Representative John J. Rhodes, Republican of Arizona, spoke against sending any such wheat present to Premier Khrushchev because, he said, "Khrushchev does not believe the Messiah was born 2,000 years ago."

The President's friend, Representative Carl Albert of Texas, Majority Leader of the House, said this would be a Christmas present for the President and would show the world whether he would be a weak or a strong President.

The vote finally turned out to be strictly along party lines. All but two Republicans voted against the measure. The vote was 189 for and 158 against.

The House was able to adjourn before 10 and the entire capital went out to meet the Christmas spirit.

Did the President really have to go through with a showdown with Congress? One Washington writer with many years of experience said, "If Mr. Johnson had dodged this one we think he would have been a dead duck; as it is, he showed steely nerve and put on as pretty a display as we have seen for some time. A strong hand is at the wheel."

Mr. Johnson's great idol, Franklin D. Roosevelt, had found a figure of enormous political appeal when he promised to help "the forgotten man." Thirty years later Mr. Johnson with another rallying cry, "The attack on poverty," was again promising to help the man who again had been forgotten—the estimated one-fifth of Americans who have not been able to enjoy the benefits of our generally affluent society. Actually a number of programs to attack various aspects of poverty were in beginning stages at the time Mr. Kennedy was shot, and a few days after the President's death, Arthur Schlesinger, Jr., revealed that Mr. Kennedy's 1964 program would have included a comprehensive plan against poverty. Just before he left the White House for the last time, Kennedy had discussed the poverty problem with Walter H. Heller, Chairman of the Council of Economic Advisers. Before them was a memo about using some of the proposed poverty program as a measure of "economic stabilization."

Four days later, on that Saturday after the Friday assassination, Mr. Heller saw Mr. Johnson for a half hour or so and the two of them discussed it and the President eagerly seized upon the idea.

On Wednesday, December 4, in a message to the American Public Welfare Association, President Johnson called for an all-out national attack on poverty. He felt that "current programs to reduce poverty and dependency in this country are not nearly enough," and said that "if the attack on poverty is to be successful in the year ahead, we must begin now to involve ourselves much more actively than ever before. Many observers, including those cynics who believed that nearly everything Mr. Johnson did was politically motivated, felt that he had a deep emotional commitment to what he named the "Attack on Poverty." This program certainly had its beginning under President Kennedy but in the emphasis and momentum it now has, it may decently be called a "Johnson Program."

Critics said the main Johnson contribution was to give the program or the segments of a program a new name and organization. That should not be belittled. It needed a new name. There is no excitement in "urban renewal," "area redevelopment" and "manpower retraining," but there is excitement in *a war on poverty*. The Johnson approach is considered great politics but perhaps it is more; perhaps it is great leadership.

In fact, the beginnings of the Poverty Program are believed to go back even earlier than the fall of 1963. According to Douglass Cater, in the spring of 1963, Walter Heller had begun to "look beyond the tax cut and ponder the inevitable down-turn in the Government's rate of spending. . . . He recognized the combined advantages of a broad attack on . . . deep-seated economic distress. . . ."

On June 3, 1963, Heller had sent a memorandum to his staff asking "specifically, what lines of action might make up a practical anti-poverty program in 1964?" Heller even made a speech

[127]

at the Communications Workers' convention, but felt that he failed to get much response "from either his audience or the press."

President Kennedy had, according to Cater, a real appreciation of the basic idea because he had been sensitive to the economic decline in Massachusetts and because in the West Virginia Presidential primary against Hubert Humphrey he "had been fully exposed . . . to poverty of a scale and severity that he had never before seen."

So the key Kennedy men believe that the late President, if he had lived, would have tried to change the pattern in which only a small part of the federal budget was devoted to federal welfare services.

The new President sent his message on poverty to Congress on March 14, with some stirring words to the effect that the objective was "total victory." The total program put together some old and new ideas and proposed an expenditure of a billion dollars.

About four hundred million of this sum would go to help some 380,000 underprivileged young people in the first year to break the cycle of poverty through job training and education in various centers and communities. Another three hundred fifteen million was to be spent in stimulating local communities through the nation into waging anti-poverty wars of their own. One novel proposal would authorize federal loans to nonprofit corporations to acquire land and develop it into family-sized farms.

The President had already named, as his "personal chief of staff" for the war against poverty, Sargent Shriver, Director of the Peace Corps. Mr. Shriver had explained that he did not plan to resign from the Peace Corps, but it was expected that if the program were approved he would resign and become full-time head of the anti-poverty program. Mr. Shriver had been working on it for weeks at the time the proposal was sent to Capitol Hill on March 15. The town had been buzzing with reports of theoretical and practical discussions and outright conflict among government agencies and experts with different opinions as to how to defeat poverty. Many of the old-line agencies such as the Department of Labor or the Department of Health, Education and Welfare felt that, to a great extent, they were fighting every day in a war against poverty, and they thus resented the newcomer.

The President did not propose a super-agency and he proposed many different projects, some of which would be administered by the regular cabinet agencies such as Labor and HEW. The rural loan project would be under the Department of Agriculture.

Already in existence is an Area Redevelopment Administration program which would be enlarged to help areas which had been hard hit by depression or the depletion of natural resources. At present the area redevelopment program is limited to giving out loans to industries locating in surplus labor areas. As Mr. Johnson described it, "The war on poverty is not a struggle simply to support people to make them dependent on the generosity of others. It is a struggle to give people a chance."

It was a certainty that the program would be the subject of much political discussion, not only before but even after election. It was also clear that the President, intellectually and emotionally, considered this very much his program. He did not in any way minimize the fact that plans for the program had been begun under President Kennedy, but there could be no doubt that he regarded this as "his baby." His tour of depressed areas in April was an enormous success from the standpoint of publicity and public reaction and he obviously expected to carry the war to the enemy.

In sum, the battle—most people felt it would eventually be a battle—between this President and this Congress promised to be one of the historic executive-legislative struggles of American history.

At the end of the hundred days most observers thought that Mr. Johnson had a good chance of doing much better with Congress than Mr. Kennedy had done, and several reasons were advanced for this belief. One, of course, was his greater legislative experience. Another was his general orientation to action. Mr. Johnson would take his case to the people and put leverage on the Congress that way, if using every means of Washington leverage failed. Some said that Mr. Kennedy would give Congressional visitors a reasoned case for his proposals and then walk them courteously toward the door. Mr. Johnson called them up the next day or used some other means of follow-up. And the man sometimes known on Capitol Hill as "Old Trick or Treat" would be prepared to get tough in a way that Mr. Kennedy would not. Very early, Karl E. Meyer of the Washington *Post* thought, "In fact, Lyndon Johnson may not only do no worse than Mr. Kennedy; he may do better."

Mr. Meyer's reasoning was that the new President would have a honeymoon period, that the Democratic majority in Congress had the duty to fall behind the President in an election year, and that Mr. Johnson succeeds to office in "the emotional afterglow of a popular President. . . ."

Ahead of us, as this is written, were major programs in the Congress.

Foremost was the civil rights bill, passed by the House but tied up in the Senate. Most observers thought the civil rights bill would pass—perhaps with minor changes—but this by no means appeared certain.

The foreign aid bill, the smallest appropriation program requested since the program began, was still not approved. Although Mr. Johnson was very persuasive, he was not capable of absolute miracles. For example, he arranged for Representative Otto L. Passman of Louisiana, the principal opponent of foreign aid, to come down and discuss the foreign aid bill. The talk was loud and long, but in the end, according to *The New York Times,* an administration official said that Johnson "got zero." There is no evidence that any more will come of this with Passman than came after Mr. Passman was taken to see John Kennedy. "Never bring that man here again," JFK is said to have told his aides.

The "war on poverty" was a program with many different packages that would require consideration by many Congressional committees. Few observers were willing to predict that the President would get most of it through.

Western Congressmen were staging a drive to put import quotas on meat. The administration is against this as a threat to negotiations with other countries, but in the end, some experts felt, the administration might give way.

The President had begun to realize that he could telephone Congressmen and Senators too often. If he gave them too many affairs at the White House, it would have a diminishing effect. Sooner or later they would resent his "coming up from downtown" and "interfering" too much on Capitol Hill.

6

"The Baker Family Gave Us a Stereo Set"

IN THE PLAY *Green Pastures* there comes a time when the actor playing the part of "de Lawd God Almighty" throws up his hands at the tragedies he sees on earth. He exclaims, "Even being God ain't no bed of roses."

Most adult Americans appreciate the fact that the Presidency is very far from being a bed of roses. The events of February 6 and February 7 give a clear idea of some of the pressures and perils of the job.

On Thursday, February 6, as part of his program to woo the press, President Johnson went to luncheon with key officials of *The New York Times.* Many important persons, kings and queens and Presidential candidates, have gone to these extraordinary off-the-record luncheons, but this was the first time a President had gone there while he held the office. The initiative for this meeting came from the White House, which in those days was using persuasion and pressure with many parts of the press.

Three days before the luncheon, Secret Service men and New York City police swarmed over the building near Times Square. They went from the sub-basement to the tower to determine where they would put their men on the day of the visit. At eight o'clock that Thursday morning patrolmen working for the *Times* checked every entrance. Each employee had his packages or briefcase inspected. By the middle of the morning 110 federal, city and plant security men were at various posts throughout the building—in the tower high above the fourteenth floor, near the machinery that controls the elevators, and on the fifteenth floor at the air-conditioning ducts that feed the board room. They were in odd little storage attics directly above the board room. On the twelfth floor they patrolled a roof that overhangs the publisher's dining room. They were also in the sub-basement pressroom and near the power machinery of Consolidated Edison.

When he arrived, Mr. Johnson went to the fourteenth floor for a brief reception and then down to the eleventh floor to the luncheon in the publisher's dining room. These two floors and the main lobby were overrun with police and detectives. They watched every office door and stairway exit. They checked every telephone booth to see that it was empty and did not conceal a crouching man.

Also as part of the preparation, three "hot" telephone lines to the White House were installed by the New York Telephone Company. There was one in the lobby, one in the foyer of the publisher's dining room with an extension in the pantry, and another on the fourteenth-floor receptionist's desk. Each phone carried a disk which said simply WHITE HOUSE. As the time of the President's arrival approached, Secret Service men guarded each phone. If anyone were to pick one up he would be in immediate touch with the White House switchboard.

Just before noon a Secret Service agent brought in a large canvas bag and took out an upholstered folding chair which he put at the President's place in the dining room on the eleventh floor. This chair is lower and wider than the normal dining chair. For a tall man like the President it is more comfortable than the ordinary chair for long banquets. Accordingly, it is carried by the President on every trip. In this case he was traveling overnight to New York, speaking at two long evening affairs, and speaking at the *Times* luncheon. The chair went with him to each stop.

During the noon hour the street outside began to fill up with

[133]

curious spectators and various formations of mounted and ordinary police, not to say innumerable plainclothes detectives. The area was blocked off with wooden police barricades, pedestrians were kept back from the entrance, and police also asked people to close windows of office buildings on the street and to stand back from the windows. No one was permitted to sit by any window such as that which overlooked the motorcade in Dallas on November 22.

The Secret Service had of course gone over the luncheon menu and checked out every cook and waiter. There was a man who double-checked the flower arrangements put in the center of the table. The flowers had to be brought in in a transparent glass container so that the decorations could be inspected.

The President's remarks, like the remarks of all guests at a *New York Times* publisher's luncheon, were strictly off the record. This procedure enables the guests to speak freely and engage in question-and-answer discussion without a feeling that the slightest remark might be made the subject of a news story. Clifton Daniel sat near the President at the table and reported the luncheon for *Times Talk,* published by the *Times* for its employees. Here are some of Daniel's observations:

> The President started talking in a very low voice, so low that people at the ends of the table had difficulty hearing at first. He seemed to be preoccupied—perhaps because of the news from Cuba. The questions started slowly. Those at the table hesitated to intrude on the President's reverie. Turner Catledge made a wisecrack. Everybody laughed except the President. His thoughts seemed to be elsewhere.
>
> At first the President looked tired, but otherwise fit. His face was tan, and there was no flabbiness anywhere. He was quietly dressed, wearing a fresh white shirt with a tab collar, a figured gray tie, pearl cuff links and a dark suit.
>
> After he had had a bit to eat, he warmed up, and in the end seemed reluctant to leave. He twice asked if anybody had any further questions.

The President was not by any means completely bowed down. He showed his sense of humor when he began to talk about the exorbitant use of electricity at the White House. He said, "Now you take the electric light bill at the White House . . ." He then fumbled in his left-hand coat pocket and came out with a piece of paper. "I think I have it right here."

One of the editors said later that the things he would bring out of his pocket "looked just like the stuff in my pocket . . . unpaid bills and unanswered mail."

While the President ate there were many telephone calls on the hot phones but he was not interrupted. After the meeting, however, he did go out to the foyer of the dining room to take a call. Then he came back and told the luncheon guests about some bad news which he had just received about Cuba. Just before he got to the *Times* the news of Cuba's decision to cut off the water supply to Guantanamo had come in. The President had received the latest word on that particular question. He urged the guests to leave because, "I have got to take another call, and this is the most convenient place because this is a White House phone."

When the President came out of the phone booth he gave the editors a little bit more news about Cuba—off the record. Then he was overheard to say one thing which could be on the record: "You have very great responsibilities here."

In the account which Clifton Daniel wrote for *Times Talk* he did not say anything about the Bobby Baker case. He did not say it was mentioned or not mentioned. As a matter of fact, the matter *was* mentioned, in an offhand, lighthearted manner. But the next day brought proof that *The New York Times,* Presidential visit or no Presidential visit, would still carry "All the News That's Fit to Print."

The very next day a reporter for the *Times* was at the White House to give people there an advance look at the ugliest story of the Bobby Baker stories.

The luncheon was Thursday, and Pierre Salinger ate heartily with the President and the *Times.* On Friday, February 7, Mr. Salinger had a personal call from a distinguished reporter for the *Times.* Mr. Cabell Phillips showed Mr. Salinger a story which he planned to publish—and did publish—in *The New York Times* the next day (February 8).

It was this story by Phillips which said that the White House was using secret documents in an attempt to strike down the principal Bobby Baker witness. The witness, who had appeared several times before the Senate Rules Committee, was Don B. Reynolds, the insurance man who had testified about Mr. Johnson's hi-fi set and the matter of the "kickback" advertising on the Johnson television station.

Back on November 22, the Friday of the assassination, it will be remembered, the rotund insurance man was being quizzed by investigators for the Senate Rules Committee, and his interrogators got from him a startling story. They were looking for information on the Bobby Baker case. That afternoon they got a whole new angle to their investigation.

Don Reynolds had made Baker a partner in his insurance brokerage business in the Washington suburb of Silver Spring, Maryland. Reynolds had wanted a partner who knew his way around town and had political connections. Someone gave him the name of Bobby G. Baker, the Senate Secretary for the Majority. Baker was a man who was said to know "just about everybody," and Reynolds at that time thought him a good choice.

Reynolds disclosed to the investigators that Baker's influence had led to a big life insurance sale. His customer: Lyndon B. Johnson.

In the course of the secret questioning, one of the investigators left the room. While outside, he learned that President Kennedy had been shot and killed. But Reynolds was not told that he was now talking about the President of the United States. The insurance man continued, unaware then that he was to become the center of a storm much larger than he had expected.

Reynolds that day was being given a preliminary interview, in the customary procedure which often occurs before a witness appears formally before a Congressional committee. (Reynolds' testimony was not given formally to the Committee until mid-January, and not released to the press until January 20.)

But as he went to bed that November night Reynolds and a few others knew that Washington would soon have a lively new "scandal." That night Washington spoke of nothing except the death of the President. But Reynolds surmised that one day soon they would be talking about a stereo hi-fi and an alleged "kickback" advertising fee on a Texas television station.

It seems safe to assume that through the December weeks of mourning and through the January return to normality, the President of the United States knew that he would soon be the subject of political attack which had actually begun—secretly—on the same day he became President. In those weeks and to the present day Mr. Johnson's life was being greatly affected by what these two very different unknown men, Oswald and Reynolds, had done on one afternoon—with bullets in Dallas, and with charges in Washington. Just what were Mr. Reynolds' charges?

According to his affidavit to the Rules Committee, Reynolds wrote $100,000 worth of insurance on Mr. Johnson's life in 1957, after Mr. Johnson had suffered a heart attack in 1955. Then, said Reynolds, Walter Jenkins, then and now a top LBJ aide, had called Reynolds and arranged for him to purchase $1,208 worth of advertising time at the LBJ Company-owned KTBC-TV in Austin, Texas. Reynolds said this was done as a "kickback." Also, Reynolds said that Bobby Baker, Johnson's ever-present Senate assistant in those days, had suggested that Reynolds buy a stereo set and install it in Johnson's home. This was the famous stereo hi-fi. And the cost was said to be $584.75.

Later, Walter Jenkins gave the committee an affidavit denying the charge about KTBC-TV, saying that he "had no knowledge of the TV advertising arrangement." This denial did not quiet the Republicans or other critics. Jenkins did not go before the committee to testify. And he gave no interviews and answered no questions.

Jenkins' affidavit and failure to testify had been a many-days' sensation in Washington, coming on top of weeks of stories and rumors about Baker. Now, it developed, the White House was determined to head off the growing criticism from the press and from Capital Hill. The Cabell Phillips story told what some of the top people in the White House had been doing for a few days before the President's visit to the *Times*.

The headline at the top of the page of *The New York Times* that day electrified Washington: WHITE HOUSE AIDES SEEK TO IMPUGN BAKER WITNESS.

The secondary headline was ATTEMPT TO USE SECRET U. S. DOCUMENTS TO CAST DOUBT IN PRESS ON REYNOLDS, WHO TES-

TIFIED ON GIFT TO JOHNSON. To many this was the ugliest development of the Baker story.

The lead sentence showed how far afield the newspapers might depart from the story which apparently White House aides wanted them to print—namely, that Reynolds was an unreliable witness. The story of what Reynolds had said or the story of his record became secondary at this point to *the story of what the White House aides were doing*.

The lead sentence was "Persons within and close to the Johnson administration have attempted to use secret government documents to impugn the testimony of a witness in the Robert G. Baker case." The story then went on to identify Reynolds as the man who had told the Senate committee about the hi-fi and so on.

Then the story explained that some reporters and editors "have been advised by persons in the White House that Mr. Reynolds is an unreliable witness." The story said that in several instances individual newsmen and news executives had been read excerpts from what were purported to be reports by either Air Force intelligence or the FBI, and these reports were supposed to contain "derogatory information on Mr. Reynolds' background and his reputation for veracity."

The news story pointed out that "Wednesday and yesterday" Drew Pearson had published articles purporting to describe Mr. Reynolds' background and characterizing him as the man "who has brought reckless charges in the past. . . ."

The White House Press Secretary, Pierre Salinger, was asked on Friday whether the White House "had a hand" in getting the Reynolds material to Mr. Pearson. Mr. Salinger answered, "I am positive it did not." Mr. Pearson also denied it.

The Phillips story, however, said that "the *Times* has established that direct approaches were made by persons in the White House to at least two publications in an effort to have them alter or suppress articles based on the Reynolds testimony."

Phillips wrote that in the case of a third publication a White House aide volunteered the information that Reynolds was not to be believed. He placed the time of these attempts at around Friday, January 17, the last day of Mr. Reynolds' testimony.

At that time the Rules Committee said that a full transcript of the hearings for those two days would be made public the next Monday, January 20.

Then, the *Times* account went on, several reporters learned that Friday afternoon the substance of Mr. Reynolds' testimony and wrote articles based on this information. At least two of them took their articles to the White House press office to see Andrew T. Hatcher, Associate Press Secretary. In at least one instance, said the *Times,* Mr. Hatcher took the reporter's copy and absented himself from his office for approximately 20 minutes. When he returned he told the reporter that the White House had no comment to offer. "Later that afternoon, however, the reporter's editor received a telephone call from a well-known aide to President Johnson.

"The aide told the editor that the story was inaccurate in certain details concerning Mr. Johnson's understanding about the source of the gift. He suggested, according to the editor, that the paper might want to kill the article outright, or at least postpone publication until the next week when the facts could be checked against the official transcript."

This editor said that he made some changes but had ordered it printed. When he compared the original article with the original transcript two days later, he found *his reporter had been accurate the first time.*

That the White House had FBI and other intelligence reports on Mr. Reynolds was known to a number of reporters, but this information had not been available to the Rules Committee when it called Mr. Reynolds to testify. So in addition to the questionable matter of using secret documents in this way with reporters, the maneuvering had bypassed the regular Congressional investigative procedure. Senators on the Hill, and not merely Republican Senators, were irritated that the Executive side of the government had known about this evidence bearing on the investigation but had not let them know anything about it. They did not like the idea of learning about it through the newspapers.

Other newspapers picked up the story so that in the afternoon the Washington *Star* reported that "several major newspapers . . . published stories suggesting that members of the Johnson administration purposely have leaked official information. . . ."

The fact that the White House aides had not gone to work until January 17 raises the question of *just when did the White House learn of Reynolds' story?* One would think that some Senator must have told Jenkins and/or the President, soon after the assassination. Neither Mr. Jenkins nor the President has ever said anything for publication on what Phillips—and later, others—wrote about White House aides using "secret government documents to impugn Reynolds." *

The February 6 column by Drew Pearson had been entirely devoted to derogatory information about Don Reynolds. The opening three paragraphs give the theme of the column:

> The more you examine the records of Don Buck Reynolds, star witness in the Bobby Baker case, the more you wonder how responsible Senators could have let such a witness testify.
>
> Especially hard to understand is how responsible Republicans, such as Senators John Sherman Cooper of Kentucky, Hugh Scott of Pennsylvania, and Carl Curtis of Nebraska, all members of the Rules Committee, could have pressed their attack in view of Reynolds's background.
>
> Reynolds came out of the Air Force as a captain, then went into the State Department as a Foreign Service Officer, a position he left under a cloud. Then he reentered the Air Force, from which he was ordered discharged, until pressure from potent solons on Capitol Hill permitted him to resign.

Then Pearson said that official records of the State Department and Air Force had material on Reynolds—about "his German mistress . . . about black market operations . . . that one of the Senators with whom Reynolds worked was Joe McCarthy . . . that a State Department report on Reynolds states . . . that Reynolds was unsuitable as a Foreign Service officer . . . that a security review board in the U. S. Air Force . . . concluded in 1953 that Reynolds' past led to a reasonable belief that he was a security risk. . . ."

The Washington *Post* at the end of the column added these two paragraphs, giving Reynolds a chance to answer Pearson's statements:

* At the morning briefing on Friday, February 7, Mr. Salinger denied that the White House had any hand in the release to Drew Pearson of derogatory information from government files.

Reynolds has denied the statements concerning the German girl, those alleging black market dealings with Russian military officers and those concerning his relations with the late Senator Joseph R. McCarthy.

He further said he had no knowledge of the State Department report on him or of the efficiency report on his duty tour. . . .

The New York *Herald Tribune* on February 13 reported that neither the White House nor the Pentagon would even say whether there was such a memo as the Air Force report which Pearson had described. Copies of this memo were part of a confidential memorandum to editors sent out by Drew Pearson in connection with his columns of February 5th and 6th. The memo was signed by Benjamin W. Fridge, Special Assistant to the Secretary of the Air Force for manpower and reserve forces. The memo, according to the *Tribune,* reportedly said in part:

> I feel you should be aware of some of the circumstances surrounding the military service of former Maj. Don B. Reynolds, who testified before the Senate Rules Committee in the Bobby Baker case the day before yesterday.

Dom Bonafede of the *Tribune,* and Cabell Phillips of the *Times* both pursued Arthur Sylvester, Assistant Defense Secretary for Public Information, to try to get him to acknowledge the existence of the memo and to release it officially. They were unsuccessful.

Jack Anderson, the employee of Pearson who sometimes signs the column *The Washington Merry-Go-Round,* blasted *The New York Times* on February 12. He said that "for three years during the Kennedy administration *The New York Times* was the number one news favorite around the White House." He said that "almost every ambassadorial appointment, almost every sub-Cabinet change, almost every piece of legislation Mr. Kennedy planned was leaked to *The New York Times,* first." So Mr. Anderson's reaction was, "It's only natural that the *Times* seethes with professional jealousy when it sees another newsman apparently getting an inside track." He wrote that President Johnson "went out of his way to have dinner with the moguls of the *Times* . . . but it didn't do any good. . . .

[141]

Twenty-four hours later they kicked him in the teeth with a front-page story accusing him of leaking the Don Reynolds documents."

Anderson also said again that "the White House did not leak the documents on Don Reynolds, on the contrary, Mr. Johnson's staff seemed rather timid and worried when they learned about the documents." He said, "I am certain of this because I know where they came from."

As the Washington *Post* put it on February 8: "How classified documents . . . were leaked to a news columnist became the center of a full-blown White House news management controversy. . . ."

The *Wall Street Journal, The New York Times* and the Chicago *Tribune* all printed stories which said the administration did indeed have a hand in leaking the documents.

L. P. McLendon, Chief Counsel for the Senate Rules Committee, said that he had wanted to get this material but had been denied it on grounds that it was classified. Meanwhile, some newsmen who requested the files also were told they were unavailable, while Mr. Pearson said, "It took a lot of sleuthing to dig out the material, the White House did not help and in fact was very uncooperative." Pearson claimed that "the White House seemed flabbergasted when I told them about Reynolds' amazing record."

An FBI spokesman insisted that Pearson never got material from the FBI, and he also denied there had been any request from the White House to make information on Reynolds available to newsmen.

On the morning of February 8, Drew Pearson once again led off with material attacking Don Reynolds but this time did not devote his entire column to it. His point this day was that "the old files of the Senate Judiciary Committee, the State Department personnel records and Air Force records contain the story of how the Air Force tried to throw out Major Don B. Reynolds in 1953 but was overruled by powerful solons on Capitol Hill."

In the same paper in which Pearson's column appeared there was an interview with Don Reynolds which said, "I believe that any and all of Mr. Pearson's comments have no bearing whatsoever on the sequence of events regarding Bobby Baker, Walter

Jenkins, Matt McCloskey and Lyndon Johnson." (Mr. McCloskey is a Washington contractor who has been awarded many government contracts and whose name has been mentioned in connection with Bobby Baker and other Capitol Hill figures.)

Reynolds said that he did not wish to engage in a point-by-point exchange with Pearson, but that on other occasions he had denied or contradicted many of the main points made by Pearson or by Walter Jenkins. Reynolds on that day said that:

> The then-Senate Majority Leader thought enough of me and my reliability to personally come to the Senators' entrance to the Senate chamber to receive his policy and thank me for having obtained it for him.
>
> I have read in his biography that he thought well enough of this policy I had just delivered to wave it around the Senate floor and explain that he had been issued a normal life policy following his heart attack.

Mr. Reynolds said that actually, in terms of insurance rating, the President "had a high hazard rating" and did not have a normal life insurance policy.

The President's first reference to the Baker case came on January 23, two months and one day after the assassination. It was six days after the Reynolds testimony, and three days after the story was released.

That day the President had called an impromptu press gathering, but *not* a press conference. The meeting's ostensible purpose was a statement on the current U. S. attitudes toward Panama. At the end of his statement about Panama, a reporter asked a question which most of the other reporters thought had been arranged in advance: "Mr. President, before you go I wonder if you could entertain another question or so. For example, how do you think things are going up on the Hill?"

The President discussed how the cultural bill had gone through, the appropriations bill had passed before Christmas, and the education bills were completed. He mentioned the civil rights bill and the tax bill. His wording was noteworthy because he used the expression "we" as "*We* finished up the appropriation bill before we went home Christmas." This was the legislative "we," a phrase he had used for years when he was Majority Leader and which stayed with him through the early months of his time in the White House.

Then to the surprise of many of the reporters present he turned to the Bobby Baker story and discussed his life insurance and the stereo set. He did not say anything about the alleged kickback in the form of advertising on the LBJ television station.*

—You are also writing some other stories, I think about an insurance policy that was written on my life some seven years ago and I am still here. The company in which Mrs. Johnson and my daughters have a majority interest, along with some other stockholders, were somewhat concerned when I had a heart attack in 1955 and in 1957 they purchased insurance on my life made payable to the company. And the insurance premiums were never included as a business expense, but they thought that was good business practice in case something happened to me so Mrs. Johnson and the children wouldn't have to sell their stock on the open market and lose control of the company. That insurance was purchased here in Washington and on a portion of the premiums paid Mr. Don Reynolds got a small commission. Mr. George Sampson, the general agent for the Manhattan Insurance Company, handled it and we have paid some $78,000 in premiums up-to-date and there is another $11,800 due next month which the company will probably pay to take care of that insurance.

There is a question which has also been raised about a gift of a stereo set that an employee of mine made to me and Mrs. Johnson. That happened some two years later, some five years ago. The Baker family gave us a stereo set. We used it for a period and we had exchanged gifts before. He was an employee of the public and had no business pending before me and was asking for nothing and so far as I knew expected nothing in return any more than I did when I had presented him with gifts.

I think that that is about all I know that is going on on the Hill, but I hope that covers it rather fully. That is all I have to say about it and all I know about it.

* Newspapers in editorials kept asking him to answer to this question. No reporter has asked him at a press conference and he has not volunteered any answer as this book goes to press.

Mr. Johnson's decision to speak out, according to some commentators, was made not on the advice of politicians but on the counsel of the President's outside advisers. Rowland Evans and Robert Novak, columnist with the Publishers Newspaper Syndicate, said that "two of the most important of these are Abe Fortas . . . and Clark Clifford."

Abe Fortas had been the personal counsel to Bobby Baker until Mr. Fortas became closely related to the Johnson administration. Mr. Fortas then resigned and Edward Bennett Williams became Baker's lawyer. According to Evans and Novak, the advisers in the White House and a good many Democrats in Congress held the opinion that "the President should not have dignified the sordid disclosures seeping out of the Senate Rules Committee with an 'explanation' that might be construed as a sign of Presidential concern. . . ." The Democratic politicians were reported to have felt that if there should have been any statement it should have dealt with the conflicting testimony between Reynolds and Walter Jenkins. The President returned to the subject two days later in another press conference and on a Saturday night at the annual Alfalfa Club dinner the President referred jokingly to the hi-fi that "Lady Bird and I used to use." Washington observers were quite surprised that the President would try to take the offensive with a campaign of ridicule.

As his February 1 press conference President Johnson was asked by Clark Mollenhoff whether he thought his assistant Walter Jenkins should testify under oath in the Bobby Baker investigation. The President said: "The general question was raised with me at my last meeting. I spoke with candor and frankness on that subject and about all I knew about it. I said then that I did not plan to make more statements on it, and I do not."

Newsweek magazine thought that no one with Johnson's political instincts "could have expected this sort of explanation to silence criticism—and it didn't." The Republicans took off just as the Democrats had once taken off when Sherman Adams was found to have accepted gifts of a vicuña coat and an Oriental rug from Bernard Goldfine.

Governor Rockefeller said, "The American people don't like to see their officials taking favors," and Barry Goldwater said that Mr. Johnson, before accepting the gift, should have demanded, "Where did you get this, Buster?" The Republican National Chairman, William E. Miller, who was later to make a slashing speech at the Press Club concerning the Baker case, said that he felt the gift was "an atrocious thing."

Senator Clifford P. Case, Republican of New Jersey, has long been an ardent advocate of a law which would require "regular public disclosure of the financial interests and transactions of top officials in both the Executive and Legislative branches." In this Congress Senator Case had again introduced a bill to require such disclosure. Co-sponsor of this bill was Senator Neuberger of Oregon.

At a Lincoln Day dinner held February 7 at Penns Grove, New Jersey, Case said:

> . . . The amazing growth in the personal fortune of the Senate's former Majority Secretary has startled the whole country. After weeks of investigation, the unappetizing story is still unfolding.
>
> When Abraham Lincoln was President the hazards of gift-giving were not so great as they now are. Hi-fi sets, after all, had not been invented. But improper stock transactions were well known. When in 1864 Lincoln received a private offer of stock in a national bank, he wrote the bank president, "I fear there might be some impropriety in it," and turned down the offer.
>
> Salmon P. Chase, Lincoln's Secretary of the Treasury, was also sensitive to the pitfall of conflict of interest. When Jay Cooke sent Chase a $4,200 profit due him from a railway stock deal, Chase returned the money. He explained that, "In order to be able to render the most efficient service to our country, it is essential for me to *be* right as well as to *seem* right, and to *seem* right as well as to *be* right."

On Valentine's Day the New York *Herald Tribune* ran a slashing editorial "Who's Hiding What?" in which it said that the President had tried "not too successfully to throw cold water on stories about the stereo set." The *Tribune* felt a far more serious charge "on which the administration is simply playing dumb" was the question of information from confidential Air Force files being "deliberately leaked to the press." The charges

[146]

about the stereo set and the TV time, if they were true, were "unbecoming" to either the President or the Majority Leader or their aides. But, the editorial said, "the deliberate and clandestine use of confidential records to smear a Senate witness who happens to be embarrassing the President is an offense of a different order."

The *Tribune* cited the opinion of the *Army-Navy-Air Force Journal* which said "No service person can feel with unquestioning trust that the privacy of his official file will not be violated."

The *Tribune*'s conclusion:

> If the White House fails or refused to order a thorough investigation of the alleged leak, and to make the facts known, the public could hardly be blamed for assuming the charges are true—and for holding the President personally responsible for a gross breach of trust and propriety.

On February 7 the conservative Washington correspondent of the *Times,* Arthur Krock, devoted an entire column to this "Perilous Misuse of 'Secret' Documents." Mr. Krock's conclusion was:

> When the method employed is an anonymous handout of this nature to the press, the constitutional rights of persons are violated also. These include perhaps millions of citizens who should be concerned about this particular example, because the Government has on file allegations about them of which they are as ignorant as they are of their sources.

Thus there remained from the Bobby Baker case two questions of a personal nature relating to the character and the judgment of the President. When *The New York Times* carried the story that the White House was using secret documents in an attempt to "impugn" a witness, many in Washington were reminded of Senator McCarthy in the bad old days of 1954. The unpleasant question lingered, unanswered: How ruthless might those in power become if once again they felt they were truly threatened?

The other personal question which would probably never quite go away related to Bobby Baker as the protégé of Lyndon

Johnson. In his heyday when Johnson used him as a trusted lieutenant, Baker was even sometimes known as Little Lyndon. Several persons have told this writer that "he was like a son to Lyndon." As one said, "Lyndon has no sons—he helped that boy as if he were a son."

No man is responsible for all the actions of a son and no employer or leader is responsible for all that a man does after he has left his direct supervision. Still, one does not have to be a Republican to raise questions about the judgment the President used in his relations with Baker.

In any case, one result of the Bobby Baker story was that Washington, which watches all appointments of a new President with a very close eye, would particularly watch Lyndon Johnson. There will be a particular concern about the men he has selected or will select to be closest to him. This is not to suggest that Mr. Johnson would be tolerant of government employees who did not observe the proper ethical code. The question here concerned his much-vaunted knowledge of human nature and his judgment of individual men. Most people agreed that he was an extraordinarily good judge of the abilities and the follies of men. That only made the question more sharp, "How did he pick Bobby Baker to be his key lieutenant and trust him with so much responsibility?"

Beneath the jokes and the smirks, far more substantial than the smoke of the election campaign, the questions were real. These questions would remain alive and smoldering as long as Baker was alive and silent.*

It did not appear that Mr. Johnson had used his influence to promote Baker's investments, but he was very close to him at the time of some of his moneymaking. And, as James Reston wrote, "He was less than candid about his close personal relations with Baker, and he seems to have been remarkably casual about where his protégé was getting money to buy the motels and houses visited by the Johnsons."

The statement on television that Baker was not his protégé and the newspaper stories to the same effect were greeted with smiles by Washington observers.

* On February 25, the day of the new administration, Mr. Baker appeared before the Senate Rules Committee and refused to answer questions.

[148]

So all the Secret Service men in the world and the personal visit of the President to *The New York Times* could not stop the reverberations of the Baker story. And the snipers of rumor and gossip continued to attack. The White House was vulnerable at the very time one wished to see it an unblemished symbol of the American ideal.

7

Abroad: "Let's Find Something to Offer"

ONE OF THE FOREMOST FACTORS in the new President's mind as he left Parkland Hospital for *Air Force One* was the knowledge that the whole world was learning of the assassination. In the midst of its tragedy, would America falter in its programs and commitments to other nations? Mr. Johnson knew immediately that the world would be watching him.

One of the sharpest questions in the minds of those who knew the White House and its responsibilities, and one of the greatest uncertainties to those who knew Mr. Johnson, was how he would measure up to being the nation's guide and spokesman in international affairs. In fact, the man himself may have agreed with the dozens of commentators who called this his weakest point.

In no given period of one hundred days of a nation's history are there likely to be any major shifts of foreign policy, barring violent emergencies—and no major diplomatic crisis occurred in Mr. Johnson's first weeks. Unless events are erupting into wars or revolution, the conduct of foreign affairs is paced on a longer time-schedule than domestic affairs. Moreover, American foreign policy has remained much the same in the past few years, and no one familiar with the United States Government would expect the change within the administration to create any sharp turn in policy. The pressures on Mr. Johnson's skill and leadership were, in fact, to maintain continuity.

What was feared at the time of Kennedy's assassination was an unfavorable reaction from abroad, where our system is frequently misunderstood. And what was feared at home was that Mr. Johnson—doing his best to carry on policies he inherited—might prove to be a poor international leader. It was not only in Washington, but in other capitals around the world, that men wondered how he would meet his challenges and make the decisions no one should make for him.

Panama and Cuba, at times, threatened to become the subject of real crises, and Vietnam held the potential, at least, of flaring into another Korea. At the same time, the usual multitude of disturbances occurred in various fever spots around the world— in Cyprus, Zanzibar, Berlin, and elsewhere. Yet these and other crises did not provide enough background for any generalizations about the new President's methods in foreign affairs.

In the beginning, several basic difficulties were seen in Mr. Johnson's position in foreign affairs.

His lack of experience was the main concern. In no area did Mr. Johnson suffer more by contrast with his predecessor, who had experience, skill and worldwide fame as an attractive young national leader.

Another difficulty was perhaps transient, but it was immediate and it was important: the assassination itself seemed a disgraceful thing, and it lowered our reputation abroad. In many countries it was erroneously but widely assumed to be a political act. Then the shooting of Oswald by Ruby made it appear that America was still a wild and violent country, at least in the West (familiar to millions around the world from stories and films).

So Mr. Johnson came to power—as a Texan—when most of the world was feeling that Texas—and a lot of the rest of America—was capable of immature judgments and raw violence. For the time being, the nation which developed the atomic bomb seemed "trigger-happy" and dangerous. To a greater or lesser number of persons in many countries we, for a time, appeared to justify the worst suspicions they had sometimes harbored. The assassination encouraged all those who had ever felt we were immature, irresponsible, or violent. In other words, many people around the globe thought of us the way Americans think when we hear of assassinations—in Vietnam or Central America.

Our tragedy in Dallas was *not* a political act. It had nothing to do with a coup, and perhaps it was not even really related to the American or Wild West tradition. But this was not immediately apparent, even to Americans. It was a main task of the new President to make our continuity and stability more apparent and—perhaps—more real.

In any case, it was vital that representatives of other countries meet the new President. Mr. Johnson was almost unknown outside this country, and he was following a man who, on the contrary, was exceptionally well-known abroad.*

Few American Presidents have been popular world heroes at the time they were in office. Washington and Lincoln have by now become legend in most of the world, but they are exceptions. In this century our power inspires respect and fear, but makes it even more difficult for our leaders to gain admiration and affection. Yet three† of our recent Presidents have been warmly and greatly loved in many countries: Wilson, Roosevelt, and John F. Kennedy.

It is true Mr. Kennedy did not live to see his program fulfilled, and it is true that while he lived we did not realize what a symbol he had become from New Delhi to Nigeria. But at his

* Astute observers abroad—for example, Anthony Sampson, in the London *Observer*—noted that many believed that Lyndon Johnson would be better able to push through Kennedy's program than Kennedy was himself. But at the same time Sampson said the atmosphere in London was that "our President" was murdered and "Kennedy had seemed closer to Britain than any previous President."

Sampson said it was only after Kennedy's death that he realized "how closely we had become identified with this exciting and romantic circle . . . Kennedy's particular line of cultivated showmanship had stimulated and inspired Britons . . . this loss will have repercussions on the faith of ordinary people that America can protect them and can deal cool-headedly with East-West crises."

† Mr. Eisenhower was popular as a general and a liberator; his work as President was not what brought him fame abroad.

death, we realized that he had become a popular figure, even a personal figure, in many different countries, even in countries behind the Iron Curtain.

To his funeral there came one of the greatest, most remarkable gatherings of dignitaries of which history has record. It was painfully strange at the funeral of this young man to see some men who were old prophets as well as present potentates. A few were men to whom fate had given many decades upon the stage of history. John Kennedy had been just a schoolboy when Charles De Gaulle, after World War I, had outlined the use of tanks in the next war. In the thirty years since Hitler came to power, General De Gaulle had survived many defeats —and several attempts at assassination. Now he survived Kennedy. A dozen African nations were unborn, and two dozen were yet mysteries of the future when Emperor Haile Selassie warned the great powers at the League of Nations that their turn would come. Only a few weeks before November, Kennedy had welcomed the aging Emperor of Ethiopia, and in elegiac language had noted how long Selassie had been part of history. Now the Emperor looked down upon the young man's grave.

These imperial old men came in their shock and massive dignity to mourn a man who was on his way to becoming, like Wilson and Roosevelt, a citizen of the world. But they also came for another reason—to meet the new man.

And the new man sensed that even in the hushed setting of the funeral day, or amid the swirl of taking office, he should lose no time before speaking and listening to the foreign visitors. He had his chance at the end of the day of John Kennedy's funeral, when he and Mrs. Kennedy insisted on meeting the foreign visitors that very day. Mrs. Kennedy received them at the White House, and Mr. Johnson at a five-o'clock State Department reception.

In the formal reception rooms of the State Department that afternoon was "the closest approximation ever seen of a world summit conference." Some 61 nations were represented as well as officials of the United Nations and other international organizations. In the funeral procession that day were 16 presidents and heads of state, 38 foreign ministers, 13 members of royal families, and 7 heads of national legislatures. As Harland Cleve-

[153]

land, Assistant Secretary of State, said, "Tragedy had brought the human family together." So in the Jefferson and Franklin rooms on the top floor of the State Department were representatives of the East, the West, and all the unaligned nations.

Promptly—three minutes after five—President Johnson took up a post at the head of the receiving line in the imposing Thomas Jefferson Room of the State Department. By his side was the Secretary of State, Dean Rusk.

First through the line were the President of Germany, Heinrich Luebke, and the German Chancellor, Ludwig Erhard. These two originally had been scheduled to arrive that weekend for talks with President Kennedy.

Mr. Johnson was heard to reply to Berlin's mayor, Willy Brandt, a cordial answer to his invitation: "I am going to come." (Mr. Johnson had already made a trip to West Berlin as Vice-President.)

Within an hour some 60 delegations had passed through, and once in a while the President was seen to take an in-between moment to rub his aching hands together. Many of the visitors he greeted with the double handshake with which he likes to meet special friends. Late in the meeting Mrs. Johnson joined her husband and she later walked over to sit with Queen Frederika of Greece.

On Saturday the President had already sent telegrams to principal nations, notably to the Soviet Union, explaining that he intended to follow President Kennedy's policies. Now he repeated the same message to many in the line. In return, the visitors expressed the greatest sorrow and sympathy for what had happened. It was with conviction that a member of the Soviet delegation said to a reporter, "We really share your grief."

Yugoslav Foreign Minister Koca Popovic said, "This is very sad and tragic. This is the general feeling of our people."

General Charles De Gaulle made a dramatic entrance after all the other guests had arrived. He was overheard in conversation with the Russian Mikoyan. The conversation ended with De Gaulle saying that it was "obviously no time to discuss politics or diplomacy, so I bid you *adieu*." However, there was no doubt that politics and diplomacy were being discussed by almost everyone present as they wandered through the Thomas Jefferson Room, as they ate in small reception rooms, or in the candlelit Benjamin Franklin State Dining Room. In an adjoining room, following the reception line procedure, the President held more detailed conversations with the heads of delegations from these countries: Norway, Sweden, Denmark, and Finland all together; Austria, Belgium, Greece, Iran, Israel, Jamaica, Korea, Liberia, Morocco, Pakistan, and with the U. N. Secretary General U Thant.

Following the reception the President went down to Secretary Rusk's seventh-floor office and had longer talks with De Gaulle and with Prime Minister Hayato Ikeda of Japan. In this latter exchange he discussed some of the economic topics which had been scheduled for the Cabinet-level conference which would now never take place. The President also had a private talk with Prime Minister Lester B. Pearson of Canada.

The President made an excellent impression on the visitors, and a later check with foreign embassies in Washington revealed that he continued to impress foreign leaders with his sense of the continuity of policy. His first steps, then, were successful.

And his first foreign policy negotiations also went well. One of the first words from President Johnson about foreign policy came through an authorized spokesman while the President was on vacation in Texas. On the last day of the year (preceding a newspaperman's New Year's Eve party to which Johnson paid a surprise visit), a spokesman talked to the newsmen for more than an hour. His purpose was to give background and an authorized view of some of the thoughts of the President.

This happened to be the same conference at which it was made clear that the President intended to keep up an outsized working schedule and that he wanted people in responsible offices to expect to work some nights and weekends. It was in that context that it was said that the President didn't anticipate that people close to him would be "on the cocktail circuit in 1964." *

* The latter remark was the subject of much gossip among government workers and there was some wonderment as to whether the new President was taking a Puritanical view of the cocktail parties which are a feature of

[155]

More important than the cocktail statement by a thousand times or so were some words about peace. And these also failed for a time to receive correct interpretation. The spokesman that day in Austin, Texas, said that the President thought it would be "muddle-headed" if the United States were to fail to take steps to keep peace because of fear of being taken in by Red tactics. The President, it was said, was interested in developing new approaches for proposals to reduce international tension.

The President that day had sent to Premier Nikita Khrushchev a New Year's Day greeting expressing hope for stretching world peace. Newsmen perhaps took the other remarks in something of the same category as the New Year's greetings to Khrushchev; they were well-meant words but not apt to lead anywhere. The spokesman said that our attitude toward Communism should be "an unrelenting peace offensive." He also referred to "breakthroughs" in the peace search, and spoke of "Red maneuvers or tactics." In this secondhand description of the President's feelings the spokesman was certainly using military expressions like "maneuvers" and "offensive" to describe peace-seeking enterprises. (Historians of the future may be puzzled by how militantly we of the twentieth century sought peace breakthroughs through offensives.)

However, even if his instinct for simple phrases was failing in this instance, the President was sending a New Year's signal that he was entering a new year and term of office with thoughts of peaceful cooperation uppermost in his mind. Historically, it is interesting to note that just about ten years after Senator Joseph McCarthy made it almost treasonable for any man to speak of peace with Russia, a practical President called the McCarthy attitude "muddle-headed" thinking.

Max Frankel, in *The New York Times* of New Year's morning, felt that Johnson had made his "first difficult foreign policy decision" when he decided to work in 1964 for a "peace-probe"

Washington life. (Washington drinks more liquor per capita than any other city in the nation.) This remark about "the cocktail circuit" was reinterpreted later has having no such implication. The intent of this statement was to emphasize work—that the President expected top officials to be working late at their desks and not to be taking off at five or six for cocktail parties.

program against the Russians. Frankel and others said that Secretary of State Rusk and other advisers had previously been urging just such a course on President Kennedy. Frankel added "President Johnson is said to feel personally and politically comfortable with a strong anti-war platform." *

According to Drew Pearson, Mr. Johnson was "restless and relentless" in probing for new peace proposals in December, and tried out his ideas on several people before taking them up with the Russians. During Chancellor Erhard's Christmas visit to the LBJ ranch, Pearson said the President urged the Chancellor, "Ask yourselves what you can do to improve relations with Russia. I am not trying to advise you. I can't be in the position of advising the German Government. . . ." But, the President went on to say the Russian people had "suffered terrible casualties at the hands of Germany," and the Russians had reason to be "jittery." He emphasized to the Chancellor that we should examine every avenue and that we cannot stand still, "we cannot keep our feet in concrete." Then, according to Pearson, early in January the President himself "began examining avenues of peace. . . . He was just as energetic on the telephone to the Cabinet regarding disarmament as he was to Congress regarding taxes and civil rights."

According to Pearson, he would phone McNamara, the Secretary of Defense, and tell him "Let's find something to offer. We can't get anywhere if we don't offer anything ourselves." This is interesting language in itself, for this is exactly the way Majority Leader Johnson used to talk on Capitol Hill.

From this restless search for something new to throw into bargaining and negotiations with the Soviets, the January proposal to freeze the strategic delivery of nuclear weapons was born, as well as the 20-percent reduction of fissionable production which was announced in the State of the Union message.

Shortly afterwards the President started working on his plan to reduce nuclear production by independent unilateral statements. Pearson implied that he himself played a part in this story when in his column he said the President knew "that Khrushchev had made a statement to me [Pearson] in an interview [August 17] that he would reduce the Russian military

* Quotes from *The New York Times,* January 1, 1964.

[157]

budget unilaterally, regardless of the Geneva arms talks and regardless of the United States."

Khrushchev did reduce by 4.7 percent, said Pearson, and in that same month, December, Mr. Johnson reduced U. S. military expenditure about the same amount.

Thus Mr. Johnson went on, said Pearson, trying the same technique of "building better trust and understanding by extending the principle of mutual example."

In his State of the Union message of January 8 the President announced a real reduction in production of nuclear weapons. This was the first substantial atomic cutback since the United States continued to build atomic bombs after the end of World War II.

There has been much discussion, not only here, but abroad, about the constantly growing atomic capacity of both the Soviet Union and the United States. Both are now able not only to mortally wound the other country but to kill and even "overkill." The new word, "overkill," describes a capacity which goes beyond the ability to destroy all the enemy cities. It means they could be destroyed twice over or thrice over. Many critics question the necessity for continuing to pile up these weapons.

Mr. Johnson said that even in the absence of the real arms control agreement "we must not stockpile arms beyond our needs or seek an excess of military power that could be provocative as well as wasteful."

The President thus put some of his characteristic personal style into the solemnity of foreign affairs. He did it on other occasions as well. For example, he tried personal telephone calls to Panama and in the Greek-Turkish dispute in Cyprus, and in the Cyprus dispute he sent a telegram addressed "Dear Friends" to President Makarios and Vice-President Bazil Kutchuk, the leader of the Turkish Cypriots. Mr. Johnson had been to Cyprus in 1962, where he had met both these men, and he now referred to those "whose hands I have pressed less than eighteen months ago. . . ."

He made a speech when the British Prime Minister was here implying they were both "country boys" under the skin. At the ranch in Texas he treated Chancellor Erhard very much as he might have treated any Western governor, and the German Chancellor seemed to be delighted.

However, in spite of his "new look" in foreign affairs, it did not appear that he had the passion for detail in foreign affairs which he brought to other tasks. He did not see as many of the experts—of the second and third rank in the State Department—as Kennedy was in the habit of seeing. And just what he did with the advice he got was a question sometimes asked, as it was in the matter of funds for foreign aid.

On March 20, 1964, the President surprised nearly everyone by sending to Congress the smallest foreign aid request since the Marshall Plan began the whole program. He asked for 3.4 billion, which was 25 percent below the last Kennedy foreign aid appeal. This apparently left no margin for Congressmen to make any cuts—a departure from the usual policy of asking more from Congress than one expects to get. Apparently it was an attempt to try economy—and candor—and surprise. Was this a self-deceiving mistake, an act of clear-sighted realism, or a maneuver of surprise which turned out to be self-defeating?

One of the President's first moves had been to set up a group of leaders to examine the foreign aid problem. In his Texas press conference the President had said that he wanted the nine-member unit under Undersecretary of State George Ball to go over the problem of foreign aid with a fresh viewpoint. Yet, said Johnson, perhaps once again with a burst of candor and realism, he had told the people some of his own views. He had asked them to come up with a recommendation and "if they are as close to my views as I hope they will be, we will probably adopt them." *

In any case, this committee had very sharp divisions as to what to do about foreign aid. Some members, not only Sargent Shriver and Ralph Dungan, were particularly opposed against proposals to dissolve AID, the Agency for International De-

* Mr. Johnson is famous for getting advice or taking soundings from numerous sources before almost any decision. But there is abundant evidence that he retains firm ideas of his own. There is some evidence, as here, that he sometimes expects to hold his main views even after he has gone through a process of seeking counsel.

velopment. In view of all the difficulties, the White House decided the Ball Committee should not make any formal report. Later, when Presidential speechwriters were working on the foreign aid message, they found they had to write many drafts to get Johnson's approval. One visitor to the President commented, "You could tell he was groping for new solutions but was uncertain which way to turn."

In all criticism or praise of Mr. Johnson during the 100 days it was usually said that this was "a quiet period" in world affairs. One could wonder just how quiet such things can be, and just a sketchy list of events in the 100 days can give a wry idea of what is meant today by "relative quiet" in foreign policy.

Perhaps the most far-reaching happening was that the French Government recognized Red China. This move, and the independent path which De Gaulle was pursuing in many other ways, offered fresh evidence that "The West" was not a monolithic bloc. Meanwhile, increased dissension between the USSR and China was becoming more and more apparent in the Eastern bloc.

In the latter part of the 100 days and soon after, the verbal attacks between Russia and China reached new heights. This division gave new hope that the Communist world movement was bitterly divided between two world capitals, and it appeared the West would profit from this division for years to come.

It is an oversimplification to compare differences among nations of the West with the split in the Communist bloc. The Communist division is greatly unsettling to Communists everywhere, and may be one of the great historic changes—providing two "Romes," and some kind of "Reformation" for the Communist dogma and faith of unpredictable consequences. Western differences are not the same for we have not had one central authority. Nonetheless, this early period of the Johnson regime did see an increasing fragmentation on both sides of the world, an increasing number of factions and viewpoints, which to many seemed less dangerous than the previous 20 years' trend toward polarization of the world into two hostile camps.

The Panama Canal Zone erupted in riots and on January 10, Roberto Chiari, the Panamanian President, suspended relations with the United States. There followed protracted negotiations which eventually brought us much ill will in Latin America.

A situation in Cyprus nearly flared into war. There was recurring trouble in the Malaysia-Indonesia quarrel, in Zanzibar, and at other trouble spots, such as Cuba and East Germany.

In South Vietnam there was another military coup, installing General Khanh in power, and apparently this coup caught the U. S. Government by surprise.

Trouble with Cuba continued and at one or two points caused lights to burn at the White House far into the night. But it later appeared that we were maturing a new view of Cuba as a "nuisance" but not a "peril." *

At home, numerous visitors from foreign countries arrived at the White House for estate visits. (Perhaps the most notable visitor was one who did not come for a conference although he came for the President's funeral—Charles de Gaulle.)

In mid-February Sir Alec Douglas-Home, the British Prime Minister, came to visit.† Some thought that the historic alliance between Britain and the United States had seldom been subject to greater strain but others thought this appraisal was greatly exaggerated. The major concern was Britain's trade with Communist countries, notably Cuba. As the Prime Minister explained after that meeting, the United States and Britain remain completely at odds on that issue. British leaders were also disgruntled with the United States for the manner in which we have treated Indonesia's President Sukarno. In January, President Johnson sent Attorney General Robert F. Kennedy as a special Presidential emissary to Sukarno, and he was able to win from him a promise of a cease-fire in the quarrel with Malaysia. To the British, the United States was more interested in propping up Sukarno, a pro-Communist neutral, than in giving good support to Malaysia, an anti-Communist democracy. It was also charged that Johnson had not consulted Britain before sending Kennedy on the trip to Indonesia.

On Robert Kennedy's return, he was ushered directly into

* The widely-discussed speech of Senator J. W. Fulbright on March 25, reviewing "myths" of our foreign policy came after the 100 days.

† Other state visitors of the hundred days were Chancellor Erhard, President Segni, Queen Frederika, Prime Minister Pearson.

[161]

a meeting with Congressional leaders and it was later said that the President had not consulted Kennedy before asking him if he could give his report with Congressional leaders present— instead of privately to the President or to the President and a few advisers. This treatment reportedly ruffled Mr. Kennedy. Thus it was said that Mr. Johnson's impulsiveness may have been shown at least twice in the treatment of the Indonesian trip.

However, this is not the first time but the thousandth time that we or Britain have done something without full consultation. Furthermore, President Johnson was intent upon maintaining good relations with Congress and consulting its leadership in foreign affairs.*

The foreign policy "honeymoon" was—like the domestic "honeymoon"—definitely over as the campaign warmed up. But perhaps there was a milestone around the end of January, when crises began to pop in various trouble spots. Then the press pundits began to notice that the President had not—apparently—been much concerned with foreign affairs.

At the end of January Douglas Kiker of the New York *Herald Tribune* wrote an explosive story that the President was involved in four different international crises and that there was "mounting evidence that he has yet to develop an effective technique for the day-by-day conduct of foreign affairs." Insiders in the capital had already been talking about the fact that the President had been almost completely absorbed in domestic affairs. The world had remained fairly quiet for a time but the crises were beginning to come in Panama, in Germany, in Cyprus and in Vietnam.

Critics said that Mr. Johnson had always run a one-man show, as many Congressmen do, and that he kept his office under his hat. It was felt that he was trying to do the same kind of show in the White House, particularly in regard to foreign affairs,

* Another item of interest in the foreign affairs field was the fact that an American ambassador, Henry Cabot Lodge, after the write-in vote in New Hampshire, became an outstanding favorite for the Republican nomination for President. Washington's gossip mills worked overtime discussing when Mr. Lodge might come home, whether he would come quietly, or whether he would be pulled home.

and so he was not getting enough counsel or enough information from a variety of persons.

This made him very dependent upon his special assistant in international affairs, McGeorge Bundy, and this particular week Mr. Bundy was vacationing in Antigua. This absence started rumors that Mr. Bundy might resign, and commentators talked of a fifty-fifty chance. It was widely printed that Mr. Bundy —like many other people—had found it difficult to work for Mr. Johnson.

The critical story by Kiker caused the President "to hit the ceiling," and it was this story and others like it which caused the President to begin to refer, in public speeches, to "belly-achers" or "alarmists." He and his chief aides began talking to selected reporters about just how much attention was being paid to foreign affairs by the White House.*

One sign early in 1964 that the campaign was gaining momentum was the appearance of a weekly newsletter published by a Republican Congressional committee, and its number one issue took off on foreign policy.*

Citing Panama as the outstanding example, the theme of the lead article followed the headline FLOUNDERING U. S. FOREIGN POLICY STILL LOSING FRIENDS AND MAKING ENEMIES.

As the campaign writers for Republican Congressmen saw it, "The long series of concessions and retreats made before Panamanian demands, starting during the third year of Franklin D. Roosevelt's administration, were blamed by many experts for the outbreak of rioting."

A minor note was the question of the budget and whether the economy measures of the new administration really were reducing expenditures. Later issues of the newsletter were to bear down hard upon Bobby Baker, the President's changing civil rights views, and his avoidance of open questioning by the press. But week in and week out the Republicans hammered away at the topic of foreign policy.

* See Chapter 8 on press relations for some of the other reporting and comment on the President and foreign policy.

* Republican Congressional Committee Newsletter, Number 1, January 17, 1964.

By the middle of February they were saying, "Long-time experts on Latin American affairs . . . foresaw a complete collapse of this Nation's hemispheric programs as a result of administration vacillation. . . ."

As this is written, Republican voices are still criticizing the President's moves in foreign policy and pointing out the various minor crises around the world. Some are criticizing our actions in relation to the unhappy, hard-fought but indecisive guerrilla warfare in Vietnam. Many Republicans accuse Mr. Johnson of having no strong foreign policy at all. As Senator Everett Dirksen, Republican of Illinois, frequently puts it, "The country is drifting on the high seas of uncertainty and confusion."

Republicans also criticized some of Mr. Johnson's remarks about the more peaceful world and prepared to make political capital out of our defeats or stalemates in Southeast Asia. Left-wing critics continued to say that we had pursued a shortsighted policy with Cuba and that we were led by men who could not treat our former "colonies" as sensibly as the other great powers had learned to treat their former possessions. Nor were the left and right the only critics. In *Reporter* magazine for April 9, Max Ascoli wrote quite sharply about the Johnson and Fulbright statements about a more peaceful world. Dr. Ascoli also was quite critical of a phrase from Adlai Stevenson who had said, "The central trend of our times is the emergence of what, for lack of a better label, might be called a policy of Cease-Fire, and Peaceful Change." Ascoli explained that up to then it had been thought that "a cease-fire was something less desirable and more precarious than an armistice, and an armistice more precarious and less desirable than a peace settlement."

Ascoli suggested that some of our leaders, like "all of us," were "still under the shock of John F. Kennedy's assassination." Ascoli also spoke bitterly about two of Kennedy's major international ventures which are frequently cited as successes—the confrontation with the Soviets at the time of the second Cuban crisis and the achievement of the test-ban treaty. Ascoli said, "Cuba, after the confrontation, had to become an integral part of the Soviet empire" and the test-ban treaty was "co-signed by an exuberant number of countries" who have no atomic bombs to test.

Was President Johnson's ignorance of other countries exaggerated? Some top officials emphasized to this writer that they thought it naïve to write, as some commentators did, of the President's "ignorance." One White House aide insisted that it was a great mistake to look at Johnson as if he were just coming for the first time to matters of foreign policy. The aide insisted that a man can't spend so many years in the Senate and not hear a great deal about the ins and outs and the details of foreign policy. It is not only a matter of defense appropriations, in which Mr. Johnson is exceptionally well-educated, said this assistant; one should also remember that, as Majority Leader, he had to understand and to fight for the major bills relating to foreign policy. Thus, he said, Johnson had heard all the pros and cons of most of the major issues of the world today.

It must also be remembered that Mr. Johnson had been associated with the White House for three years, attending nearly every important meeting. In times of crucial decisions, like the two Cuban crises, he was with the people who knew the situation best, and he lived with them on a day-to-day and sometimes hour-by-hour basis, as the major decisions were made. State Department people also insist we should not dismiss those trips which he took to Southeast Asia, Africa and Berlin as entirely formal or ceremonial affairs. In each case he was going to a troubled area. He had to learn something in advance, a task which he attacked with his customary drive, and he took the opportunity to learn while he was overseas.

Thus White House and State Department people make the reasonable point that one can exaggerate how new the foreign affairs field was to the new man.

This still left aside, of course, the question of his interests and whether he was going to be as skilled in foreign relations, as he was in domestic politics. His habit of talking nearly every day—to groups, to reporters, to visitors—could cause trouble in domestic affairs but could be really dangerous in the world at large.

In foreign relations an off-the-cuff remark can cause repercussions around the world. Mr. Johnson's liking for impromptu statements had in the past struck many persons as particularly dangerous. His off-the-cuff invitation to Bashir the camel driver turned out to be a success. But at least one overseas remark of his still causes faint reverberations.

While he was still Vice-President and on his Asian tour, he referred in an offhand speech to President Diem of Vietnam as the Churchill of his country. Mr. Johnson made this public statement because, he said, he was trying to make some headway in dealing with the dictatorial premier (who was later assassinated). What he meant by that statement was later explained and "clarified." His point was that in Vietnam there was no one except President Diem who had been able to rally the country to a sense of national purpose. He did not mean to suggest that President Diem had anything like the greatness of a Churchill. But despite the explanations, the verdict of serious observers was that the phraseology and the statement were inept.

Time and again in speeches discussing the rest of the world the President goes back to a line about all the world envying us. As he told a gathering of Texans at the White House on February 29, "There is not anyone in the world who wouldn't like to change places with you, economically and socially. There is no citizen in the world who has the freedom, the luxury and the high living standards you have today."

Earlier that same month (February 11) he had told the IRS tax collectors:

> My plane has landed in many continents, touched down in more than 30 countries in the past few years. The wheels have never stopped and the door has never opened anywhere that I have not looked upon faces which would not have liked to have traded citizenship with me.

And the President has been making this statement for years, *even in speeches abroad.* He has been told that it is not well-received by people of other countries, but when he gets on his feet to speak extemporaneously he is likely to drift back to such old standbys.

Nearly always the President spoke optimistically about world affairs, as in this passage from the February speech to the tax collectors:

[166]

We have problems in the world. We are living in a frustrating period, an exciting period, a developmental period. I have seen times when the skies were grayer. We don't have on our hands this morning a missile crisis in Cuba. We don't have Laos; we don't have the conference in Vienna that we faced the first few months of President Kennedy's Administration—the Bay of Pigs—all of those were major problems.

In talking of international differences, Mr. Johnson frequently brings these down to the size of the country, even to the size of a small town or negotiations between individuals:

So, regardless of what you hear and regardless of what some of the belly-achers say, we are a much-loved people throughout the world. We are respected and we appreciate it.

* * *

. . . Even in our own country we do not see everything alike. If we did, we would all want the same wife—and that would be a problem, wouldn't it!

We must make allowance for the other fellow. A good way to treat him is just to assume that he wants to do for his own people what you want to do for your own. Try to find an area of agreement instead of an area of disagreement.

These speeches made some think of the homely flavor of Abraham Lincoln—who might well have made the remark about "we would all want the same wife—and that would be a problem." Yet these same touches prompted others to say that we now had the worst White House prose style since Warren Harding. But the country heard its leader when he said on the topic of discrimination, "The best way for you to understand how the other fellow feels is to put yourself in his place for a while and see how you would feel. . . ."

Over and over again, on the topic of foreign affairs, Mr. Johnson mentioned not just one country but the more than 100 with whom we have to deal; for example, "of the 113 nations in the world, 50 of them have had new governments in the last three years."

In spite of the remarks which could be made about the President's style, it gradually became clear that he had an extraordinary ability to speak to ordinary citizens in homely and direct terms. More and more persons understood how friends of his could say that not even Khrushchev could win a discussion with Johnson. The President lacked the eloquence of a Roosevelt, or a Churchill, but his seemingly direct manner made his points readily understood and remembered. In his speeches he was being understood by the voters and in his private office he was succeeding with some difficult negotiations, such as in the settling of a five-year-old management-labor railroad conflict. Perhaps, as Jack Valenti prophesied, he might indeed be known in history as "The Great Persuader."

But could this ability really count for much in international affairs? The capital's sophisticates snickered at the Texans who said Lyndon would outtalk Premier Khrushchev. The ability to persuade masses of persons is not ordinarily a talent which "travels" well, and the "howdy, folks" manners of the President seemed unsuitable for summit meetings and sometimes even for greeting heads of state on ceremonial visits to Washington. Lacking experience in foreign affairs, and lacking a commanding eloquence, Mr. Johnson's era at first seemed sure to be one in which America's voice in world affairs would be diminished.

But was it correct to assume that the homespun persuading ways of Lyndon B. Johnson would not help to bring him victories in international affairs? Certainly the deadly game of international power is different in some vital respects from the wheeling and dealing game of the U. S. Senate. Very seldom are Congressional struggles concerned with life-and-death decisions as foreign policy may be. But yet it began to appear that Johnson's homespun manner might in the end be a positive asset with many of the homespun persons with whom he may have to negotiate. A very small part of the world is Ivy League or Old School Tie. Khrushchev and Mao, like Johnson, came from down under, and both rose through years of service to their cause. Moreover, underlying the Johnson style is something more solid than style, than manners: there is the personal experience of decades of negotiation.

But there is another persuasion factor which may be of overriding importance to the judgment of history. The first 100 days gave some indication that the new man could on occasion be an excellent leader, or "explainer," to his own people. He might not quicken a listener's pulse when he spoke, as Kennedy or Roosevelt—or General MacArthur—might have done. But it appeared that without rhetorical flourishes he was still able to make his point. This led to a very provocative and interesting line of speculation. In foreign affairs a democracy often falters, not because of ignorant leaders, but because of ignorant followers. Wilson, for example, had been idolized by masses in Europe, but then was unable to make enough Americans understand the choices before the nation. In 1964, in Johnson's case, it appeared that just *because* of his homely manner and *because* of the absence of special phrases, and *because* of a rather flat delivery, Mr. Johnson was in his first weeks gaining acceptance for some new ideas about America's position in the world.

It appeared he might not be the man to lead a crusade. But in an age when crusades could be wildly dangerous, he might be just the man *not* to lead a crusade, and even to hold back the dangerous crusaders.

For some time many advanced scholars and well-informed diplomats had been saying that the U. S. needed to reexamine some of the fundamental ideas on which our policy in the cold war is based. For example, did we really think we could never —not ever—put some real trust in agreements with Russia— not even when mutual self-interest seemed to indicate a real basis for cooperation? For another example, it was even daringly suggested that the world tomorrow might not be completely divided and torn into a cold war. For years we had been told that for generations we could expect the world to be divided between two huge contenders, with all other peoples more or less affiliated with one side or the other. Now that picture of the world seemed less likely—hundreds of millions of people had not been involved in the cold war and perhaps were not going to be. In another new development, it became more and more obvious in 1964 that China was really and truly dividing itself from the policies of the USSR.

More and more nations were becoming reluctant to be firmly identified with either side, to be partners of either Russia or the U. S. The world was changing. The balance of power was changing and it appeared less and less likely that our atomic power could help us—except in desperation. For example, we did not wish to use it in Cuba or Vietnam. The world had had many small wars since 1945, and perhaps would have many more. But it seemed the big powers could no longer use their power—sometimes it seemed they no longer even wished to threaten use of it!

Millions of Americans had once rallied—at least with words and cheers—to the idea that "in war there is no substitute for Victory." In 1964 very few realists wanted to rally for that slogan with guns and bombs as well as words. In the latter half of the twentieth century it began to appear that a stalemate, or a coexistence—with humanity and progress—would be a handsome substitute for victory—if victory meant turning the world into a radioactive ruin. The early polls and even the primaries in 1964 indicated that in America's villages they understood the President, who said it was no longer a simple business to "send the Marines."

It was ironic that in the spring of 1964 Washington gave all honors to salute the passing of the "old soldier," General MacArthur, while the men who managed the military and diplomatic policy of the nation were turning decisively from the strategy he represented. A dozen years before this, a plain-spoken homespun man from Missouri, also a President-by-accident, had fired General MacArthur for challenging the authority of the civilian Commander in Chief, the President. As the General's funeral procession went down Pennsylvania Avenue one gray rainy day, another plain-spoken citizen had been thrust by fate into the chair which sits higher than those of all our generals and admirals. Johnson's language as well as his words indicated America was not dreaming of glory through arms, or through bombs, or through any form of military "victory."

From the White House, at the time MacArthur was speaking grandiosely through posthumous published interviews, there were coming bluntly spoken simple sentences which made clear our government's sincere desire to be calm and cautious in the world of the H-bomb. A few years later, a Secretary of State had spoken of how we might deal with those we regarded as dangerous. John Foster Dulles had threatened any Communist

[170]

move anywhere with "massive retaliation." That no longer seemed a believable alternative in the time when Russia and other nations had super-weapons.

There were still in 1964 critics who found it puzzling that with all our strength we were reluctant to use it. The new man in the White House seemed determined to teach his countrymen something about these matters. His ability to make progress in this persuasion might turn out to be—it was possible—on a par with FDR's gradual awakening of the country to the European crisis in 1939 and 1940. In 1964 President Johnson, while speaking toward the restraints of power, was engaged in the same general task as was Roosevelt in 1940, when he was leading us toward the development and use of our power. Both men were attempting to understand the real world and the changing balance of power.

Many intellectuals interested in foreign policy criticized Mr. Johnson for failing to understand some particular area of international affairs. But many international observers also gave him the highest praise for being exceptionally lucid and emphatic on the broad outlines of the present U. S. position in the world. Ironically enough, in these views of our new position, he was serving as an "explainer" for views generally held by John Kennedy. In this respect he was campaigning for the Kennedy program beyond anything he had done in 1960. And it appeared that now, as in 1960, he was reaching some of the men in the street who did not understand some of the same things when enunciated by JFK. And now he could speak to the entire nation, and perhaps he was going to be well understood by the rest of the world.

Perhaps the most favorable early statement made about President Johnson's philosophy of foreign relations came from the most respected commentator in the national capital, Walter Lippmann.

He wrote that the President had "put his finger on the crux of the whole problem of our inability to have ourselves followed, often, indeed listened to in so many parts of the world."

Mr. Lippmann quoted with approval key sentences from the President's television "conversation":

[There are] people who feel that all we need to do is to mash a button and determine everybody's foreign policy. But we are not living in that kind of a world *any more.* They are going to determine it for themselves, and that is the way it should be. And we are going to have to come and reason with them and try to lead them instead of forcing them.

Lippmann said he believed "these are . . . among the most important words spoken by an American President since the Second World War." Lippmann reasoned this way:

. . . They recognize the reality of things. They recognize the profound change which has taken place in the power balances of the globe since the end of the postwar period. These words are the key to most of what so many find so puzzling—for example, the policies of General de Gaulle, the evolution of Latin American attitudes toward this country, our frustration in Southeast Asia.

Lippmann said that his own impression or conviction was that "our people are in the mood to believe these words when they hear them from a President whom they trust completely."

In the actual telecast, the President made these remarks without any special emphasis. Perhaps this quiet manner only underlines their importance, if one accepts the general Lippmann view. It means these beliefs are now taken as basic, and they are accepted as such by our top policy-makers. The President, in a "common sense" view of the balance of power, makes the basic assumption that American power cannot be so overwhelming that when we meet a crisis it is merely up to us to be "decisive" or "firm" in order to get our own way. His emphasis is on negotiation and not threats of retaliation, for "we are going to have to come and reason with them and try to lead them instead of forcing them." *

* In a speech March 24 to an AFL-CIO meeting, the President once again returned to this theme of caution. "The world has changed and so has the method of dealing with disruptions of the peace," he said. "There may have been a time when the Commander in Chief would order soldiers to march the very moment a disturbance occurred, although restraint and fairness are not new to the American tradition.

"But the world as it was and the world as it is are not the same any-

So far as open criticism was concerned, the President enjoyed a "honeymoon" in the foreign area as in others, and he also enjoyed some good luck. In the first place, during the period of mourning, political criticism was absent. That meant a lessening of pressure to be "bold," to "stand up to them," and in other words relatively less of the pressure for "hardness" which is easier to achieve in campaign words than in the field.

By coincidence, apparently, it was also a relatively quiet period in the world. The Russians, it was believed, would not wish to start major trouble at a time when our leadership might be uncertain. As a high State Department official told the writer, "That's how we would treat *them* at such time—carefully and deliberately." But as the weeks went by, it became apparent that the relative quiet was significant of more than this. The Russians, for whatever reasons, were going to continue to explore the paths of cooperation. Apparently they had really changed course after the "eyeball-to-eyeball" confrontation in Cuba.

They were showing more and more evidence to justify the faith and work which the Kennedy administration had put into U. S.-Russian relations. Spokesmen for the White House felt there had been steady growth since the Cuban confrontation, and they felt that a new note of reasonable cooperation with us was continuing in the Johnson administration. In late April came the announcement of a mutual cutback in atomic bomb material, and this was hailed as a major step toward a new era and a new "thaw" in the cold war. High spokesmen—and commentators like Sevareid and Lippmann—began to talk about America facing a new period of international quiet in which we could work on problems at home.

It was much too early to say whether this was a transient phase. But it was clear that the President—and the nation—after a year in which we had had some atrocious luck, had been favored with a period of good fortune. Men who had been fearful of what might have happened to us with a new President untried in foreign relations, began to breathe sighs of relief.

---

more." He continued: ". . . once upon a time even large-scale wars could be waged without risking the end of civilization but what was once upon a time is no longer so—because general war is impossible."

They felt that the thermonuclear world remained terribly dangerous but that the new President had been granted a learning period. President Kennedy in his first 100 days had not had such good luck, for he had inherited the Bay of Pigs operation which turned out to be a disaster. The new President's references to that previous 100 days of JFK showed that in his own way he, too, was breathing a sigh of relief.

So far as foreign policy was concerned the early period was marked by a crossing of fingers, a knocking on wood, and then this sigh of relief. The capital—and much of the world—had the keenest possible interest in what would develop in the future, when our luck would inevitably change.

8

"What Is Your Biggest Problem?"
"Being President."

IT WAS QUITE A SURPRISE PARTY, for all the guests were surprised. The new President had decided to meet the press at a time and place he could choose on a moment's notice. No one advised him to do it this way; his own experience and instinct led him to the decision. The President seemed quite pleased with the meeting itself and with the early press results. And the press people were as pleased as children at a party—a surprise party.

It was a sunny Saturday morning two weeks to the day after President Johnson had spent his first morning as President.

The White House press room had the unnaturally subdued atmosphere which characterized it during the period of mourning. In addition the press room had a Saturday morning mood: nothing very important was likely to happen. The only known events-to-be were rather private and personal—on this day Mrs. Johnson was going to move into the White House and Mrs. Kennedy was spending her last hours as a White House resident before moving to a private home in Georgetown.

From the East Wing offices for the First Lady there was to be a little bulletin about the time Mrs. Kennedy departed, about how she had called the switchboard operators to say goodbye and how she had left a note and a bouquet of flowers for

Mrs. Johnson. Still later there would be an opportunity to photograph Mr. and Mrs. Johnson on the White House steps.

Few reporters came in and out that morning. Of course, on duty all the time at the White House when the President is in Washington are certain reporters from the wire services. They are the irreducible minimum of the White House press corps. Among other things they are sometimes called "the death watch." Even when it is known that the President is not to meet anybody, that "the lid is on," the members of the death watch may sit around smoking endless cigarettes, reading and rereading the newspapers and keeping in touch with their offices through the direct-line telephones which belong to the different agencies and newspapers.

On most days the White House Press Secretary holds a briefing at noon and again at five o'clock, but ordinarily on Saturdays the five-o'clock briefing is skipped. In this case, on December 7, the eleven-o'clock briefing was late as usual, and it was a few minutes before twelve when reporters casually strolled into Pierre Salinger's office. Some noticed that the Press Secretary was wearing a coat that morning. Ordinarily he stood at his desk coatless and informal in a colorful striped shirt.

As the press started its questions, Mr. Salinger said, "The President would like to have you come in and have coffee with him." Self-consciously, and in a hurry, the newsmen followed Salinger down the hall to the President's office. So began a new chapter in Presidential press relations. This sudden invitation was in some ways unprecedented. Other Presidents had on occasion called in reporters, but the resulting conferences were rarely put on the record. FDR and Truman had met reporters in their offices, but on a regular schedule.*

Some thirty reporters followed Salinger into the oval office. The President shook hands with each of them. The room was overcrowded, and a little maneuvering was required to seat them all. Actually there *was* coffee, but later reporters could hardly remember anyone drinking it. The President sat in his own rocking chair, a new one; he leaned forward a little and

---

* Press conferences steadily grow larger. In Truman's time they were moved to the old State Department building; in JFK's time they went to a large auditorium at the new State Department.

opened the conversation which the press was too startled to begin.*

He started the questioning by saying: "If there is anything you would like to ask me I would be glad to answer."

The first question was, "This will be your first night here?"

"Yes."

"How do you feel about it?"

"I feel like I have already been here a year."

Then for about twenty minutes Mr. Johnson talked, an interesting fact which people remembered later. Little space or intermission was left for questions. In any case, no critical questions were asked.

However, in this, as at other spot conferences held later, the President did give out quite a bit of information which was national and international news. This first day he touched on the legislative program, his problems in establishing continuity and in achieving a sense of unity. He mentioned the economy drive and how he was working with Secretary McNamara on cutting down the number of civilian employees in the Defense Department. He discussed how he would try to work on a free flow of information in press conferences "after the period of mourning" and said that he wanted to work out "what would be the most effective way, with your counsel and cooperation." He discussed his calendar and visitors and he gave out quite a few details on how the budget might shape up. He mentioned the forthcoming visits of the Prime Minister of Canada and the President of Mexico.

He was asked, "Are you going to be spending the weekends in the country?" and his answer was, "I expect I am going to be at this desk pretty much straight through."

He was asked what was his biggest problem, and he replied, "Being President."

One of those present that day was a young and pretty girl reporter, Mrs. Judith Martin of the Washington *Post*. She was

* The night before, while swimming with Salinger in the heated White House pool, the President had said that he would like to have the reporters in for such a meeting when his crowded schedule permitted. On this morning the President had arrived at 9:41, and a short while later the meeting was called.

quite bowled over by her accidental arrival at the first Presidential press conference and began her story, "Lyndon B. Johnson has the distinction of being the first President of the United States to buy me a cup of coffee." She ended it by saying, "Speaking just for myself, I had a lovely time, and I hope that you and Mrs. Johnson and Lynda Bird and Lucy Baines and the beagles will drop in and have some coffee with me whenever you're in my neighborhood."

Most reporters at first liked the idea of such spot conferences. Some did not. Those who represented small news bureaus or "one-man agencies" had to cover the whole town and could not stay at the White House all day on the chance of sudden news. Radio and television did not like it because it could not be recorded. The foreign journalists, most of whom are tied to the State Department as their base of operations, did not like it because there was no chance for them to reach the White House in time.

Only later was it observed that such press conferences included the regulars, the men who cover the White House all the time, but could not possibly include a representation of the Washington press corps, most of whom must cover other areas and cannot stay on watch at the President's office. But at the beginning it appeared the most open, natural, and charming form of press conference one could imagine. And it also seemed tasteful and quiet and suited to the period of mourning.

Before the first 100 days were over, this Johnson technique of informal and spontaneous press meetings would be severely criticized.

In January, Richard L. Strout of the *Christian Science Monitor* wrote that the impromptu system "tends to keep the initiative in the President's hands. . . ." He said of one sudden meeting that "the circumstances were not favorable for asking the follow-up press questions with which Washington buzzes." Mr. Strout wrote:

> Anyone who knows the Washington press corps knows that this hands-off relationship is not going to endure very long.
> Then it will be a test of President Johnson's tact and temper which every President faces.

And this probably will be the key to the next fall's Presidential election as much as the name of the Republican candidate.

Some students of the Presidency, like Sidney Hyman in his book *The American President,* argue that use of the President's facilities for managing "the slippery imponderables of public opinion" is the ultimate test of a President. How, then, did the new man change White House press relations? And how important is the press at the White House?

In the two-story wing which houses the office of the President, the main entrance is now commonly known as "the press entrance." If one stands in Lafayette Square and looks at the White House, one sees in the center the Executive Mansion and at either side two small, low office buildings known as the West Wing and the East Wing. The West Wing houses the President's office; it also contains the press room and the offices of the Press Secretary and his secretaries. The entrance which gets the most usage—"the press entrance"—is the main one at the front of the West Wing. (Actually there are many entrances to this small West Wing, and not all of the doors are observable. A President and his visitors still have some privacy. A side entrance faces onto Old State and there is an underground entrance, a tunnel between the West Wing and the EOB. There are back entrances opening on the lawn and there is an entrance which goes through the White House, a sort of long arcade from the East Executive Wing.)

On the first floor of the West Wing, more space is allotted to the press room and the Press Secretary's office than to the President's office itself and the secretarial rooms immediately adjacent. Nothing quite like this partnership—press and President—exists anywhere else in the world. As Douglass Cater has noted, "No television idol, axe-murderer, or foreign head of state lives in the glare of continual publicity that is the accepted fate of our President." *

When one enters the West Wing, one is, of course, stopped

* Douglass Cater, "The President and the Press," *The Fourth Branch of Government.* Houghton Mifflin (Boston, Mass., 1959).

at the gate for clearance. Then, upon entering the lobby itself, one meets a guard or perhaps a captain of the White House guards. One nearly always sees some television or still-camera men and their gear, and, inside the waiting room where official visitors sometimes wait, a crowd or a scattering of reporters, comparing notes, telling stories, and relaxing like "indolent courtiers," in Cater's phrase.

The White House press room proper is very small, crowded, and so cramped as to be uncomfortable. Adjacent to the waiting room and press room is a little office where three secretaries work, and beyond it the office which Mr. Salinger (and now Mr. Reedy) shared with their secretaries during the first 100 days. The Press Secretary's office, the waiting room, the lobby, and the press room itself take up a good part of the first floor of the West Executive offices, and so it is no wonder that this front door of the West Wing is called "the press entrance." In the middle of January, 1964, the porch canopy was rebuilt and neon tubing was installed so that night and day a delegation standing under the canopy could be photographed for television and by cameras without flashbulbs.

This floodlit door, this press room, and this waiting room are symbolic of the fact that *the Presidency is a voice*. As Theodore Roosevelt put it, and as Kennedy sometimes quoted, the White House is "a bully pulpit." It is also an information or publicity center. A President is the voice of the Government, the voice of the people, and sometimes the voice of a political party. Nearly every day he announces something or pleads some cause and the press is there to listen, to report, to praise and to criticize. The West Wing is thus a loudspeaker, and on some days when TV has strung cables and lights all around, it appears to be an impromptu broadcasting studio. If the President—with or without his Press Secretary—decides *this minute* to make an announcement or to reveal a secret, it can be announced to reporters before you have finished the next page of this book. Before you finish this chapter that news can be coming out of teletypes in San Francisco and out of radio receivers in London, South Africa, and Calcutta.

It is a hot question as to whether White House correspondents are "courtiers" to a man who may be termed a "monarch." And it is a more perplexing question to understand just how much power they have and how much they really cover or really criticize.

It is far easier to walk in off the streets and cover Congress than it is to cover the White House. No reporter can just stroll into the West Wing. All White House correspondents have to be cleared before receiving a card permitting them to come and go through the White House gates.

Even after he is inside the working wing of the White House, in his own press room or the waiting room, a reporter *never* just opens a door to the inside and walks in to see a staff aide. Those last few steps are not taken unless one has an appointment. There are uniformed policemen, plainclothes Secret Service men, and ushers to keep people from the corridors outside the President's office and the offices of the other White House aides. The President and his staff are seen by appointment only.

In the press room one might expect that reporters would constantly be on the phone ringing offices elsewhere in the building. They are not. If a man wants to "work a story" in the White House, his best bet may be to stay in his own office and get on the phone to query people or make arrangements to meet them. In that way he has more privacy and his interview has less chance of being known to some colleague in the press.

Much of what the White House does, particularly what the President does in his function as Chief of State, is perfectly open and publicized. *Much of it is nothing but publicity.* It has no other meaning than to call attention. The President is merely doing something in order that a picture may be taken, or so that a few words may be said on behalf of the Red Cross, against cancer or for the Boy Scouts.

But on the other hand, most of the work that is done in the White House is not publicized until it is in its final form, except for certain accidents, leaks, "plants," and "trial balloons."

What did Congress do today? All its main actions are in the record.

What did the White House do today? Generally, no news-

[181]

paperman knows, except for those actions which are arranged as set pieces for him to observe.

There is ample room for argument about the way in which Presidents use and misuse, manage and mismanage the news. And the same is true of the way news is managed in the only place in which JFK said it could be managed—in the offices of publications themselves. But there can be little doubt that the press is a prime instrument of control and of self-control in our society. Explaining and reporting are part of the self-government process in a democracy.

As he took over the Presidency, Mr. Johnson, it appeared, was fully aware that the press would be important to him. He approached it with a show of great certainty and great energy. Whether his certainty was justified and his energy well-expended became one of the great question marks of his first months in office.

His opening was dramatic and seemed to sweep all before it.

Perhaps no man could ever hope to surpass the tremendous wave of press approval which President Johnson received on his first appearance before Congress. The Washington *Post* suggested that his speech belonged "in a place among the best of the State papers in American history . . . it would be hard to improve upon it by the alteration of a single sentence or a single sentiment." The New York *Herald Tribune* raved: "fine words, fitting words, at times inspiring words . . . he showed himself not a fluke of history but a President." The San Francisco *Chronicle* predicted that he would be a "strong President, and faithful to the Kennedy principles and policy." Many commented upon the fact that his delivery was slow and measured and dignified and that even his accent was subdued. Many observers agreed with the Boston *Herald* that the President had "demonstrated a sense of the grandeur of language that we did not think was one of his talents."

The next night the President gave a Thanksgiving message. This time the man mainly responsible for the text of the speech was not Theodore Sorensen but Horace Busby, Washington business newsletter editor and former staff member of the Johnson office. Privately news stylists and Presidential observers felt that the Thanksgiving speech was not the equal in style—and delivery—of the Congressional speech.

Reaction to the first spontaneous informal press conferences —for the impromptu character of that Saturday "coffee break" soon set a pattern—was almost entirely favorable. Joseph Kraft, former *Times* man and now an independent commentator, wrote that the "snap news conference" had "served the interest of the President, the press and the public alike." He thought that the President spoke casually but with clarity and candor and "there was none of the frantic fuss that used to tie up the whole Executive branch on the eve of a televised news conference." Mr. Kraft noticed that in the absence of TV cameras there was none of the usual striking of poses. He wrote: "The fatal connection between cameras and posing was underlined in Wednesdays' conference when, toward the end, the photographers came on the scene. At precisely that moment, the President removed his glasses. It was the one self-conscious act of the session." Chalmers Roberts of the *Post* felt "the new President has concentrated on creating a mood and an atmosphere, rather than on giving out hard news."

Mr. Roberts commented that the new President "is off in the right direction" and that flexible format was important but not nearly as important as "that the President be available to the press at reasonably regular and frequent intervals and in a manner which can accommodate those who want to see him in the flesh."

An early-day *Editor and Publisher** article, however, deserves special mention for forecasting that Mr. Johnson would probably operate with a personal approach and a "unique blend of rewarding his friends and ignoring his enemies." The article further said:

> Mr. Johnson has shown himself to be exceedingly sensitive to news stories, calling up individual newsmen and berating them at some length.

The *E & P* story, written before Johnson's Presidential press career had started, is also interesting for this passage about Mr. Johnson's temper under pressure:

* *Editor and Publisher,* November 30, 1963.

[183]

Newsmen who know him best, however, say that he has mellowed noticeably since his days as an irascible Senate Majority Leader. Says one:

"I recall a session at the Capitol with newsmen when, thinking photographers had finished taking his picture, Lyndon then put on his glasses. Jut at that moment a flash bulb went off. Lyndon was furious, angrily told the photographer not to use the picture.

"As Vice President he has gotten over a lot of this. Remember that he hasn't been under his old-time pressure. But since he had a heart attack a few years ago he's naturally had to take it easier, anyhow.

"Just how he'll react with the old-time pressures on him again—and then some—is anybody's guess."

Concern about sensitivity to criticism was voiced by few others at that time, although it is possible to cite examples from men and publications at opposite ends of the political spectrum.

James Reston wrote in *The New York Times,* five days after the assassination, that Johnson was "tyrannical with his personal staff, disorderly about administration and apoplectic about characters who write sentences like this . . . more thin-skinned about press criticism than anybody . . . since the last President Johnson . . . he has tended to regard dissent as perversity . . . as if criticism were not a duty in a free society but a crime."

I. F. Stone, in the first issue of his liberal biweekly newsletter after the assassination, said, "His vanity, his thin skin and his vindictiveness make even the mildest criticism, or approach to objectivity, dangerous."

A *Newsweek* column sounded this note quite sharply, in February. It began with a quote from "a Washington reporter who knows the President":

He has almost everything it takes to be a great President—intelligence, experience, drive, and a heart in the right place. But he lacks one of the essentials—a thick skin. This deficiency can be his undoing if he doesn't overcome it. He should never read a newspaper.

With this quotation as his text, Kenneth Crawford in *Newsweek* wrote one of the sharpest criticisms of the way the President's "thin skin" was causing him trouble, but Crawford also emphasized that "the press, too, can be hypersensitive when it suspects that an attempt is being made to use it."

Though White House aides are no longer the sphinxes they were a generation ago and are far freer about giving out degrees of information or degrees of intimation, they are not garrulous. As recently as the Eisenhower regime it was difficult if not impossible for correspondents to call up an assistant at the White House, or a key official, and obtain any bona fide answers.*

In the early days of the Johnson administration all the persons who had some interest in briefing the press comprised quite a list, and of course one reason for the size of the list was that the White House staff to some extent represented a double team. There was also a tremendous amount of news; events of historic importance occurred daily.

Among those who regularly met the press were, of course, Mr. Salinger and his assistants, Andrew Hatcher and Malcolm Kilduff. Then the special technical people, such as McGeorge Bundy for national security, or Ralph Dungan for Latin America, would meet in various contexts, sometimes social, with the reporters assigned to their particular areas. As long as he remained, Theodore Sorensen kept up a certain amount of "backgrounding" of the press, a job which he had also done for Mr. Kennedy. George Reedy from the beginning was a regular source for backgrounding and for keeping in touch with magazines, book writers, and special information projects. Jack Valenti and Bill Moyers, the one a professional advertising and public relations man and the other a man who had had special public relations experience with the Peace Corps, often saw press people. Valenti and Moyers, of course, were also key people in deciding who would be brought in to see the President

* In the days of James Hagerty the news in many respects was more managed than it has ever been since, because the key Eisenhower people were required to check out strictly with the Press Secretary every contact and every luncheon with members of the press.

After the first 100 days, Mr. Johnson began to move in this direction, too. Although he held many more impromptu "appearances," the doors to aides and access to real information became even more difficult.

or who would have an interview or semisocial contact with him.

When Eric F. Goldman joined the staff, one aspect of his mission was to meet with scholars and writers, and this included of course some newspaper and magazine writers. Way over in the East Wing, Fred Holborn, whose main duties were handling the President's correspondence, also met regularly with reporters and seemed to enjoy their company either at luncheon or in the press room of the White House. In addition, the First Lady had her own press operation, and it gradually became apparent that Mrs. Johnson's press secretary, Mrs. Liz Carpenter, was in fact an adviser in her own right to the President.

Accordingly, at first it appeared that the new man was maintaining the open-door policy, and that his informality might even open more doors than ever before.

Almost exactly a month after the assassination, at the time of the President's Christmas holiday, *Time* magazine wrote of the press relations on the Texas trip: "If there was any lingering doubt that Lyndon Johnson likes his press relations on the easy-going side, these doubts were removed last week. The guest list of the LBJ ranch seemed to be limited not so much by Presidential hospitality, which was boundless, as by the number of correspondents. . . ." *The New York Times* reported, "Members of the press have never seen anything like it.* The President of the United States held a news conference with a haystack as a rostrum. In the background smoke drifted up from barbecue pits. . . . After the conference the President rode off on a horse."

The President invited Tom Wicker of *The New York Times*, Douglas Kiker of the New York *Herald Tribune* and Phil Potter of the Baltimore *Sun* for a fish fry. The next day the President himself drove the Presidential Lincoln and took Wicker on a ride—at times they went 70 miles per hour. High Sidey of *Time* magazine had a chicken dinner and a boat ride up the

---

* Actually, those correspondents who were old enough to remember Franklin D. Roosevelt had seen a lot of the same. President Roosevelt would have off-the-cuff conferences very easily—when his car stopped, or in a swimming pool, on vacation, in an airplane—wherever and whenever he felt like it.

lower Colorado River with Lyndon Johnson for a guide. James Reston of *The New York Times* called from Phoenix, Arizona, and asked if he could come over. The President not only invited him but sent his own plane to intercept Reston and his wife in Dallas. Marianne Means, the Hearst papers' correspondent at the White House, received a special invitation and had a hard time getting away. The President insisted that she sit next to him at dinner and before one flight of three helicopters left the ranch the President sent Jack Valenti to pick Marianne out of one helicopter and reinstall her in the President's. Miss Means is a personable blonde as well as being a good reporter.

When the President had been in office for about a month he was at a White House party which was attended only by four women reporters, one of them being Isabelle Shelton of the Washington *Star*. The President spoke to them, decided to take them on a spur-of-the-moment tour of his White House offices. He showed them his office, the small "think-tank" next door, the Cabinet room, the swimming pool. He kept up a chatty running commentary for close to an hour and dropped some very solid news. He disclosed that the military was seeking a $9-billion increase in the defense budget for the next fiscal year, which would bring the total budget far above the $102.3-billion ceiling President Kennedy had informally established. Actually, that very day Mr. Johnson said that he was bringing the budget down to $102.2 billion, and later evidence indicated that Mr. Johnson was then making up his mind that he didn't want to be a hundred-billion-dollar President.

In this informal tour Mr. Johnson gave out several such nuggets of real news, and in numerous asides indicated that he knew exactly what he was doing. "You're as good as the men reporters," he observed, "and I want your bosses to know it. . . ." Or he would say, in referring to the military request for a $9-billion increase, "Nobody has written it, you've got it."

The party itself, which the four women attended, was held on December 23, two days before Christmas, and was a famous White House reception for Congress and Cabinet, which the President had decided to hold only that morning. It attracted some 200 legislators despite all the holiday absences and a tremendously heavy snowfall. It was at that party that Mr. Johnson stood atop a gold and velvet chair in the middle of the State Dining Room and made a speech urging Congress to cooperate, saying, "The eyes of the world are upon the United States tonight," and making an emotional appeal that the nation must show itself strong and resolute.

Earlier in the receiving line he had told the Republican leader, Rep. Charles Halleck, "Charley, I'm sorry if anybody here said anything ugly about you—we can disagree without being disagreeable."

Thus the whole day was a lesson in the Johnsonian drive, the Johnsonian persuasive ability, and the Johnsonian impromptu method of handling news with a few reporters to whom he had —apparently—just decided to unburden himself on the spur of the moment.

But the aides closest to him have told the writer that the main "impromptu" press conferences are scheduled days ahead. There is plenty of other evidence that Mr. Johnson was giving the press a great deal of calculation.

On that same day of December 23, Washington had a record snow. The snow came down in the big flat flakes from 8:30 A.M., and continued all day and much of the night.

But the flurries outside were nothing to the flurry of activity inside the White House. This was one of the key days in the relations between the White House and Congress, and in the middle of it the President also turned to the question of getting more and better publicity. The rest of the city was concerned with Christmas and with snow and with getting Congress out of town. But at this moment, *Congress was being coaxed back into town,* sometimes one Congressman at a time, by phone calls from the White House, including a few President-to-person calls.

On such days government employees hope that the White House will declare a "holiday" to avoid the traffic tie-up, and the word finally came that government employees in nonessential categories would be dismissed at 2 o'clock. Long before that, many workers had begun to leave, and they drifted home through most of the day so that the usual rush-hour traffic jam never materialized.

But in midafternoon the key public relations officers of the Cabinet departments were trudging to the White House. There they filed into the "Fish Room," * which on this occasion was set with board table and chairs. They were greeted by their host, Pierre Salinger, but were told that the President would soon join them.

Mr. Salinger explained that the President was keenly interested in publicizing government activities to the country. He was also specifically interested in seeing that everything that could be announced from the White House, or which could be helped by a White House announcement, be forwarded to the Office of the President. (There was no emphasis on politics or "the campaign," but it may be assumed that all present knew how important it was to the campaign to keep information going out of Washington. Nor was there mention of economy, but by this time no one in Washington needed to be told that all economy stories should be referred to the White House so that the President himself could speak of the new saving.)

The purpose of the meeting represented no radical departure in Presidential information procedures. Cabinet departments have always referred to the White House any story which could be more usefully broadcast from the higher rostrum, the louder amplifier. But the meeting itself—the time, the place, and the main speaker—was new to the old pros.

Mr. Salinger asked those present to produce story ideas for the White House the very next day, which was Christmas Eve, so that he could take them to Texas and possibly make some governmental announcements from the Texas holiday headquarters. Mr. Salinger explained that Mr. Johnson wanted to keep the pot boiling even during the holidays.

The President then entered the Fish Room. He greeted the group by saying that while he understood from Pierre that they were all a hardworking bunch of men, in his opinion they were hardly doing anything at all. He spoke jokingly, but some present failed to be amused at being thus addressed by the President of the United States. Mr. Johnson referred to the story that had

* In this room President Roosevelt had kept a tank of tropical fish, and later President Kennedy had decorated a wall of the room with a sailfish he had caught off Acapulco.

[189]

lately appeared about his lighting the White House Christmas tree, and he said, "Well, we did get a good play on that." He spent only a few minutes with the group, and his casual but pointed remarks were felt by some to be undignified. One listener, who had seen President Kennedy under somewhat similar circumstances, commented that Mr. Kennedy could be very down to earth, while simultaneously preserving a certain dignity which kept one aware all the time that he was the President. He thought that JFK's approach might have gotten the same point across without his "coming on like the mayor of a small city and saying now we got to get more publicity for City Hall . . . I don't see my name in the paper as often as I would like to."

The meeting was at the end of the period of mourning, and in a philosophical sense it underlined the White House attitude that it was now proper—and essential—to beat the drums. And it was one more early indication that Mr. Johnson would follow news (and publicity) more closely than had any other President.

Within the first two weeks after the assassination it was noticed that President Johnson kept a sharp eye on the White House news ticker. One day a White House reporter was in a phone booth in the West Wing lobby dictating a story to his office. The reporter had barely come to the meat of his story when Mr. Salinger knocked on the phone booth door with the astonishing comment, "The President says to tell you you've got the wrong emphasis in your lead!"

Such hot news is phoned in to the wire service bureau and is written and put on the wire even before the reporter has finished it. The reporter's first paragraphs had gone to his office and to the ticker and were coming back into the President's White House office *before the reporter had finished phoning from the lobby.*

Another reporter was nearly knocked off his chair in the press room when he received a call from the President himself. His office had inserted the name of Adenauer in a story about the visit of the German Chancellor and the President called to correct him: "That's not Adenauer who's coming to see me, it's Erhard."

Such telephone calls from the President rapidly lost their

novelty. The technique, in fact, was already well-known to those who had covered Mr. Johnson at the Capitol.

As Richard Harwood of the Louisville *Courier-Journal's* Washington Bureau reported, "Cecil Holland's account of Johnson as a budget-cutter appeared in the Sunday edition of the Washington *Star*. That afternoon he got a call from Texas. It was the President, who spoke half an hour praising Holland for the story."

Strangely enough, although it sometimes seems that reporters print nearly everything they hear, it was almost impossible to find in print any direct transcription of what the President said in his frequent press phone calls. One newspaperman with personal knowledge of such calls, however, emphasized to this writer that they were by no means all negative, nor was it true that the negative ones did not accomplish something. The very day he gave his joint Congressional speech, the President made some phone calls to newspapers. To one Washington newspaper he expressed great appreciation for its editorials on his problems in succeeding to the Presidency.

In another later instance the President urged an editor to veer off the trivialities of the Bobby Baker case and go to work on a certain problem in Congress. The newspaper management thought the latter point well taken and for days pursued the subject Editor Johnson had suggested. (They continued to pursue the Baker story, however.)

Mr. Johnson is an I-want-it-done and do-it-now man. Thus it was that one influential newspaperman was taking a bath in a San Francisco hotel when the phone rang. He ran to it dripping and stood there getting a chill while the President gave him a long-distance scolding. This newspaperman was impressed but essentially unflattered. He was annoyed and frozen. He also thought it undignified for the President to call coast-to-coast to a newspaperman about a relatively unimportant few lines in a newspaper story.

For people experienced in press relations, the methods the new President was using raised several questions. How personal can a President be with reporters and editors in view of the number of newspapermen interested in the White House?

[191]

Another question concerned television and radio—they were missing the "spot" conferences.

For it seemed sometimes that the President was using methods adapted to his personality and Senatorial experience which were inappropriate in the White House. How many press men could he see personally—with the best will in the world? How many not seen would then become resentful at being left out?

The first line of the first press conference that Mr. Johnson held was only half serious, but in retrospect may have been more important than was realized. He said, "I told Pierre a little earlier in the morning I was going to buy coffee later in the day but I didn't really know how much coffee I was going to buy. He has more friends than I anticipated."

A reporter answered, "More people work on Saturday than you think."

There are 2,500 members of the White House Correspondents' Association. Many of them, of course, are not regular working reporters, and the actual maximum attendance at the largest regular press conferences approximates 350.

Later, when the President said that he had been seeing people and that he wanted to hear from reporters and would try to see them individually whenever he could, his remarks were greeted incredulously but silently. Not everyone realized that even in his first two weeks in office he had been seeing reporters alone for special interviews. Experienced men could not believe he would try to see reporters individually, day after day.

Reporters chafed under the fact that they had to wait around and sometimes got news and sometimes didn't. (The attitude of some White House aides and even some reporters was that it wouldn't hurt a few complacent veterans of the press to learn to cover news on a spot basis and to have to wait around or to move swiftly in an impromptu manner.)

The television question was partially solved in the first weeks. The Johnson television formula was seldom going to feature large, live conferences. In his first months in office his predecessor, Mr. Kennedy, had startled the country by agreeing to have his press conferences televised. The nation thus had an extraordinary chance to see its leader in action, answering questions and displaying his knowledge, charm, and wit. Mr. Eisenhower had done it for film, but film can be cut and edited. No other President had done it live.

As the Kennedy conferences grew larger and larger, reporters frequently complained that they were being turned into exhibitionists and actors. JFK was charming and masterful in these conferences, and it was felt that the arrangement in his case gave more and more command to the President so that the press conference could be planned as a finished performance. It was carried off with polish and wit but less and less spontaneity, under the spotlights, the glare of the camera, and the huge size of the crowd. But if the Kennedy press conference was a show, it was a good show, for unquestionably JFK was a virtuoso. There would be little question that Kennedy and Roosevelt were far and away the best press conference performers the White House has ever seen.

It was thought reasonable to assume, then, that Mr. Johnson did not adopt the same format as JFK simply because he did not want to invite invidious comparisons.* In addition, however, it must be said that many press relations experts agreed that even under JFK the large TV conference was not accomplishing its desired purposes.

Douglass Cater in his book on the press in Washington, *The Fourth Branch of Government,* took for granted that the press conference had generally failed under the administrations of Truman and Eisenhower. The conference itself, he thought, "tended to aggravate their problems" as leaders and he thought it "compounded a difficulty of leadership for the President in an era when he deals with issues incapable of easy or quick solution." Cater cited as an impossibility pessimistic prediction another writer's idea that "the day is not far distant when the President will have his own television theatre."

> There will be . . . nothing to prevent the President from having a press conference a day, if he likes, and flooding the tele-

---

* Mr. Johnson in April held a conference using the same format and same auditorium formerly used by JFK. It was his most successful conference to that time. So much for comparisons, invidious, odious, or imaginary.

vision screens with prepared answers to questions written in advance. Thus, while the other "equal" branch of the Government, Congress, is arguing its case to virtually empty seats, the President would be in a position to use the carefully prepared and televised conference to overwhelm the weaker voice of Congress.

Then, years after Cater's book, after some 60 days in office the new President announced a startling innovation being considered for television arrangements at the White House.

The three television networks were to be given permission by President Johnson to build a permanent TV studio within six feet of the door to the President's office. The TV facilities, which might cost approximately a million dollars, may be installed in the Fish Room just across the hall from the Presidential office. The Fish Room is smaller than the Cabinet room and is used for all kinds of meetings. Already, like some of the rest of the White House, it is perpetually being arranged and rearranged like a stage setting or a hotel banquet room. Sometimes, even as important visitors are arriving in the outer lobby, the huge round tables in the lobby are upended and rolled into the Fish Room for a meeting. At other times the room is more like an eighteenth-century drawing room.

At present, when the President wants to make a televised report from his desk he has to vacate his office six or seven hours ahead of television time so that technicians can install equipment.

The new arrangement would also provide for cables from the central headquarters to go out to the Rose Garden, to places where foreign visitors are received, and to other key points. Thus, official arrivals and departures and the comments of key visitors as well as the President's impromptu statements can be instantly transmitted onto all three networks.

The proposal for a studio startled observers in the Capitol, but it was no different in principle from other government facilities and services for the press. The permanent TV cameras will be just one more step in making the White House a glass bowl for America's number-one gold fish. As this book goes to press, details are still being worked out, but the TV wiring has now been started.

Still pictures had earlier been the subject of Presidential attention. One of the first "new men" to come to the White House with Mr. Johnson was a photographer, and within a few weeks he was appointed an assistant in the press office—the first photographic press secretary in history.

Few people are aware of this appointment, because the Johnson man's term in office lasted only a few days. And though this one man's appointment and departure are but a small story, it is nonetheless one which tells much about the President's interest in thrift, in history, and in publicity.

In those early days of the new President, Mr. Johnson thought quite seriously about the importance for history of notes and records. One of the first things he did was to ask Lady Bird—and then Cliff Carter—to make some notes on the day of the assassination.*

Before becoming President, Mr. Johnson had come to know the work of an exceptional photographer with the United States Information Agency, namely, Yoichi Okamoto. The two men met in August, 1961, when Okamoto was picked to go with Mr. Johnson to Berlin. In the course of events, Mr. Okamoto was assigned to the transition as part of the U.S.I.A.'s coverage. As would be expected, the U.S.I.A. put out many special publications to explain to the world our method of Presidential succession, in order to reassure the world that our government would continue to function as before

The U.S.I.A., formerly directed by Edward R. Murrow, and now by Carl T. Rowan, is entirely a federal government news agency. It is created for the express purpose of giving information and propaganda about the United States to the whole world, its best-known division being the "Voice of America." The U.S.I.A. also operates as an information and education service, sending to our overseas exhibit centers and libraries all

* Nevertheless, some items did get away. Today no one can find the piece of paper written in the President's own longhand in which he composed that first message to the nation which was broadcast from Andrews Field, "I will do my best. That is all I can do." It was written in longhand, then Jack Valenti saw that copies were typed. The records office has a typed copy with some revisions in the President's own handwriting, but the original was lost. Another lost item is the Bible which Judge Hughes held while the President put his hand upon it.

kinds of news and feature stories about politics, industry, agriculture, art, science and life in the United States. An experienced writer is assigned by the U.S.I.A. to the White House at all times. Okamoto became the first man assigned to cover the photographic story of the White House, and in addition his prints were useful in many ways.

As the early days went by, the President was quite pleased with the work of Okamoto, and he began to ask for the photographer to attend nearly every meeting and event. Okamoto would take a few pictures at the beginning or the end of interviews, even if there was only one visitor in the oval office with the President. When the prints came back, the President or one of his assistants would select what seemed to be the best pictures. Many times the President would send an autographed picture to his visitor. As any politician can well imagine, these photographs in themselves became a part of the personal touch—a touch of thoughtfulness or a touch of manipulation—by which the President made his face-to-face conversations with visitors still more effective.

The shy, quiet Okamoto thus became privileged to see history close up, a privilege seldom granted to anyone not directly participating in great events. Okamoto responded by taking magnificent photographs and by keeping his mouth closed.* Finally, since the Press Office had long wanted to have a photographic adviser, Okamoto was officially named an assistant to Mr. Salinger.

This exciting assignment came to an end overnight.

Two or three reporters, including a writer for *Newsweek* magazine, had written news features about the President's photographic shadow. One night Richard Harkness, a news commentator for NBC, mentioned rather critically that while the President was talking a lot about economy in government, he was using a photographer to take an extraordinary number of pic-

* When this writer asked to see Okamoto for his personal comments on the transition, he was told that Okamoto was the most silent man in Washington, and the White House correspondent for U.S.I.A., Mr. Robert Cahn, said, "Okie won't even tell me anything; he won't even say what they have for lunch in there."

tures. And the figure mentioned was "11,000 frames," meaning individual negatives.

To one not familiar with the work of news photographers—and of course this includes most of the television audience—the number 11,000 sounds simply enormous. The average magazine, however, will take perhaps 2,000 or 3,000 frames on a major picture assignment. This figure merely refers to the number of negatives exposed. Many are exposed almost at random because in fast-moving events sometimes a stray shot will turn up a better photograph than the most studied exposure. Not all of these frames are ever turned into prints—the latter are far more costly than negatives. In other words, to have worked for weeks at the White House and to have taken 11,000 frames was normal professional procedure.

Of course, the question of economy is by no means the sole issue involved. It is questionable whether in a democracy, even for the sake of history, "a court photographer" is necessary and desirable. In previous times the White House had used photographers from the armed services. (An Army photographer was with Kennedy in Texas and took the photographs of the swearing-in aboard *Air Force One*.) The U.S.I.A. made films of the visit of Mrs. Kennedy to India and to Pakistan, but these films were *forbidden by U.S.I.A. rules from being shown in the United States,* under the basic principle that most Americans would not wish to have their elected leaders use taxpayers' money to make an impression on the taxpayers, even with beautiful propaganda films.

If the issue had been brought up and approached in this light, many elements of the press would no doubt have been the first to criticize the use of this excellent photographer. Immediately after the Richard Harkness broadcast, however, Okamoto was summarily sent back to the U.S.I.A. The press was given no explanation, and the incident was frequently mentioned in the many critical conversations bubbling along in February in Washington. The historian of the future will have to be satisfied with the early photographs of the transition and probably will be so grateful for them that he will not pause to curse the later darkness—or Harkness.

"LBJ Loves the Press: Or Does He?"

The title comes from an early February headline in the Louisville *Courier-Journal,* and seems a good plaintive background for the question: When is the honeymoon over?

In the case of the honeymoon between the new President and the press, various mumbles and grumbles began to be heard in January, and by the middle of February there was a good-sized flurry of Presidential criticism from newsmen, columnists, and editors.

Then on February 12 a panel of newsmen on a television show examined the topic of White House information policies and concluded that the honeymoon was definitely over. The three panelists were all professional newsmen, and their comments soon became a live topic of discussion among press and Washington officials.

The program was moderated by Edwin R. Bayley, a public affairs editor of the National Educational Television network. In opening the show Mr. Bayley said that the President had been irritated by stories about him, that he had seemed more sensitive to criticism than most Presidents, and that White House aides "had called reporters, editors and publishers to object to stories or even a few lines in a story."

The other participants were Peter Lisagor, Washington Bureau Chief of the Chicago *Daily News;* Charles Bartlett of the Chicago *Sun-Times;* and Philip S. Potter, Washington correspondent of the Baltimore *Sun.* Bartlett had been a personal friend of the late JFK. (With Stewart Alsop he wrote the famous *Saturday Evening Post* article which put Adlai Stevenson in such a precarious position.) Potter is a personal friend of LBJ and occupies a similar position to President Johnson that Bartlett held with Kennedy. Mr. Lisagor, a veteran Washington reporter, is also personally known to the President, and thus his critical comments were all the more interesting.

One day the new President had had lunch at the home of Marguerite Higgins, a news columnist. Among those present at that informal "surprise" luncheon was Lisagor. After this and other close-up views of the President, Lisagor said on the program, "I think he would like to make cheer-leaders out of all

[198]

of us, and we're fighting hard to preserve our virtue, because soon enough, I think . . . we'll all turn into our natural state which is to be common scolds and he'll have to deal with us then."

Philip Potter had had numerous personal contacts with the President, before and after his White House days, and was repeatedly described in the press as "an old friend." Potter agreed that the honeymoon was over: "I think the President's making a difficult transition from legislative leader to President. As legislative leader he'd hide things close to his chest. . . . In the Presidency, he's got to make his aims and objectives known to the public to gain their support, to get programs through Congress. So he's made himself very accessible to the press, perhaps too accessible."

In summing up the broadcast, Mr. Bayley as moderator expressed the thought that as the honeymoon ended, the antagonism between the press and the Presidency could be "serious." His concluding remarks might almost serve as an appraisal of the early period, particularly since they carried a justifiable note of uncertainty about predicting the future:

> What I think we have is a situation that could have serious consequences to President Johnson. We have a press corps accustomed to the disciplined, intellectual approach of President Kennedy; we have a new President, concerned about his public image, who is trying hard, perhaps too hard, to make news. He has made himself more accessible than any other modern President. He has introduced the coffee conference, the Saturday conference, the sudden appearance on the Hill or social gatherings, the six-hour monologue at the ranch, and skinny-dipping in the White House pool.
>
> As Majority Leader of the Senate, Lyndon Johnson was quite effective with reporters, with whom he had long, informal chats. He still tries to see reporters individually, and said in his January 25 press conference he had granted 30 or 40 separate interviews. . . .
>
> Every President has been irritated by what the press does about him. Mr. Johnson has seemed more sensitive than most. He and his aides have called reporters, editors and publishers to object to stories or even a few lines in a story.

[199]

No one at that first Saturday morning press conference in early December imagined that the little informal get-together would be a prototype of many to come, but in fact the pattern was soon established, and most of the early conferences were held on a Saturday. The only exceptions were the second press conference held on a Wednesday, December 18, and one in Texas on Friday, December 27. Only toward the end of the first 100 days did the President have a larger conference with some slight advance notices, with television permitted and with a larger space for reporters than is possible in the West Wing.

On February 1, the President met the press in the theatre of the East Wing, and on February 29 he held his first live television conference with an audience of approximately 300 reporters in a large State Department meeting room. He had been in office 72 days before that conference in the theatre of the East Wing, and it was called only after press criticism by commentators and editorial writers had begun to grow in volume and sharpness.

Actually the President's pattern with the press began to change one week earlier, on January 25, the day of his fourth press conference.

It was a Saturday, a day of drenching rain, a good day to stay at home or in the newspaper office—a bad day to go to the White House press room—unless something was likely to happen. As of 11:30 that morning Malcolm Kilduff, the Assistant Press Secretary on duty in Salinger's absence, was telling reporters that the noon briefing was not expected to contain anything very special. The word was that the place was quiet, "the lid was on." In the White House lobby some 35 reporters waited for the briefing which was running an ordinary, normal "late."

Then, without any prior word to Mr. Kilduff or the official stenographers, a conference was called, and literally three minutes later it began. The reporters filed into the Oval Room and found the President seated in a rocker having a cup of coffee with an old friend who also happened to be a newspaperman, Harry Provence, editor of the Waco, Texas, *News Tribune*.* The reporter for the Washington *Post* found the President

* In March, Fleet Publishing Corp. published Mr. Provence's *Lyndon Johnson: A Biography.*

"unusually relaxed and at ease" although on the other hand he, at one point, showed "irritation" with the press. Mr. Johnson told reporters that he would soon make decisions on foreign aid, "if you all just don't jump the gun on me, and have me having a closed mind on this and having already decided it, with each one of your leads coming out saying that this is what the President has done." He continued, "So don't write that it is all finished and settled and concluded; or that the President has made his decision or that he has made a wise one or an unwise one."

The President also seemed somewhat irritated that his press conferences were called "quickies." He said, "I don't know what you call formal ones. . . . I guess I'll have to wear a white tie. . . . Some of you, I think, feel that I don't see enough of you individually. I will be glad to do that." He added that he had seen thirty or forty reporters and that some of them wanted to ask about his Cousin Oriole or about "what I think of my wife."

In retrospect, perhaps the most important thing said was that another press conference would be held the following week. This, of course, was noticed by the press—it meant "advance notice." Still there was no word as to an exact time, and all that week reporters paid special attention to the morning and afternoon briefings. Tension began to build up as the days passed.

On Thursday there seemed to be a more solid rumor than on most days that the press conference was imminent, and reporters began to crowd the West Wing. There were various encouraging signs, such as the way the official stenographers scurried to and fro, and there was something in the manner of the press secretaries—all dressed to the teeth. On Friday more reporters waited and then on Saturday, although no word had come from the press office, the lobby began to fill up around noon. Altogether, a man who wanted to make certain of going to that press conference that week might have spent three or four days waiting. Accordingly, there was a good deal of grumbling among the press at the idea that they had to watch the White House hour by hour on the chance the President might press the buzzer.

Eventually at 1 P.M., Saturday, the press was told that the conference would start at 3 P.M. This was the first press conference announced in advance by the White House, and the announcement was a scant two hours in advance on a Saturday afternoon.

Of course, when considering how the press gets pushed around by the White House schedule or the lack of a schedule, one might take into account some of the other things going on. The week before there had been a state visitor, the Premier of Italy. This week the President had recorded a key speech to the Geneva Disarmament Conference which proposed a plan to "freeze the number of atomic delivery weapons." The Panama crisis was still simmering along and General de Gaulle had recently rocked the power structure of the world with his decision to recognize Communist China. On Wednesday the President gave to Congress his astonishingly low 97.9 billion "American Dream" budget. The ladies of the press that week were not heard to complain. That Friday night the President had dropped in unexpectedly at a big dinner being given to Mrs. Johnson's press secretary, Elizabeth Carpenter, by the Women's National Press Club and the American Newspaper Women's Club.

By two-thirty, two dozen reporters were on hand, and by a quarter of three the theatre in the East Wing of the White House, which can accommodate about 90 people seated, was so crowded that late-comers had to stand along the wall at the side. Mr. Hatcher, Associate Press Secretary, had already told the press that there was no earthshaking news to be expected and that the conference was just being held because reporters had asked for it and the President had promised it. To many of the persons present, that was the tone in which the President walked through it, as if it were a chore he was performing in a careful and controlled way, but with irritation lurking beneath the surface.

About that first big press conference Chalmers Roberts wrote in the Washington *Post* of Mr. Johnson speaking calmly and of a "hitherto largely domestic-oriented President wading deep into foreign affairs." Mr. Roberts thought it was generally "a good baptism . . . the nation began to get a better idea of its new President's handling of foreign affairs . . . given less cramped quarters and more notice next time the nation should learn a lot more, as it is entitled to do."

On February 28, the President announced through his press office that the next day—for the first time—he would have a press conference which could be recorded as it happened by television and radio. This was also the first conference of which there was a real advance notice, although it was less than 24 hours.

This day marked precisely 100 days since Mr. Johnson's arrival in the White House.

He started the conference with lengthy announcements and, like the first big press conference (of February 1) where he had discussed such weapons as the Red Eye, he had a military weapon to announce, the very secret "advanced experimental jet aircraft, the A-11, which had been tested in sustained flight at more than 2,000 miles an hour."

The second question concerned "the possible political impact of the Bobby Baker case." As he had often done before, the President said that this was a matter which the Senate was considering.

When asked about foreign policy and if during his first one hundred days he had seen any encouraging signs that the world was traveling toward coexistence rather than to strife, the President answered, "We must be concerned not just with our foreign policy in the twentieth century but with the foreign policy of 110 or 120 other nations, and we are today dealing with serious problems in many places in the world that seriously affect the peace."

Mr. Johnson also repeated commitments he had given before that "it's important for the people to know the problems that confront me" and then he spoke on press information:

> I shall have my press secretary hold daily briefings, at least two a day, and make available all information that can be available to the press. From time to time, I will see individual members of the press about press business, and I may see some of my old-time friends socially, occasionally, and I hope without too much criticism.
>
> And other times, I'll have them in my office too—if I have any announcements that I think are worthy of their attention and of taking their time.

Other times, I'll have a meeting like this to reach the folks who the press may not be able to reach through the ordinary newspaper or magazine media, so that we can have radio coverage and television coverage.

The entire transcript of this press conference was carried in major city newspapers. James Reston in *The New York Times* thought that the President approached his ordeal like a man going to the gallows, that he had gotten through it with "no runs, no hits, no errors—and several issues left stranded." Reston—and some other reporters—thought there was no particular reason for announcing the new plane, the A-11. Other commentators explained critically that the President knew that the story would dominate the headlines, as it did, even in Mr. Reston's *New York Times*. Mr. Reston, like others, also felt there was a great scarcity of real information and that the Johnson political technique was mainly "to minimize or evade trouble."

Later in the day, some idea of the President's own reaction to the press conference was revealed in a talk which Mr. Johnson gave in the State Dining Room to a crowd of 200 Texans, including the musicians of the Houston Symphony Orchestra who had come to perform at Constitution Hall. He told them that he had had a busy day, beginning with a breakfast conference with the Secretary of State, followed by a meeting of the National Security Council, and then he referred to the press conference as a meeting of the "war department." The President said, "It was a press conference of their desire, held where they wanted it. . . . Afterwards I saw many individuals so I could get many things I had confused in the conference clarified."

Mary McGrory in the Washington *Star* wrote that "the most memorable thing about the long-delayed confrontation—is that it is over—the President had avoided the meeting as long as he could, he had taken refuge in a series of substitutes. . . ." But, thought Miss McGrory, "the moment that would provide the most vivid contract between him and his predecessor, President Kennedy, could not be put off forever." She noticed the President "smiled only twice and then warily. He seemed uneasy, he

[204]

did not look at his questioners, he stared straight ahead and in many cases he did not answer their questions." *

David Lawrence, the conservative editor of *U. S. News and World Report*, thought that "President Johnson handled himself just right . . . presented himself simply as an earnest, dignified President of the United States."

Meanwhile, the public opinion polls were beginning to indicate that this is exactly how the public saw Mr. Johnson. And no politician—or statesman, for that matter—needs to be too concerned about press relations in Washington when his public relations are demonstrably going well. Whether the press sniping of Washington was going to grow and become a major factor impeding the Johnson program was an interesting but iffy and highly debatable subject.

But of course not all the press agreed as to which was the sensitive party—the press or the President.

At a time when other reporters were becoming quite sharp about what they called LBJ's system of playing favorites, Betty Beale, famous society writer for the Washington *Star,* wrote a strong defense of the Presidential policies.

Miss Beale started off with the old saw, often applied to White House inhabitants: "They're damned if they do, damned if they don't." Then she wrote:

> This columnist never thought she would live to see the day when the press criticized the President for being nice to the press! The press corps as a group has never before had it so good under any previous President. Perhaps there lies the rub.
>
> The Lyndon Johnsons have not changed one iota since entering the White House. They have always regarded reporters as people and they like and are kind to people they come in contact with—whether it's a camel driver on a dusty street in Karachi, a weary reporter in a cubby hole in the National Press Building, or a Chancellor of a European State.

* In fairness to Mr. Johnson, all Presidents evade or fail to answer press conference questions. All of them bring out stories like the A-11 to make news even though the news may not be closely related to the White House. It is the President's press conference after all, although some of the press feel it should be the press's Presidential conference.

The question other reporters would ask Miss Beale, of course, is whether the President really was "talking to the press" or whether he was in fact talking just to "a few." It was not clear to all of the Washington press corps that everyone was getting "an even break."

The columnist T.R.B., writing in the *New Republic*, was particularly sharp about "Press Pals." He said that the President had picked up the phone and congratulated a reporter on an early budget story, then had grown angry at an AP reporter. The columnist thought that "it is distressful to find that Mr. Johnson, after all these years, does not know the press better. His proper indicated attitude is one of polite aloofness."

T.R.B. thought that it was one of Lyndon Johnson's big faults that he read newspapers. (It is reported that he reads 15 a day.) He wrote that "he ought to stop right off. . . . He is one of the most thin-skinned and sensitive men who ever paced the Lincoln Study, and he should not be permitted to see criticism because he writhes under it. . . ."

The worst personal publicity the President had in the early weeks came as a result of taking some reporters on a speeding automobile ride near his ranch. *Time* wrote:

> A cream-colored Lincoln Continental driven by the President of the U. S. flashed up a long Texas hill, swung into the left lane to pass two cars poking along under 85 m.p.h., and thundered on over the crest of the hill—squarely into the path of an oncoming car. The President charged on, his paper cup of Pearl beer within easy sipping distance. The other motorist veered off the paved surface to safety on the road's shoulder. Groaned a passenger in the President's car when the ride was over: "That's the closest John McCormack has come to the White House yet."

Newsweek had a similar story, but did not mention the beer, and newspapers ran stories from coast to coast.

So far as the President and the press are concerned, several items about this are interesting. This was a social occasion, after a more-or-less official press get-together with the President. The reporters who were in the car with the President—they did not include anyone from *Time* or *Newsweek*—did not immediately write any stories about this, and neither did reporters in other cars following Mr. Johnson. The story broke several days later after another incident of speeding, concerning Mrs. Johnson's car (not being driven by her).

Experienced Washington press relations men felt this was another instance in which the President failed to realize that it is almost impossible for a President to have social relations with the press. If what he does on those occasions makes news some reporter sooner or later is almost certain to write it.

Once this story was out, of course, many columnists and editorial writers criticized the Chief Executive for his driving habits.

How far can a President go in making friends among the press? This is a difficult question, and it is far from clear that friends in the press are very useful to a President in the long run. Strangely, the real game of press relations seems to be to obtain goodwill from people who are kept at a distance.

A President presumably arrives at the White House with friends, but it is very difficult for him to keep up his relationships with any but the very closest. He is too unapproachable. His schedule is too full. Even his relaxation has to be so calculated and so scheduled that it is not possible for him to seek out the old and develop new friendships. And if it is difficult for a President to make friends, generally, it is particularly difficult for him to maintain and have friends in the press. A reporter should be doing *his* business, which is to report the news, and he needs some distance and objectivity from it in order to do a good job. Some go further, and say there should always be a definite note of conflict between President and press. T.R.B. in the *New Republic* in February wrote: "There may be a few exceptions; but these White House confidants are immediately known, and dangerous. People read particular writers and say 'Aha, that is what LBJ is thinking.'"

There was no doubt in Washington that many people said "aha" when they read William S. White, Les Carpenter, Philip Potter, Drew Pearson, and Gerald Griffin.

An article by Philip Potter in the Baltimore *Sun* (February 15, 1964) is an interesting example of the kind of story which could filter out of the White House to a selected few. This article was originally filed as a news story, but the editors of the *Sun* found it more interpretive than editorial and therefore placed it on the editorial page. They gave it a three-column headline and a position at the top of the paper, and although it may not have been much read in Baltimore (editorial pages, it is said, are read by less than 10 percent of the newspaper readers) it certainly was in a position to be well-read by the newshounds of Washington, those who watch for indications, intimations, and inspirations. This was the only such story by Potter given this special treatment in the first months of the Johnson regime. It is reasonable to conclude Mr. Potter decided it shouldn't become a habit.

This story contained no direct quote and was not "pegged" to any specific event, with one exception. Its key sentences were flat declarative judgments or were presented as if they were straightforward reporting of observations from unknown but reputedly "top-rank" officials.

The lead sentence of this story, or "plant" or "leak," said:

> Published reports that President Johnson's sureness of touch in handling domestic problems does not carry over into the foreign field are sharply refuted by State Department officials, White House aides who have worked with him on foreign problems and by Robert F. Kennedy, Attorney General.
>
> Kennedy, who worked closely with his brother, the late President, on many foreign problems, including the crisis caused by the placing of Soviet missiles in Cuba, told this correspondent this week that Mr. Johnson is making "effective use" of the machinery he inherited for dealing with foreign problems.

Another judgment by Mr. Potter was:

> There is no validity at all to reports that McGeorge Bundy, special White House assistant in charge of national security affairs, has found it difficult to work with Mr. Johnson and that in consequence there is a 50-50 chance he will quit.

Another judgment was attributed to a "top-rank official," who apparently had told Mr. Potter "that if the staff had been relatively as well-coordinated at the same stage in the Kennedy administration there would never have been a Bay of Pigs. . . . If anything, Mr. Johnson's way of working is more orderly than Mr. Kennedy's and he is staying closer to developments." This reporting, that a top official thought Mr. Johnson more orderly than Mr. Kennedy, was followed with the inane but believable statement: "The President's staff has been instructed to notify him immediately when anything important happens anywhere in the world."

The article went on to say that "staffers of long experience with Mr. Kennedy say they sense no difference now in the way appropriate officials are called into consultation, relevant facts are assembled and alternatives in policy are discussed." Then follows another inane but this time unbelievable statement: "The President, it is said, has no difficulty in making up his mind what to do or in rendering decisions."

In this entire column, under the heading "Making Foreign Policy," there was not one word implying any criticism of the new President, nor was there one line suggesting that he had difficulty in getting the White House staff to work well together nor even any great complications in dealing with other countries.

Some of the Potter sentences have to be read quite carefully before one understands just what in the world they do mean, other than that the President is against evil and for good. For example: "The President's firmness in upholding American prestige without exacerbating relations with friends or foes is stressed by his foreign policy advisers."

At first glance this sentence suggests that the Baltimore *Sun* is reporting that the President is succeeding in upholding American prestige, without, etc., but actually the line says only that the President's firmness is stressed—by his advisers. Thus the story, if that is what it is, returns to its essential theme of reporting in the Baltimore *Sun* the line which the "top official" apparently wish to be reported.

The famous columnist, Drew Pearson, also wrote quite favorably about Mr. Johnson.

Mr. Pearson's stepson, Tyler Abell, is an assistant postmaster general. One of Mr. Johnson's actions in the first month was to promote Mr. Abell. In addition, Mrs. Abell is assistant to Liz Carpenter, who is the First Lady's press secretary.

On December 18, 1963, Pearson discussed the visit of fourteen top correspondents to the White House, the tour which included the bedroom and a glimpse of the President's pajamas. Pearson said, "The fourteen top correspondents departed feeling that their country has a friend in the White House and that the White House is not a national museum, but a home."

On December 26, Pearson reported on the topic of Bobby Baker's income tax returns which, he said, President Johnson had made available to Senate investigators. Pearson said copies of Baker's returns had been shown to Jack Anderson, Pearson's associate, by Baker himself more than a year before, and that they "show none of the fabulous profits he is supposed to have made on his back door business deals." *

Early in the administration, a few days after the assassination, Drew Pearson had written about the Bobby Baker case:

> In addition to his many great assets, President Johnson has some problems. The No. 1 political problem at the moment is the Bobby Baker investigation. It was Mr. Johnson who picked Baker as a bright young secretary and developed him.
>
> My investigation of the Bobby Baker case shows that Mr. Johnson is in no way involved with Baker's financial operations. But the two were personally close, and guilt by association is popular these days.

Another columnist who had personal contact with the President more than once during the first weeks of the regime was Robert G. Spivack. Mr. Spivack has long been known as an independent writer, and he is not classed as a personal friend of the new President.

In the first week in January, however, Mr. Spivack wrote a

* Not until April 11 was it known that Mr. Baker had signed his accountant's name to his 1961 federal tax returns. Mortimer Caplin told this to the Senate Rules Committee Chairman, Sen. B. Everett Jordan (D., N. C.) after FBI laboratory tests were reported to him. Accountant Milton L. Hauft had previously said his name had been "forged," but he did not say by whom. Caplin did not use the word "forged."

series "based on interviews . . . with President Johnson's closest friends." In it he said that the President was not a rough-hewn character, as frequently described, but that he worked with Congress on a basis of friendship and understanding and sympathy and "developing a mutual respect . . . the only basis on which a President can work with Congressmen and Senators who are proud of their privileges and prerogatives."

About press relations, Mr. Spivack explained the hubbub as follows:

> Certain columnists were regularly spoon-fed by the previous Administration. Often they were also the ones who played to the hilt the popular Washington game of "who's in" and "who's out." When the new President took over he tried to make them feel at ease. But they found that his habit of saying grace before each meal, of expressing solicitude about their relatives, of not beating about the bush was just too homespun—certainly it was not Ivy League style.

Then Mr. Spivack brought up the subject of Boston-Austin feelings, and he strongly implied that Johnson's critics were Easterners from the Hamiltonian tradition, whereas the friends of Johnson were Westerners from the tradition of Andrew Jackson. Mr. Spivack in the column of February 21 did not refer to any interview or session with Mr. Johnson. He did not quote him. For all we know, he may have gotten these sentiments from friends of Johnson's, from years of watching him on Capitol Hill, or by telepathy. All this writer knows is that Mr. Spivack did see the President, and he did write like this:

> He makes no apologies for his humble beginnings. He also knows something about American history and that it was Alexander Hamilton, the ideological father of the present-day Republican Party, who once said of the masses, 'Your people, sir, are a beast.' It is ironical, of course, that this bit of snobbery came from a man who was an illegitimate child.
>
> When people speak of the new President as being in the Andrew Jackson tradition he is pleased to plead guilty. Jackson, in his time, was criticized for opening the White House to what the Eastern press called "the rabble."

Mr. Johnson feels that his first 100 days already produced more recruits than any since FDR's first 100 days. Roosevelt was able to get whatever he wanted because the country was in dire straits; today it is, generally speaking, in good condition.

Does this mean that Mr. Spivack has had private seances with the President and is now another brainwashed victim of the treatment, *aha!*

A proper procedure would be to read Washington columns with care and skepticism and a sharp sense of what are feelings and what are facts.

Despite all his efforts and his major success in reaching the public, there was growing criticism of the President's press relations as the 100 days ended.

It was not just criticism of too few press conferences and too much attention to selected individuals. It was not just related to the quite special treatment given to the Bobby Baker case and the surprising manner of handling information about the opposition witness, Don Reynolds. The issues involved, it was felt by seasoned observers in the press, were more important.

Chalmers Roberts, for many years a careful reporter of international affairs and of the White House for the Washington *Post,* expressed this criticism quite bluntly. Mr. Roberts' thesis, certainly debatable but not unique to him, is that a President's foreign policy or an administration's program in foreign policy is judged not only by formal statements and by activity in the usual diplomatic channels. A President—and the nation—is in part understood by the world through the medium of the answers given to questions which are brought out at press conferences. Thus, to Mr. Roberts, the lack of more complete press coverage was a hindrance to the understanding of the new administration's policies abroad.

Mr. Roberts also pointed out that Presidential candidates had been opening up on President Johnson. Nixon had spoken about "the worst series of foreign policy failures" since World War II. Goldwater had called him the "great compromiser" and referred to "eroded strengths, ailing alliances and threatening disasters." Rockefeller thought the situation in Panama was "completely tragic." To this type of attack, Roberts said, the President merely "runs up a temperature" and calls his opponents "alarmists" and "belly-achers."

Roberts referred to the unique material cited by Philip Potter of the *Sun* which apparently came from Mr. Johnson or some source close to Mr. Johnson:

> As of a week ago, he [Mr. Johnson] had participated in 175 separate White House meetings and made 188 telephone calls on foreign affairs. . . . Dean Rusk, Secretary of State, had been to the White House 51 times for sessions on national security affairs; Robert S. McNamara, Defense Secretary, more than 80 times. . . .

Roberts thought "this sort of statistical defense about as meaningless as the Republicans' generalized attacks." The main point of Roberts' critique was that "Mr. Johnson had been dealing in generalities in foreign affairs under a controlled system of news . . . he has not really exposed himself to questions."

More than that, if one looks at the timing of the press conferences, it appears that the choice of Saturday and the choice of surprise press conferences is designed to make the most of Sunday newspapers and to get the minimum number of reporters. It is not a way of answering diverse questions from many segments of society; it is a way to reach the major correspondents for wire services and networks.

This means that the major outlets and the most people can be reached through twenty-five or thirty main channels. But a larger press conference, using four or five times as many people, does not by any means mean four or five times as much audience, although it does mean four or five times as much chance of embarrassing or direct questions.

And what can be said of the way in which reporters and groups were often kept waiting, given hints of announcements which were about to be made, and then told that there would be no announcements, and the like? It may (and then again it may not) give us some idea of the smoothness of the administration or organization of the new team. Once again it would seem a little harsh to judge the administrative ability of a man by the first three or four months. Nonetheless there is a question when individuals, reporters and press conferences themselves are so unsmoothly managed. Here is an area in which it is known that the President is greatly concerned and yet here is one which did not run at all smoothly in the first four months. If this is how people are treated in an area which means so much to him, what happened in other areas in which the President did not have such an overwhelming interest?

The final questions about Mr. Johnson's use of his press relations machinery will be decided by certain tests—by elections and by the support which Congress gives to programs he has advocated and publicized.

Millions seemed to feel after the first television press conferences and the television "conversation" that here was a hard-working and humble man who understood certain fundamentals about poverty, economy, hard work, and the sincere desire of people everywhere to have peace. The opinion polls indicated the public liked the man and his program.

Still ahead of the President, after his first months of office, lay the acid test of the campaign. These months would test the President and his staff with formal speeches, press conferences, and television. Much of what we have noted here will seem like mere Washington chatter if the November election ratifies what the pollsters find. The new President did not seem to have any press or speech-making problems so far as the people are concerned.

9

From Camelot to Johnson City

MANY FELT IT WAS like going from the saintly Abraham Lincoln to the coarse-grained Andrew Johnson. Some even saw it as worse—like going from Woodrow Wilson and scholars to Warren G. Harding and scoundrels. And nearly everyone thought that no two men could be more different in background, appearance, and style than John Kennedy and Lyndon Johnson.

Top people of the New Frontier had favored French restaurants near the White House—Le Bistro or Chez François. Now it was claimed that Washingtonians would have to eat in chili parlors. Weeks later people still grumbled that we had gone from Camelot to Johnson City. Emotion blended reality and fantasy and people could not remember that they had ever disliked anything about John Kennedy. Many were sure they would never like anything about the new man.

But Washington tended to overlook two main facts about these two men. One was that they were after all very much alike in what they did in government. They had quite similar beliefs in their philosophies. They followed the same path to the top, for both were practical and professional politicians.

The second fact was that Mr. Kennedy held the intellect and abilities of Mr. Johnson in high regard, as symbolized in the much-quoted statement, "If I didn't want the job myself, I'd get behind Lyndon. He's the ablest man I know in American

[215]

politics, and he really cares about this country as I want a President to care." When Mr. Kennedy chose Mr. Johnson as his running mate, there were several very basic reasons for the choice. But one of them was consideration of the grim possibility that Mr. Kennedy might not live out his elected term. A newsman heard JFK say, "And you just have to think of what might happen."

These considerations make clear that Johnson's selection to be Vice-President was no political accident—as the selection of the number two man has sometimes been in America's past. The Dallas shooting was a kind of wild accident. In that respect, Johnson came to the White House accidentally, but the reasons for his being there in case of tragedy were as rational as the act in Dallas was irrational.

Both men had served in the Senate together, and in many ways they were cozy club members. In part of that time John Kennedy was very much a freshman—and looked it. Lyndon Johnson was the Majority Leader and the most senior faculty member in terms of poise and power—and he looked it. (Robert Kennedy was a junior staff employee—not nearly so influential as another junior staff employee—that other Bobby.)

Then, in 1960, LBJ and JFK were rivals in a hard-fought primary campaign. Their combative partisans—and to some degree they themselves—made unusually nasty charges against each other. Cries of "foul"—of religious prejudice or sectional prejudice—were common. Then the two were candidates together, after John Kennedy picked Lyndon over the protests of many in his own party and notably against the advice of his brother Robert.

Then for three years Kennedy and Johnson worked together, and it is important to know they really did just that. Of course, the Vice-President's role was quite subordinate. In fact, at times it was so quiet and so much in the background that the energetic Mr. Johnson became quite restless. However, all observers are agreed that at no time did the Vice-President seek to undercut the President. The older man gave unquestioned loyalty and obedience to the man who had bested him at the Convention in Los Angeles.

When the President was shot, Lyndon Johnson shared the horror—and the pageantry—with which the Kennedys and the nation said farewell. Then he became President as a substitute and as a successor. He remained closely aligned with John F. Kennedy because he was the inheritor of the Kennedy program. Beyond that, on his own, he made himself, by his powers of persuasion and his good sense, the inheritor for a time of the extraordinary Kennedy staff, and he worked with the Kennedy team. Meanwhile, for months and perhaps for years, he would be haunted by what might be called the ghost of Jack Kennedy, by the inevitable, endless comparisons.

And then it became obvious to everyone, early in 1964, that Mr. Johnson still had to consider the Kennedys as formidable and unpredictable powers, not necessarily allies, in the political campaign of 1964 and the political currents of other years ahead. Some of the most dramatic chapters in the relationship of Johnson to the Kennedys may soon be written. To understand the history of '64 and beyond, we will look at some of the record and once again review some of the comparisons. Some of these are invidious and oversimplified, but they are part of the story of that winter and spring, in which we said good-bye to so much of Boston and said hello to so much of Austin.

In *The Making of the President 1960,* Theodore H. White makes a great point about the "conflicting recollections" concerning the selection of the choice of Johnson for Vice-President. White wrote that within days or indeed hours after the event "anyone at the Biltmore Hotel in Los Angeles could have his choice of three or four certified versions of the transaction, all purporting to be the only truth, all interlocking yet all conflicting."

The day of selection—the day after the nomination of JFK—was a day of weariness for everyone. That was one reason people's "recollections of their own role blurred and faded in exhaustion . . . in exhaustion and cross-purpose." According to the White story, when Kennedy went to sleep he had left his lieutenants with the impression that the Vice-Presidency was a choice between only two men, neither of them Johnson. The main contest, most thought, was between Senators Henry Jackson and Stuart Symington. (Hubert Humphrey might conceivably have been in the running, but twenty-four hours earlier he had decided to support Adlai Stevenson.)

It is true that Kennedy had made the favorable remark about Lyndon B. Johnson being so well-qualified for the Presidency, but in White's words "the poison of the stinging contest for the nomination had so changed his mind later that his remarks about Johnson in the final pre-convention weeks were of the same colorful bitterness as Johnson's remarks about him . . . and yet the underlying respect must have continued . . . for . . . on the Sunday before the Convention opened, Kennedy, seemingly idly, remarked to Washington publisher Philip Graham that if he thought Johnson would accept the Vice-Presidency *he might offer it.*"

Graham had taken that word to Johnson and Johnson's answer to the feeler, just before the Convention, was simply "a single earthy expletive."

But, according to White's chronicle, when Kennedy after his nomination returned from the Convention to his apartment he found that Johnson had sent "the warmest and most cordial telegram of congratulations." The telegram may have started Kennedy thinking. In any case, the next morning he began his day with a phone call to the Johnson suite.

A generally accepted version of what ensued goes like this.

It was 8 A.M., July 14, in the Biltmore Hotel, when the nominee called Lyndon Johnson's suite. Lady Bird answered the phone because Lyndon was asleep. Then Mrs. Johnson woke her husband. He talked to Kennedy and agreed to meet him two hours later but (according to Helen Fuller's account in her authoritative book *Year of Trial*)* he really was not sure why Kennedy wanted to see him.

That day at 8:30 John Kennedy conferred with his brother Robert, but the decision was not yet absolutely crystallized. At 10 o'clock he saw Johnson and asked him, and Johnson accepted, but both men still had some thinking to do. At 10:45 Kennedy met with Pennsylvania's Governor David Lawrence, an example

* *Year of Trial—Kennedy's Crucial Decisions.* New York: Harcourt, Brace & World, Inc., 1962.

of the type of big-city leader who had not liked Lyndon Johnson and had to be won over to the idea.

At 11:15 A.M. Senator Henry Jackson was told by Kennedy that Johnson was his choice.

At noon Liberal leaders who were strongly against Johnson called on Kennedy. They included Alex Rose, New York Liberal Party leader, U.A.W. Chief Walter Reuther, and David McDonald, President of the Steel Workers. Adlai Stevenson also came by during the noon hour. These men were either won over or reconciled to the choice.

In the middle of the afternoon John F. Kennedy, all by himself, made the final decision—and once again phoned Johnson's suite. None of his friends, not even his own brother, knew of that ultimate decision until after it had firmly been made and a public statement was on the way.

At the time that Jack Kennedy made the announcement, Robert Kennedy was in Lyndon Johnson's suite at the Biltmore Hotel. From that suite a phone call went upstairs to Mr. Kennedy. "Jack, Bobby is down here telling Speaker Rayburn and Lyndon that there is opposition and Lyndon should withdraw." According to Helen Fuller's history, Kennedy's voice came back calmly, "Oh, that's all right, Bobby's been out of touch and doesn't know what's been happening."

"Well, what do you want Lyndon to do?"

"I want him to make a statement right away. I have just finished making mine."

Miss Fuller relates how the day before the Democratic National Convention opened, two newspapermen friends of Kennedy went to see him and gave him a strong argument about the qualifications for Johnson. He came from the right region, he had the right religion. It would be difficult to run a campaign later or to get along with Congress, if he had to contend "with a vanquished and embittered Johnson." Miss Fuller added however, "And most important of all they emphasized Johnson's exceptional ability."

To their astonishment Kennedy told them he had considered the same factors and had come to the same conclusion. The newspapermen were the more astonished not only because of the bitter competition between Kennedy and Johnson but also because Robert Kennedy had assured one of them only a few days before *that Johnson would not even be considered for Vice-President*.

It was calculated in 1960—as it is now in 1964—that the Democrats cannot win the Presidency unless they pile up huge majorities in the industrial cities of the North. To do this they have to have support from labor and minority groups. There can be no compromise with the South's position on civil rights. It was thought then that Lyndon Johnson in some respects was Mr. Compromise himself and that to have him on a national ticket might be fatal.

Miss Fuller and others have said, however, that the real basis for Kennedy's selection of Johnson was "the basic respect" the two men had for each other.

Mr. Joseph Alsop has also reported that he heard Kennedy say that in the selection of a Vice-President "you just have to think of what might happen." On the Johnson side of things, that Thursday afternoon only a few hours before the Convention would nominate a Vice-President, Johnson's wife and his political mentor, Sam Rayburn, "were somewhere between negative and neutral toward the idea of Johnson in second place."

After Mr. Kennedy had announced his decision to select LBJ in the morning, pressure on JFK did not slacken but on the contrary mounted. Supporters of Senator Symington were putting on the heat. Walter Reuther and Arthur J. Goldberg were protesting and Kennedy, after various calls, took a few minutes to think it over and then sent the message to tell Lyndon that the decision was final.

That was about 2:45, but the opposition to Johnson still did not give up.

About 3 P.M., Robert Kennedy came back to see Rayburn in Johnson's suite with the word that a call would shortly come from John Kennedy. With Johnson, who was nervous and on edge, were Governor Price Daniel of Texas, Senator Robert S. Kerr of Oklahoma, Speaker Rayburn, and a man not known much outside of Capitol Hill—Bobby Baker, at that time Secretary of the Senate Policy Committee. Kerr, Rayburn, and Daniel were objecting loudly to Johnson's acceptance.

By four o'clock the call had not yet come and Johnson, reportedly now "extremely nervous," was with Mr. Rayburn, John D. Connally, Jr., later to be Secretary of the Navy and still later to be Governor of Texas, and wounded on that day in Dallas. There were also Mrs. Johnson; James Rowe, Washington lawyer, who remains a close adviser of the President; the late Philip Graham, publisher of the Washington *Post;* and Baker.

At this point Robert Kennedy appeared, saying that there was a lot of opposition and that Johnson should withdraw for the sake of the party. It was then that someone called John Kennedy and got the word that Bobby was "out of touch." Then the phone was given to Johnson and he heard John Kennedy read to him the statement he was making, announcing his choice.

Then Robert Kennedy, very serious and dead tired, in Johnson's presence listened to his brother on the phone and was heard to say, "Well, it's too late now" as he half slammed down the phone.

Then with some urging and coaxing from those with them, Lyndon and Lady Bird were pushed into a hall blazing with television lights. The cameramen asked them to stand on chairs, and Johnson read his statement of acceptance. One reporter said that their facial expressions changed from fatigue and discouragement to show "enthusiasm and confidence." Miss Fuller summarized:

> By choosing as his running mate the man whom he considered, after himself, the best man for President in 1960, Kennedy acquired a possible antidote to religious bias in the South; he removed a potential rival for power from the Congress with which he would have to work as President; he took the first step toward restoring the Vice-Presidential office to its original importance; and, consciously or not, he created a Democratic heir-apparent to follow him in office."

None could have imagined, in that convention scene, the day when Johnson would phone from Dallas to ask Robert Kennedy about taking the oath of office. But we choose a Vice-President —in convention or wherever—for that main simple life-and-death reason. That is the Vice-President's reason for existence: to be there in case.

Many months later—it seemed an era later—in March of 1964, Charles Bartlett, a correspondent who had been close to John Kennedy, wrote about troubles between Robert Kennedy and President Johnson. He said that, as a matter of fact, Johnson had been selected by something of a fluke, in that John Kennedy had not expected Johnson to accept the number two spot. This story had been told before but not in print, not in such a pointed manner. Is it true? Available evidence is conflicting.

In Theodore White's book, he writes that after the day of selection in Los Angeles was over, "the impression of the Kennedy staff on this day of action was that the subject of the Vice-Presidency came up almost casually in a general exchange of courtesies and political talk and that it was only during the course of the visit that Kennedy realized that the Majority Leader would enjoy a change in rank and status."

White quotes one of the headquarters staff as saying numbly, at the end of that July 14th day, "It was always anticipated that we'd offer Lyndon the nomination; what we never anticipated was that he'd accept."

In interpreting different stories it must be understood that before a convention, men who are running for President almost never tell the truth as to whether they would accept the Vice-Presidency. In many cases they do not know the truth. As Hubert Humphrey said (before the campaign of 1960), "It usually happens in the late hours of the convention after the man has been nominated and he calls someone and asks him if he would run with him and he says, 'we need you on the ticket.' "

Humphrey pointed out that the man who is receiving the phone call knows that he may be listening to the next President and thus: "You really don't know what you would say to that until you get the phone call."

These remarks of Senator Humphrey's were made about five years ago. In the aftermath of the assassination of President Kennedy many people have gained a new sense of the importance of the Vice-Presidency. Almost for the first time in American history has there been campaigning for the Vice-Presidential nomination. So—to return to the Los Angeles story—up to the time of the Convention, Lyndon Johnson had always said that he would *never, never, never* accept the nomination for Vice-President. It had always been assumed that he had an excellent position of power in Washington and that it would not make sense for him to leave his Senate post—a place of great respect and leadership—to go to the relative "nonentity" of the Vice-Presidency.

Lyndon Johnson as a campaigner with Kennedy in 1960 made an undoubted contribution, and in some ways his work was unique and surprising.

The election, of course, turned out to be so close that any group or any man who was able to deliver some extra votes could claim with some justice that without A, B, or C, the President could not have been elected. There was more truth in this statement when it was made by Johnson men—as it often was—than by others. Because of his particular characteristics and regional support, Johnson won more electoral votes than any other Vice-Presidential candidate could have. The kind of campaigning he did was in sharp contrast to that of President Kennedy, and in this year of 1964 many more professionals are willing to admit how much it appeals to the average voter.

The fall of 1960 was the first time that many national reporters got a chance to see Johnson away from his official habitat on Capitol Hill. One of them wrote that past observers "would hardly recognize him as a campaigner for Vice-President . . . partisan and aggressive and anything but subtle . . . he has mixed folksy humor, biting sarcasm about the Republican Party and frontal attacks in the Harry Truman style." This writer, Anthony Lewis in *The New York Times,* thought this quite a contrast from his work on the Hill as "a subtle parliamentary strategist."

When Johnson campaigned in the East his five-gallon hat and his raspy voice startled people and his folksy manner reminded some of Southern evangelists. A listener in Queens said, "I'm converted but I don't know what to."

Johnson had already been gaining attention for his changed, but forthright, convictions on civil rights. In this campaign he gave the same speeches in the South that he gave in the North. As he told one audience, "What I say here today about the civil rights plank I will say tomorrow and every day everywhere I speak in the South."

Speaking in Richmond, Virginia, he said, "I did not come down here to promise Virginia exemptions from the obligation to carry out the decision of the Supreme Court but instead brought an invitation to join the nation in extending civil rights." He asked, "A hundred years of debate among ourselves is enough, I think, don't you?"

Traveling on his special train, in one five-day period he made forty-eight stops and saw more than twelve hundred local Democratic leaders. They conferred with Johnson individually or in groups and they always had their photographs taken with him by the train photographer.* Those five days which started his campaign in 1960 aboard "the LBJ Special" were not too impossibly different from the first five days in Washington in 1963 where he had *more* than forty-eight appointments and saw hundreds of officials—and also saw to it that they later received photographs of themselves with Johnson.

As President, John Kennedy treated Lyndon Johnson as "a proud and sensitive man would best know how to treat the man who had lost out to him."

Mr. Kennedy also continued the increasing number of measures that had been taken since FDR's sudden death to see that the Vice-President was well-informed about the Government and given some important jobs to do. Kennedy gave Johnson a tremendous office in the Executive Offices Building next door to the White House. This was a favor that President Eisenhower had never granted Mr. Nixon. It appealed to a man who likes some of the trappings which go with office. (LBJ's office as Majority Leader was so large and grand that it was the frequent target of Washington wits.)

In Kennedy's first month in office he wrote Johnson a letter describing the responsibilities the Vice-President would carry in his administration. This letter was never made public but is described as a most unusual document, assigning some executive duties to the Vice-President and providing a staff for him.

* This experience helps explain the role of photographer Okamoto when Mr. Johnson first went to the White House.

Richard Nixon had been invited to many important meetings and in the Eisenhower regime had even on occasion presided over the National Security Council. But essentially his job was advisory. For the first time, under Kennedy, the Vice-President was given specific things to do.

Johnson was a special representative of the President in certain diplomatic contracts with nations abroad. He was Chairman of the President's Committee on Equal Employment opportunities. This gave him an opportunity to work for civil rights and to meet civil rights leaders. His special assignment was to enforce the prohibition of racial discrimination in any hiring by the Government or government contractors. He also had the job of coordinating the United States program for the exploration of space. And he was Chairman of the Advisory Committee to the Peace Corps.

Thus Mr. Johnson was given an opportunity to gain experience and friends and reputation in precisely those areas in which he had been the weakest before, notably foreign affairs and civil rights.

Many people would agree with Helen Fuller that Johnson was most at home in the area of fair employment enforcement. On this committee he came to know the Secretary of Labor, Arthur Goldberg, who had been bitterly opposed to Johnson's nomination. Surprisingly, they became warm friends. Through the Peace Corps he became well acquainted with Sargent Shriver and helped to guide Shriver's extraordinary campaign on Capitol Hill to gain acceptance for the new and much-criticized Corps.

In the field of international affairs most commentators would agree with Helen Fuller that "Johnson found himself singularly unprepared" by the time he was Vice-President. Johnson himself has said that at the time he ran for President "I had not read a book all the way through since I graduated from Southwest State Teachers College." He had been abroad on a Pacific tour of duty in World War II. He had once taken a trip to attend an interparliamentary conference in London. And that was all.

In his first year as Vice-President, Johnson went to Africa as the President's envoy, his real test came on an extended trip through Southeast Asia—to Vietnam, India, Pakistan, and other trouble spots.

When Kennedy asked Johnson to visit the Far East, Johnson realized that his relative ignorance of foreign affairs was poor preparation for this mission. Privately he admitted that he was worried about the trip, that he didn't know much about the area. He began to work on reports and memos with his customary energy. He put in hours of listening to briefings. Then he took off on the 29,000-mile journey to the Philippines, Japan and Southeast Asia.

Descriptions of his visits are mixed. Even then he would use the line that he knew that just about all foreigners would like to be American citizens if they had the chance. State Department advisers winced then and later winced even more when he spoke the same line in the White House. Johnson also broke the rules which State Department protocol had laid down for him. When he saw a crowd he liked to wade right into it with Texas style, handshaking and talking. The crowd nearly always responded with enthusiasm. At the end of his trip he said, perhaps with Texas expansiveness, that he had never seen a hostile face or heard a hostile voice. (He couldn't, Washington wags said, see some of the State Department advisers behind him.)

His advisers had told him not to shake hands or touch any heads in Asia. He couldn't stop shaking hands. The Vice-President irritatedly replied, "Dammit, I haven't patted anyone on the head!"

The whole world noted with some amusement, and generally with approval, how Johnson met the camel driver Bashir Ahmed and invited him to come visit the United States. As Washington will never forget, Bashir took him up on the invitation and the Vice-President arranged an impressive schedule for him in the United States. Bashir visited the Texas State Fair and went to Kansas City to shake hands with Mr. Truman. It was said at the time that Mr. Kennedy and his aides were not amused by the "corny" publicity. But Bashir was a great hit with most people in Washington and throughout the country. More people, it seemed, cared about LBJ and his camel driver than about Pablo Casals or the cuisine at Le Bistro.

The President also sent Johnson on a fast trip to Berlin in August, 1961, when Mayor Willy Brandt reported that morale in Berlin was sinking and rioting might occur in the city. Johnson was a tremendous hit in Berlin. He treated it like Dallas or Los Angeles or Karachi. He frequently left his automobile and plunged into dense crowds. He passed out ball-point pens bearing his name, and the West Berliners were particularly pleased with his distribution of dozens of gold-edged cards of admission to the Vice-President's gallery in the Senate.

The trip was a success to the extent that a goodwill mission could substitute for a change in German policy and specific action. Insofar as Johnson's representation was concerned, it was an extraordinary success.

Of the early period of Johnson as Vice-President, Helen Fuller wrote:

> Lyndon Johnson grew in grace. The volume and variety of work Kennedy gave him attested to that.
> The Vice-President served as a cheerleader in gloomy West Berlin, as a broker with business to break down discrimination in employment, as a mediator between competing groups in the field of space, as a balloon-floater for the President on controversial issues. . . .

Basically, this was the general verdict up until the time Mr. Johnson became President. Then everyone judged him in a new light—as a President—and inevitably, they made a thousand comparisons with the man who had picked him.

A major point of discussion was the difference in their sophistication and literacy. John Kennedy, it sometimes seemed, read almost anything. And for relaxation he might read Robert Frost or Ian Fleming. He enjoyed many different kinds of theatre, although it seemed he would have been just as happy to leave the ballet-going to Mrs. Kennedy.

Mr. Johnson never reads for relaxation, only for information. Mr. Johnson has practically no interest in music or the theatre. He never watches television dramatic programs, although he carries an alarm clock on his wrist, an alarm wristwatch which he uses to remind himself when a newscast is coming up. The new President, however, is a swift reader who likes to dive into memos and reports to try to get at the heart of a problem, or to find an ingenious solution to a conflict. He does not have the range of interests which led Kennedy to read so many different publications and even to urge upon people, for example, that they too should read the *London Observer*. Magazine men were often surprised that Kennedy was familiar with what had been written or editorialized about in recent issues of their magazines. But no President ever watched the news more closely than Mr. Johnson.

It is Mrs. Johnson who does a great deal of general reading, including fiction, and a few years back, Mr. Johnson asked her for outside reading. For a time, she gave him summaries and marked copies of three books a week. On becoming President he has asked people to prepare reading lists or to send him the books they think he really should read.

The President has said that when he has to know the contents of a bill or report he can scan it and fix it in his mind perfectly well. In fact, when he needs to remember a point, he can cite it and paraphrase the whole page and what followed the key passages. But once a task is done he may remember little of a report on which much work was done, and a large decision based. His associates say "he is oriented wholly to the job at hand." However, his associates also believe that he will learn to do "whatever work is necessary to handle the Presidency."

It may be that they are wrong, but this writer does not believe they are practicing their press agentry—they are describing a man they believe has enormous capacity. From long before November 22, men close to Johnson have believed "he might be one of the greatest Presidents this country ever had." One of his greatest capacities, as they see it, is a tremendous understanding of the processes of government. That includes the reading (and the writing) of government reports. They believe few can equal or surpass his ability to get "the gist" or "the essence" from his reading.

One man said that Kennedy looked like a movie president, but Johnson, however, looks like a real one. Then he added the unkindest cut of all—"Real Presidents are not usually good-looking." The two men in their looks, their age, and their style of speaking were different, and in many ways strikingly so.

When President Johnson concluded his first speech to Congress by quoting from the old hymn "America the Beautiful," most people who heard it (including those of the television audience) were sincerely moved. As Washingtonians looked back on it, however, they realized that quoting that verse in that way was something President Kennedy would never in this world have done. The conclusion was too emotional *—and the hymn would probably have seemed trite to him.

The new President's speeches sometimes rose to rhetorical eloquence, but more often his style was staccato, with short sentences. But it seemed to be convincing. It carried conviction. It was understandable. It didn't soar. But it punched home the message.

As one speech after another and particularly as impromptu speeches began to be made by the new President, certain words like "compassion" began to appear over and over. This was quite interesting to some Washingtonians who felt that the New Frontier had lacked the genuine idealism and emotion which had marked political causes in the past. There were those who felt that in particular the New Frontier brought in many experts, but not partisans who cared about causes. The new men were not, as in FDR's time, the kind who had a passionate desire to clean up social conditions. And more than once, it was mentioned to this writer—before November, 1963—that the new men admired excellence and technical skill in social engineering, but they did not feel personally or idealistically about people. Many had never known anyone living in poverty or poor housing or under conditions of race prejudice. So their views were those of a responsible elite, but not of veterans who had seen hardship. In the new President's speeches, as in his entourage, was evidence of human understanding of poverty in personal terms. Meanwhile, the Washington wisenheimers thought "compassion" was becoming as overworked as "vigor" had been before.

* To many people the late President Kennedy had seemed colorful and charming but a little cold. After his death many close friends and admirers said this was not true at all. In particular, Mr. Sorensen emphasized that those who thought that about the late President had just not known him, that Mr. Kennedy did have strong and warm feelings, but that he shrank from showing them.

In the new year, the opinion polls indicated Johnson's prose was understood, and Washington took note. In private conversation and once in a while in print, it began to be said that the LBJ style might in the end make the Johnson administration more strongly popular at the grass roots than was the Kennedy administration. The youthful appearance and manner of the late President, as well as his eloquence and appealing programs such as the Peace Corps, had won him a strong following among young people, not only in this country, but abroad. That might never come to Johnson, but older voters might still give him huge majorities.

While Mr. Johnson was not a great deal older than Kennedy, in appearance and manner and method he suggested an older generation. Much had been made of Mr. Kennedy's youth. Though he was not as young as he appeared, he certainly had a youthful and spirited style. To many persons abroad, as well as at home, he represented a striking contrast with the older rulers, in some cases left over from World War II leadership. In this respect it was discouraging to youth to see the torch that had passed to a new generation suddenly at Dallas passed back to an older person. In this respect the youthful appearance and youthful style of the late President would be mourned by millions for years to come.

But at a closer view, it began to be noticed that the White House now did not have less but more dash and bustle. And the atmosphere was not more conservative and formal, but more informal.

Douglas Kiker, of the *Herald Tribune*, summed it up by saying, "Under Mr. Kennedy the White House was exciting, but somehow a little cold. Under Mr. Johnson it is warm, but somehow a little corny."

Both these men believed in personal direction. Both liked to be accessible to their staffs and to people outside the White House. There is no comparison, for instance, between the diversity and number of people who came to see Kennedy and Johnson, *and* the number who would be brought in to see Mr. Eisenhower. The traffic count, however, was higher under Mr. Johnson in the early weeks than it had been under Mr. Kennedy, and not solely because of the emergency. By March it had settled down somewhat, but was still high.

The big State Dining Room, the East Room, and even the living quarters where the President's family actually lives had now become places very much tied to the work of running the country and keeping the Democratic party humming.

It has been written that the new President seems to have no sense of privacy, whereas Mr. Kennedy had a distinct (and for a politician, a rather unusual) sense of privacy and withdrawal. In his first months in the White House, Mr. Johnson's apparently wide-open hospitality left no doubt that things were going to be different. At the moment that Mr. Johnson was showing some reporters the upstairs of the White House and they caught a glimpse of the President's pajamas laid out upon his bed, a French reporter said, *"No one* has ever seen de Gaulle's pajamas."

It was true that the Kennedys had brought a far wider range of people into the White House, particularly people from universities, the sciences, and the arts. Mrs. Kennedy had done imaginative and energetic work in restoring the White House and in making clear to us that the White House was *our* national residence. Yet, in the first hundred days, much more was opened up under the Johnsons.

Millions would remember Mrs. Kennedy's memorable television tour through the White House. Yet as one Washingtonian said, "It is true she was on television, and in that way saying the White House belonged to all of us . . . but it looks as if the Johnsons are going to let *all of us go through it in person.*"

In his workday, President Johnson is different from President Kennedy and all recent predecessors in the number of hours he puts in, either with government officials or with his staff aides. He can get along and still feel energetic on very little sleep. He starts his business day at seven o'clock in the morning or earlier, when Jack Valenti brings him orange juice and secret intelligence reports at the same time. Even before, at six or six-thirty, he is likely to awaken and start to read the ten to fifteen newspapers he sees each day. He frequently has breakfast meetings before nine.

His day is ordinarily scheduled and frequently he goes along from meeting to meeting, reception to reception, and continues with meetings after dinner until midnight. The day may be broken by one or two swims and they may be broken by phone calls or poolside conferences.

It is not uncommon for him to continue with staff members' meetings after midnight. But usually after the 11-o'clock news on TV he has a reading period until one or so.

This schedule gives him about five hours' sleep, and he averages about that—and often a short nap during the day. He is a man who can take a nap very easily and in a small room adjacent to his oval office he has a very comfortable reclining chair where he can tilt back and fall asleep in a moment.

Mr. Johnson has spent some sleepless nights in the White House, but ordinarily he sleeps easily and well. He says, "It's impossible for a President not to worry a little, but when my head hits the pillow at night, it's like dropping a curtain. I go to sleep."

President Kennedy, on the other hand, once he was past the period of organization, worked a White House day which ran from about nine-thirty in the morning to about seven-thirty at night (except, of course, in times of crisis). When Mr. Kennedy left the office for the Executive Mansion, he put aside the ordinary business of government. (Of course, a President never really puts aside his responsibilities; he is always "on call.") Mr. Kennedy almost never took staff members to the mansion itself for dinner. His idea of a relaxing evening was not to spend it discussing politics—or methods of reorganizing the State Department. Mr. Kennedy's dinner table knew many other topics besides politics. His dinner companions were most likely to be there because they were old friends or interesting people, and not merely because they were politicians, Although many of his friends were politicians, many, like William Walton, the artist, had only an amateur's interest in politics.

In contrasting the two men, it is often said that both of them were strictly politicians. That was their career and that was, to a great extent with both men, their hobby. Mr. Kennedy had a second career—he was a writer. But he wrote almost entirely about government and politics. He did enjoy many different sports, and he could relax in many different ways, and the main distinction between the two in this respect is that Mr. Johnson does not have such a need to get away from politics. Mr. Kennedy would lay his work aside. But Mr. Johnson enjoys politics and talk of government so much that he has practically no urge to get away from it. He does enjoy getting to Texas and his ranch, and he enjoys the outdoors, but even when he is there, he is most likely to have with him someone who can talk politics.

In any case, it had always been thought that the Presidential schedule of appointments was even less flexible than a railway timetable. Each day the President's public calendar is published far and wide. The public calendar includes all his major meetings—be they with the Secretary of State, or the Prime Minister of Italy. The President's staff also maintains more private schedules—for use by the inner circle. In any case, White House staff assistants always considered that the major appointments might as well be written in marble. That's the way they had always been; a President's appointments were sacred.

President Johnson sometimes treats these schedules as if they were made of rubber. He has a tendency to let all his appointments run overtime. He adds new items after the day is started. He gets on the telephone during, before and after appointments, and if the mood strikes him, he may leave the White House to go on some errand he considers important—either to visit someone who is sick, to make an appearance at Capitol Hill, or to make a surprise appearance on the other side of the White House, or even on the other side of Washington. Like Franklin Roosevelt and Theodore Roosevelt, he positively likes to do things which are going to startle people or create a sense of drama.

Often on a trip or on the way home from a speech he has headed for a crowd of people or abruptly turned into a store or a hotel. More than once some woman in the crowd has said, "Oh, Mr. President, are you trying to scare people?" He would probably not mind scaring people if he thought they would get a delicious thrill out of telling the story later. There is a strong suspicion among those close to him that he likes to keep his work and schedule a little unsettled on the theory that it keeps people on their toes. There can be no doubt that he has enjoyed surprising Washington reporters with his impromptu press conferences and with the apparently spontaneous way in which he will walk up to a group of reporters at a social event in the Executive Mansion.

Many Presidents have liked short appointments and have seen their problem as one of getting a man to state his case in a hurry and leave to make way for the next one. Mr. Johnson, on taking over, was more concerned with stating his case to the visitor. He is a good and quick listener, but there is no question that he, unlike Mr. Kennedy, would generally rather do most of the talking. So it is that a committee or delegation can come to the White House for lunch at one and then receive a tour of the place, perhaps even a swim, all the while being bombarded with Johnsonian arguments and persuasions.

He does not see as many staff people within the White House as often as Mr. Kennedy did. But on the other hand, he is also a great believer in memos. As one Kennedy staff man has said, "I am not in that oval office nearly so much, but I know he reads my memos." Thus, he said, he now has a permanent record of his work with the President which he did not have before. And when he does see the President, there is no "distance" between them. They are co-workers, although there is not any doubt who is boss.

Johnson likes to drive his staff. (It is small comfort sometimes to feel that he is driving himself just as hard.) A man who has spent most of his life helping Johnson says, "When you work for Johnson you're on duty twenty-four hours a day. Any time the phone rings after 11 P.M., I know who it is, so I reach for the light and a cigarette, a pencil and paper. I feel a fast surge of blood to my head because I know the test is coming. He's going to throw 100 things at you, asking your opinion on this and telling you that, and you know you've got to be ready for anything."

Why do people put up with such arduous working conditions? The answer: "You have great faith in what this man is doing. When you go home, beat and whipped, you feel you have contributed a little bit by helping him."

While a number of people have worked for the President for

years, however, he has not developed the long-time cohesive staff that Mr. Kennedy and some other Presidents have built up. Some people work for him and then go to another job and then go back to him. Bill Moyers is one such example; Horace Busby, another.

One long-time veteran of the LBJ staff "used to come crying to me twice a month," another Washington figure said, "but finally I told him, 'Go on—you love it.' " Apparently, some do love it, and even take a fierce pride in working for a perfectionist. It does seem, however, that the JFK staff was led; the LBJ staff is led, and it is also driven.

Many experienced commentators made the point that Johnson might well be able to do more with Congress than Kennedy had. To some political experts, this is the main judgment on a President: What is he able to get through Congress?

When Johnson's markedly different approach had gotten excellent results earlier in his administration, several commentators said he was improving upon Kennedy's record in this respect. I. F. Stone, an independent and frequently left-wing commentator, wrote what may have been the most blunt comment of all. In the first issue of his newsletter after the assassination, Stone wrote, "Perhaps the truth is that in some ways John Fitzgerald Kennedy died just in time." Stone concluded (December 9, 1963):

> He died in time to be remembered as he would have liked to be remembered, as ever young, still victorious, struck down undefeated, with almost all the potentates and rulers of mankind, friend and foe, came to mourn at his bier. . . . The Kennedy administration was approaching an impasse, certainly at home, quite possibly abroad, from which there seemed no escape.

Thus many felt (though not many as strongly as Stone) that Kennedy had not gotten the most he could from Congress, and that Johnson was going to get a great deal more.

In the future, as we have said, the story of the Kennedys and the Johnsons will include more about Robert Kennedy and others of the Kennedy family.

On the day Johnson was selected to be Vice-President, it was Robert Kennedy who spearheaded the last-ditch bitter fight against him, according to the main accounts. Robert Kennedy was the number two man to President Kennedy while the Vice-President remained to a great extent informed but not in the thick of things.

After that fatal day in Dallas, there ensued the early period when the President consolidated his control of the Government, and Robert Kennedy was in a state of personal and professional shock and suspension. Later came the movement to write in Robert Kennedy's name for Vice-President in New Hampshire. This was disowned by RFK but not before it had caused further bad feeling between "Kennedy men" and "Johnson men." Rumor had it that at one point RFK and LBJ were not speaking to each other, although both men denied the stories of a big break between them.

By late March there was much Washington gossip, some of it in print, about the breakup of the White House staff and its relationship to Robert Kennedy or to supporters of Robert Kennedy. Drew Pearson wrote (March 24) that "what most people don't realize about the atmosphere around the White House is that after the 1960 election it was Brother Bobby who picked most of the White House staff." He said that the President brought in Sorensen and O'Donnell, but "Bobby, who had managed the campaign and knew first-hand the abilities of various Kennedy supporters, picked the majority." Consequently, said Pearson, "This is a factor which has contributed to a sometimes hostile attitude toward LBJ around the White House."

Pearson said that sometimes "new members of the staff wonder whether the Kennedy holdovers are working for LBJ or Brother Bobby."

It would be a difficult problem but perhaps not impossible for the Attorney General and the President to quiet all such comment absolutely. It would hardly do for the President to say anything stronger than his comment in his television interview when he explained he was sure the Attorney General and he understood each other. The President—in spite of all the phone calls he had made to press people—could hardly take time out

[236]

to make a specific statement without making the situation worse.

It was the same kind of situation in which Robert Kennedy had found himself when, as was widely reported, he had wanted to call off the write-in movement in New Hampshire and had consulted Kenny O'Donnell about it. He was told that it would only call even more attention to the write-in vote and consequently cause more dissension in Democratic ranks and more possible embarrassment to the President.

In any case, because of Mr. Pearson's relationship to the new President, Washingtonians read such comments with great interest and wondered how much of this had come rather directly or even with urgings from the White House itself. On this same day, Walter Lippmann wrote that "Washington is having a fairly mild case of the unease which invariably accompanies a change at the top. . . . For no succession can be wholly smooth, human nature being what it is."

Lippmann thought the succession could "be kept smooth enough if the principals and the supporting casts, the mind-readers and the key-hole peepers, the inside dopesters and the tale-bearers, can be made to remember that the molehills, which they would work into mountains, are normal."

And Mr. Lippmann concluded:

> It would have been better if the Attorney General had disassociated himself at the outset and completely from any organized attempt to usurp—that is the right word for it—the prerogative of the President in office to say the final word about his own Vice-President. The mistake has now, it would appear, been rectified. But it was a mistake, and it is the reason why the inevitable unease of almost every succession has threatened to become inflamed and angry. All the rest of it, such as the transition from a Corinthian to a Dorian style, is only interesting.

In the spring of 1964, no one in Washington could predict whether these two men would become bitter enemies or political partners—or both.

10

The Faith of a Juggler

Q. Mr. President, some reference was made to your first hundred days. How do you size up your hundred days generally?

A. Well, I have been reasonably close to the Presidency during the thirty years that I have been in Washington, particularly the last three years. But I have had many different impressions in the last hundred days than I had before I came to this awesome responsibility.

I am deeply indebted by the spirit of unity in this country, by the many people of all faiths and all sections who closed ranks and were anxious to unite the country following the tragic affair of last November. I am quite pleased with the manner in which the executive personnel have carried on following the death of their great leader, how the Cabinet has functioned to a man in this crisis.

I think the continuity and the transition and the organization of the budget and the various messages, and the outlines of the program have created confidence in the country and in the world. I am pleased with what the Congress has done in the field of passing ten of the fifteen appropriation bills in the first hundred days that were carried over from last year, and in passing the education bills that made this Congress known as the great-

est education Congress in the history of our land; in the passage
of the civil rights bill in the House of Representatives after it
had been considered there for some six or seven months; in the
passage of the tax bill in the United States Senate after it had
been there almost thirteen months, and now finally enacted into
law.

While I have been lavishly praised by some, and I think
lavishly criticized by some, I think generally speaking the
American Nation has conducted itself as you would expect it to
in a crisis and would get very good grades.

Insofar as I am concerned, I am rather pleased with what has
been accomplished in the first hundred days as a result of men
and women of good will working together.

—from the President's Hundred Days
Press Conference, February 29, 1964

Mr. Johnson took over the Presidency with great composure and command. Moreover, and this was surprising to many, including some who knew him in the Senate, he showed great subtlety and taste in delicate matters.

Mr. Johnson went instantly to work and showed extraordinary presence of mind in those first few hours and days. He is a perfectionist and he "loves to think of everything." So we might expect him while still in Dallas that November Friday to start making lists of people he should be in touch with on the next day. But surely it was remarkable that he thought of asking several people to make notes of the afternoon's events. And it was amazing that he took care to see that photographs were taken of the swearing-in and that he asked Kilduff to try to get some sound recording of the ceremony. These things all show responsibility and political sense. And they show how ingrained in politics or how intuitive this political man is under great stress.

Memory fades, and we forget now how well and how surprisingly well the first steps of transition were accomplished. Everyone had trouble doing his job that day. Case-hardened reporters, veterans of war correspondence, got on the phone that day and found themselves unable to speak coherently to their news desks—while the men at the other end of the wire also wavered in spite of the jobs they had to do. But the new President did not waver in the job he had to do. Predictions are risky; but surely his reaction to the crisis has earned him a page in history.

Lyndon Johnson became President as a result of violence and an assassination. That was not in itself unique. It had happened three times before. But there were unique things about it. He was the first Vice-President who had been on the scene of the assassination at the time. He was the first to understand that atomic decisions had fallen with appalling swiftness into his hands.

He came to power as a substitute for a man who had himself been elected by an exceedingly narrow margin.* We may surely conclude that no matter how much surface poise and command he showed, he must have felt himself somewhat a substitute. He has not mentioned it. But other Vice-Presidents who came to power have spoken of this natural feeling.

When Mr. Kennedy was installed, by a razor's edge, he himself devoted months to building up a "firm base" of support at home. Thus he came to feel more secure as a President who was no longer merely representing a thin electoral margin. There can be no doubt Mr. Johnson was consciously trying in his first months to build such a firm base. And apparently he succeeded.

Mr. Johnson was older than Mr. Kennedy by about a decade.

---

* In 1948 Lyndon Johnson himself won the Democratic nomination for U. S. Senator by only 87 votes. This won him for a time the nickname of "Landslide Lyndon." He had been a member of the House of Representatives for eleven years. He had already made one previous bid for a Senate nomination and lost by a narrow margin that time.

Nearly a million votes were cast in this 87-vote victory election in 1948. In the first go in the primary his opponent was Coke R. Stevenson, a man who had three times been Governor of Texas. In the first round, Stevenson got 477,077 votes to 405,617 for Lyndon Johnson. There were other candidates in the primary and they had won enough votes to keep Stevenson from capturing more than 50 percent of the total votes. That forced a runoff primary, and with only a month to go Johnson campaigned with terrific intensity. The preliminary returns gave Stevenson a lead of 854 votes, narrow enough to touch off numerous charges and countercharges of irregularities. There were three separate investigations and five court actions before it was decided that Johnson had won. That election was closer than the Kennedy-Johnson victory over Nixon and Lodge.

This is not unique in our history, but not unnoteworthy either. Many Vice-Presidents have been older than the men for whom they served as an understudy. But Mr. Johnson looked his age, and Mr. Kennedy looked younger than his, and in any case, Mr. Kennedy was the youngest President the United States ever had. Youth was thus one of his main characteristics. In the 1960 campaign, it was said that Mr. Johnson seemed to be campaigning at extraordinary hours and with extraordinary drive, almost as if he were competing with the vigor of the younger man. And in taking over, Mr. Johnson seemed intent on showing that there was to be no diminution in the expenditure of energy and the amount of work done at the White House.

Mr. Johnson came to power later in the term of his predecessor than any other Vice-President in American history. As has been mentioned before, this was one of the dominant factors which affected nearly everything he did in his early period in office. There was a great deal of urgency in some other matters, such as the deadline on preparing next year's budget. But the basic urgency that fell on him that November day, and which would remain with him every hour until the November election, was the campaign. It was his responsibility to lead the voters through disunity and confusion and to support for his administration.

Every President, even the duly inaugurated man, has a certain problem of change of pace as he comes in following another President. A man who comes in as a substitute has a different kind of problem of gaining support. Mr. Johnson was the first to follow an extraordinary family, one which in many ways had been America's first "royal family." It was difficult for the American people not only to accept the tragedy, but to think of anyone other than Mr. Kennedy being President, nor anyone other than Jacqueline Kennedy being First Lady.

Moreover, no President before Kennedy had ever appointed a brother to the Cabinet, and when Mr. Johnson came to power, he found that many people in Washington, and presumably Robert Kennedy himself, felt that Robert Kennedy would have been a more logical successor than the man who was legally in the position to succeed.

There is a common phrase, "palace politics," meaning the

kind of politics which goes on in places of power. We are not a monarchy, and so we do not have a palace. But in the winter of 1963 and 1964 we came closer to genuine "palace politics" than we ever had before in American history. In this period we experienced a tremendous emotional reaction. Many people had a deep and bitter feeling of basic frustration and disappointment—because the American people had elected a Kennedy to be President, a Kennedy should be there. But instead we had a quite different man. No American President had ever had to deal with this particular kind of poignant but unsettling emotion swirling around ambitious men. Historians of the future may well find that the principals in this part of the drama were not as bitter—nor ambitious—as the men around the principals.

There can be no doubt that in recent years we have greatly improved the position of the Vice-President. Today our government procedure is designed to keep the Vice-President well informed. In fact, few White House experts believe that there is anything further which can be done in an institutional way to improve the Vice-Presidency. Up to the time that Mr. Truman had to take over during a war, the Vice-President had been treated as an afterthought—and that is what the office originally was in the writing of the Constitution. Now there is no guarantee that the President will keep him informed—but the new tradition has been established. The Vice-President now is a member of the National Security Council and it has become tradition, with the force of law, that he should have ready access to any important information.

This writer asked all key officials interviewed if they knew of any major surprise which had confronted the new President. There was none. Mr. Truman, in 1945, faced many surprises, including the news that we were making an atomic bomb. There was no such bomb of any kind which turned up in the briefings and the official sessions for Mr. Johnson. There were, of course, many new things, many surprises in events of national and international affairs. But his access to information had been sufficient. No major information had been withheld from him. No one had "forgotten" to tell the Vice-President something of overwhelming importance.

It should be emphasized that this arrangement and understanding can never be entirely provided by legislation. Mr. Eisenhower kept Mr. Nixon informed to some extent, and during the Eisenhower illnesses, Mr. Nixon sometimes presided at official meetings. But there is and probably always will be an element of personal relationship which is essential to maintain smooth communication. It was Mr. Kennedy who had the idea that the Vice-President should have a suite of offices in the Executive Office Building itself. There is no law providing for this, but it is certainly likely that this office will be maintained, particularly if Mr. Johnson is the next elected President.

As this book goes to press, there is considerable discussion among political experts of whether we should continue the tradition of letting the nominee for President choose who is to be his running mate. It is true that the nomination is always voted on by the convention, but in recent times the nominee has always clearly designated his preference. There has been only one recent exception. That was the case of Adlai Stevenson who, with characteristic hesitation, apparently could not make up his mind at Chicago in 1952. It was he who revived in modern times the previous practice of having an "honest, wide-open contest." This seems quite democratic, and it may be, but in fact in former generations it sometimes led to the selection of a man who had been a deadly rival of the Number 1 nominee. Now we go by a different custom. While there is no justification for the practice in law or in convention procedure, it has become a tradition for Number 1 to choose Number 2.

In the light of recent events, it seems that this is a sound tradition. Anyone familiar with work in an organization knows that you cannot very easily legislate the arrangements by which an official can be informed. We cannot trust organization charts if the temperaments of the President and Vice-President lead them to be indifferent or even hostile to each other. As one White House aide told this writer, "Even giving the man an office just over there across West Executive Avenue would not mean anything unless there were a good relationship between the two. He could sit over there and read official reports all day and still be completely ignorant of the guts of what we were doing over here."

[243]

A historian intimately familiar with recent White House history and a scholar of the White House for many years have both emphasized to this writer that the relationship between the two men will probably remain the clue to a smooth transition under stress. Thus very simply for the smoothness of this transition, we give all credit to Mr. Johnson, but we also pay respects again to John F. Kennedy. He chose his own Vice-President, and the whole nation is indebted to the fact that the two men understood each other well.

What emergency plans are ready if Mr. Johnson should be attacked by an assassin tomorrow—in Detroit—or in Dallas?

This writer asked all the key people of the old and new regimes about Dallas: "Did you put into effect any emergency procedure? Did you use any part of any emergency procedure—perhaps a part of civil defense alert plans?"

The answer was uniformly negative. Since the Presidential communications were in Dallas on November 22, there was an immediate switchover of power. There was no alert—as rumored—of the Strategic Air Command, nor of any other military command. Important senior officers of the State Department remained at their posts or went to their offices as soon as they could, but no general alarm was sounded. The use of the State Department's emergency operations room—for people working on the thousand details of the funeral—was the closest anyone anywhere came to using any pre-planned emergency procedure.

People did what they had to, what they could do, or what seemed best at the time—in a great hurry and under emotional stress. In view of how much was done, and how swiftly, it is surprising that there were not more mistakes or accidents. The Dallas police, for example, under great pressure, made great mistakes. Not catching Oswald—on first sight—cost the life of a police officer, and not guarding their prisoner cost Oswald's life. Both incidents were related to the shock of the unexpected.

In Washington there were no comparable errors and disasters resulting from the unusual and emotional events of late November.

We may not always be so lucky as to have international calm

at such a time. The questions about how men can be prepared —as Vice-President or as Secretary of Defense or State—to cope with sudden black catastrophe remain essentially unanswered.

The point has great relevance for all—including you and me —who must think about how our top officials must prepare to meet sudden crisis.

Too often these days we plan our weapons systems and conduct our diplomacy as if we would always be capable of hair-trigger responses. Many believe our computers will keep up with disaster and we will keep up with our computers. Men write of atomic crises as if we and they would always conduct ourselves rationally. And writers on national strategy write chapter after chapter with only an occasional—and parenthetical—reference to "madness or miscalculation."

In this writer's judgment Mr. Kennedy's death was a historical accident triggered by madness. The excellent transition accomplished by Mr. Johnson was something of an accident—for although Mr. Kennedy admired him, no one really thought Mr. Johnson might have to take over. It was unthinkable. So it had not been thought about.

Our recovery after the assassination was fortunately favored with cool weather, in terms of actual climate, diminishing the chances of racial unrest, and with "warm weather" in the cold war. We cannot, however, assume that the succession machinery now provided—nor any system which human beings can provide—will in the future do as well with sudden events brought about by disease of mind or body, by sheer accident or miscalculation, or the other things men used to call fate. A look at wars in modern times shows that one does not have to look far for crises begun or brought to disaster by madness or miscalculation.

We can—and must—think about such things without lowering our respect for Mr. Johnson, or for human beings, or for fate.

As Mr. Johnson worked along in the early weeks, it was obvious he was perfectly familiar with the main outlines of the job and he knew from "political instinct" just what people he should see. He knew what to say, what to do, and what meetings to hold. He knew the problems before the country. He had been well informed, he had experienced assistants who were personally acquainted with the White House and with the staff of Mr. Kennedy, and he had a profound understanding of the philosophy and the details of our form of government. And he had the physical and emotional stamina to meet all the challenges thrown at him.

But what may have been more extraordinary and may seem historically more important was his instinct to see so many different representatives of so many different power groups in American society. Even before the assassination America had been perhaps more disunited than it had been at any time since the divisive debate over isolationism or intervention in the European war in 1940. The shadow of the 1964 election and the particular talents of Mr. Johnson were well adapted to pulling the country together and gaining in real unity as well as in the appearance of unity.

As the months have gone along and the actual campaign time has come closer, Mr. Johnson continues to see many different delegations and to make speeches with an astonishing frequency. This in turn has led to his regime being completely accepted as *the Johnson administration*—a transformation which was thought impossible last December. It is an intangible but real achievement, built with subtlety and artistry.

What were the new President's mistakes? Most observers— including this writer—did not find that he had neglected any major instrument of the Presidency. There was some criticism of his appointments and attitudes in foreign relations. There was much apprehension—so far unjustified—of what he might do, through ignorance, in some unspecified future foreign crisis. Perhaps the most persistent problem before the President's desk every day was his use or misuse of press and publicity.

In the first 100 days his tactics in press relations were quite wrong and they did harm to him and his program. His attitudes toward the press—and the ill will already somewhat needlessly created—still seemed capable of causing major damage in the future. He seems to swing from underexposure to overexposure. His basic attitude in the early weeks was that information and public relations could and should be manipulated to a great extent through personal contacts and personal persuasion.

Linked with this way of handling press relations was the unsavory and unsuccessful attempt to get major segments of the press to discredit an opposition man, the insurance man Don Reynolds, star witness in the Bobby Baker case. The use of investigative material and secret reports in this manner was "worse than a crime—it was a mistake." The best men in the Washington press corps thought it unworthy of the White House. This episode was unique in the hundred days, however, and is now being written off as something which could only have happened with inexperienced men, sorely tried in a new environment.

Citizens in the capital were immensely irritated by the way the President turned out the lights in the White House. They thought he had left that beautiful white shrine dim and gray. George Reedy insisted that it was all in their imagination— that the *outside* lights at the White House were the same as ever. The President constantly referred to the light bill, without ever being specific.

Many Washingtonians considered the lights business a grandstand play designed to impress unthinking people. Was this gesture—or obsession—a mistake? It did not seem to be a political mistake, although columnists and tourists complained in increasing numbers. From his own words, the President seemed to regard the lights business partly as a way of telling government workers that he was not kidding when he asked them to stop waste and save money.

Another "mistake" concerns the President's remarks, related to his personal religious beliefs, at the "Prayer Breakfast." That was the occasion when he proposed—not as a government project nor as a Presidentially sponsored project—"a memorial to God." At the risk of seeming blasphemous or intolerant, many people spoke out against this idea, which seemed to die a quick and deserved death. A few people judged it to be not an ingenuous proposal but a disengenuous and shameless attempt to please a segment of religious people. The result was a small flurry of letters to editors from private citizens, generally saying that God needed works more than monuments. Not many

Washingtonians thought Washington needed another monument for such a purpose.

As discussed elsewhere in this book, there are many other areas where the President was criticized, and where history may judge that he made mistakes. But there was—as he sometimes rather boastfully implied—no foreign affairs disaster like the "Bay of Pigs" in his early record. There was no domestic disaster in the first 100 days. And he did not make any big public blooper to cost him votes.* Commentator after commentator said that in the first 100 days at home his record was virtually perfect. This writer agrees, except to say that he needlessly irritated the press of Washington and that the hostility in some cases will be a source of concern for years beyond the 100 days.

In the private files of the President's first 100 days there is an extraordinary Okamoto photograph which shows the persuader at work. The scene might be upstairs at the White House or perhaps at an embassy, at a large reception. The picture shows two men seated on an eighteenth-century couch. One man is listening with his back to the camera. The other person is a tall man whom we all know. He is leaning forward intently. He is lifting a hand to make a point, and the lines of his body show that he is not yet in sight of winning. This, and not the presentation pictures, or those of formal addresses, is the photograph of this President at work.

Mr. Johnson works terribly hard at persuasion, and he succeeds incredibly well. Understanding his "treatment" is difficult for everyone, even those who have often been through it. The skills of the negotiator, the conciliator—or the wheeler-dealer —are not easy to sum up. Being persuasive at short range is far more complicated than being eloquent, or even being ingenious. The record of what the President himself said, in short speeches and in bits and pieces, through the railroad negotia-

* Soon after the 100 days were up he made two small-sized bloopers. One was driving with reporters at 80 miles an hour. The other was pulling the ears of beagles "to hear them yelp." On both of these occasions he acted impulsively to show off in front of people—and cameras. How much do these incidents tell us about his judgment as a President? His impulsiveness was shown in many more important ways. Yet in major decisions he has generally taken time to get plenty of advice.

[248]

tions would fill several chapters in a book. But the record of how he decided to say what he said, and when, and to whom, would be far longer.

That railroad negotiation was summed up by one participant as being dominated by the persuasive skills of Mr. Johnson. A reporter asked Roy Davidson, President of the Brotherhood of Locomotive Engineers, what had made the difference between the success of these negotiations and the failures of many bargaining efforts in the past. For reply he merely pointed to the President: "There's your answer." Credit is due to others, to all the participants. But nonetheless, the settlement was a triumph for the President.

This victory and other lesser achievements simply cannot be shrugged off as merely superlative wheeling and dealing. Nor is his simply a technical skill—a set of acquired professional tricks from the profession of politics. Years of watching the technique of others and perfecting the Johnsonian "treatment" are, of course, fundamental to his artistry. And there sometimes seems to be in him an inordinate desire to please, and to be liked, a drive which seems disturbingly like that of a vain actor who loves crowds, *all crowds,* if they applaud. There seems also to be a cold calculation in the man, a consciousness always awake and driving, almost shameless in its determination to have something for everyone. One imagines some kind of computer in him which is always whirring away, mixing and blending a menu for every week, almost for every day: something for labor, something for business, something for the Negro, for the South, for the city, the country, the rich, the poor, the women, the old—and for the adolescent school drop-outs!

Yet in the final analysis there seem to this writer to be too many extraordinary success stories in Johnson's record for his ability to be dismissed as calculation and technique. Too many times he has won over people who were themselves calculating and on guard against a professional bag of tricks. And there are too many stories of Johnson's sympathy expressed when no political end was in sight. He may at times be corny and even common—but he is not insensitive. He does care a great deal about people, and not just about votes.

He can be resistant to some ideas, and at times insensitive to some kinds of feelings (ask the nearest beagle). But despite an occasional blind spot, Mr. Johnson is tremendously sensitive to human emotions. Some of his public expressions of emotion and sympathy may be contrived. Many of those which are genuine are expressed in corn and cliché. But he has genuine sympathy and understanding which in small groups he conveys well, and he conveys sympathy and understanding beyond words. This is the secret ingredient of his mysterious "treatment." One reason that people falter when they attempt to describe Johnson's persuasive ability is that it is done with well-worn words—and without words. His understanding comes through without words and often it comes through in spite of them.

Thus in the railroad negotiations President Johnson used many words—without any special majesty. But he also used the desires of the two sides—of which he was superlatively aware —to make an end to a struggle of which he knew they were tired. In the negotiations he virtually "locked the door" on the negotiators. He used the majesty of the White House. He used the building, the meeting rooms, the privacy, the tradition, and the power of the White House. He used persuasive tactics and he used bullying tactics.

But there is human understanding in the railroad story as there is in many other stories of President Johnson in action. In him is a strange blend of emotion and sympathy and sleight of hand. Yes, there is also vanity, and Mr. Johnson is a vain exhibitionist who just naturally likes to juggle. Yet it may be that history will find this mixture as acceptable in the White House as Our Lady found the juggler in the garden of Notre Dame.

We are amused. We are astonished. We are sometimes taken in, as his hand is quicker than our eye. But here is more than prestidigitation. Here is dedication, a man working his hardest not just with skill but with faith. No responsible ruler in the atomic age can rely merely upon information, manipulation and skill. For technique is not enough in this age when a bomb can blow out a city as a bullet can blow out a brain.

The Hundred Days:
A Chronology*

Friday, November 22:

12:29 P.M. In the motorcade going down Elm Street in Dallas, Texas, the fourth car held Vice-President Lyndon Johnson, Mrs. Lady Bird Johnson, U. S. Senator Ralph W. Yarborough (D., Texas), Texas Highway Patrolman Hurchel D. Jacks, and Secret Service Agent Rufus W. Youngblood; the second car held President and Mrs. John F. Kennedy and Texas Governor and Mrs. John B. Connally, Jr.

12:31 P.M. Three shots were fired. The first and third struck the President; the second bullet struck Governor Connally.

12:36 P.M. Five cars arrived at the emergency entrance of Parkland Hospital, three and a half miles from Elm Street.

12:38 P.M. President Kennedy and Governor Connally were wheeled into "trauma rooms," emergency treatment rooms, No. 1 and No. 2 at Parkland Hospital.

1:13 P.M. Secret Service Agent Emory Roberts returned from Trauma Room No. 1 to inform Lyndon Johnson that President John F. Kennedy was dead. Not knowing whether the assassination was an individual incident or part of a plot, Agent

---

* The author is indebted to Miss Cathy Friedman for her suggestions and assistance in the preparation of this Chronology.

Roberts advised the new President to return to Washington. President Johnson first called for Kennedy aides Lawrence O'Brien and Kenneth O'Donnell. O'Donnell, following Johnson's advice, telephoned Attorney General Robert F. Kennedy, brother of the late President. Johnson sent Cliff Carter to find Jack Valenti, a public-relations adviser; Mrs. Elizabeth Carpenter, Mrs. Johnson's public relations secretary; and Marie Fehmer, Johnson's personal secretary.

Dallas Police Chief Jesse E. Curry drove Johnson, Agent Youngblood, Texas Congressman Homer Thornberry, and Texas Congressman Albert Thomas from Parkland Hospital to Love Field.

1:30 P.M. When the President's car arrived at Love Field, the plane *Air Force One* was waiting for them near Gate 27.

1:30 P.M. Officer J. D. Tippitt of the Dallas police force got out of a police car and approached a suspect. The man pulled out his gun and shot and killed Officer Tippitt.

1:35 P.M. Johnson called Attorney General Robert F. Kennedy, offered his condolences, then asked the Attorney General about Johnson's taking the oath of office immediately. Robert Kennedy telephoned Deputy Attorney General Nicholas de B. Katzenbach, who stated that any officer empowered to administer a federal oath could do so. Kennedy thus informed *Air Force One.*

1:40 P.M. The nation was informed, through Malcolm Kilduff, that the President was dead.

2:00 P.M. Officer M. N. McDonald arrested Lee Harvey Oswald in Dallas, Texas. Oswald, arrested for the murders of President Kennedy and Officer Tippitt, reached for his gun when Officer McDonald approached him in a motion picture theater.

2:15 P.M. Johnson attempted to contact Federal District Judge Sarah T. Hughes, a political supporter, through U. S. District Attorney H. Barefoot Saunders. Saunders contacted Judge Hughes at 2:15 P.M.

Mrs. Kennedy and the body of the late President arrived at the plane.

2:38 P.M. Thirty people witnessed Johnson take the oath of office: "I do solemnly swear that I will faithfully execute the office of President of the United States, and will, to the best of my ability, preserve, protect, and defend the Constitution of the United States." "So help me God," added Judge Hughes, a phrase not included in the official oath. "So help me God," Johnson repeated.

2:47 P.M. *Air Force One* left the runway at Love Field.

6:00 P.M. *Air Force One* arrived at Andrews Field in Washington, D. C. The press met the plane to receive Johnson's words: "This is a sad time for all people. . . . I will do my best. That is all I can do. I ask for your help—and God's."

6:17 P.M. While Kennedy's body was taken to Bethesda Naval Hospital, Johnson entered the Presidential helicopter with Secretary of Defense Robert S. McNamara, White House National Security Assistant McGeorge Bundy, and Undersecretary of State George W. Ball. The helicopter landed on the back lawn of the White House at 6:17 P.M.

6:55 P.M. The President met with Undersecretary of State W. Averell Harriman and chairman of the Senate Foreign Relations Committee, Senator J. William Fulbright (D., Ark.).

7:05 P.M. Former President Harry S. Truman telephoned President Johnson.

7:10 P.M. President Johnson telephoned former President Dwight D. Eisenhower.

7:29 P.M. President Johnson telephoned Sargent Shriver, Director of the Peace Corps and brother-in-law of the late President Kennedy.

7:40 P.M. President Johnson met with Congressional leaders. He talked with Senator Edward Kennedy, brother of the late President; John W. McCormack, Speaker of the House of Representatives; Senator Richard B. Russell, Chairman of the Senate Armed Services Committee; and Justice Arthur Goldberg, Justice of the Supreme Court of the United States.

9:00 P.M. The new President was driven to his home, The Elms, in the Spring Valley section of Washington, D. C.

Saturday, November 23:
The new President conferred with Attorney General Robert Kennedy, Secretary of State Dean Rusk, Secretary of Defense Robert McNamara, and bipartisan Congressional leaders.

John McCone, CIA Director, gave President Johnson an intelligence briefing in the Situation Room of the White House.

Cabinet members and various White House staff members met with the President early in the afternoon for a 25-minute meeting.

President Johnson issued a national mourning proclamation for the late President Kennedy.

Sunday, November 24:
A parade from the White House to the Capitol accompanied the late President's coffin from the East Room of the White House to the rotunda of the Capitol.

Lee Harvey Oswald was shot by Jack Ruby, a fifty-two-year-old night club operator. One bullet was fired as Oswald was being transferred from the jail in City Hall in Dallas, Texas, to the county jail in the Criminal Courts Building, about thirteen blocks away. An ambulance rushed to Parkland Hospital with Oswald, who died at 12:40 P.M.

Monday, November 25:
The body of policeman J. D. Tippitt was buried in Dallas, Texas.

The body of Lee Harvey Oswald was buried in Fort Worth, Texas.

In Washington, at St. Matthew's Cathedral, Richard Cardinal Cushing, of Boston, Massachusetts, said Mass over the body of the late President, John Fitzgerald Kennedy. At the conclusion of the Mass, Cardinal Cushing blessed the coffin and said, in English:

> "May the angels, dear Jack, lead you into Paradise. May the martyrs receive you at your coming. May the spirit of God embrace you, and mayest thou, with all those who made the supreme sacrifice of dying for others, receive eternal rest and peace. Amen."

Three cannons fired a 21-gun salute, taps were heard over the hill, and the American flag was raised above the coffin as John F. Kennedy was buried in Arlington National Cemetery in Arlington, Virginia.

President Johnson was host to the royalty and rulers of 70 nations. A reception was held at the State Department for these notables who had come for the funeral of the late President and to meet the new President.

President Johnson met with a group of Governors and asked their cooperation, saying:

> "Our country has suffered a grievous shock. The transition while a term is still going on is always a difficult test for

democracy. It is doubly difficult in these days of quick decisions on matters that involve the fate of humanity."

President Johnson ordered an investigation of the assassination of President Kennedy and the murder of his alleged assassin.

Tuesday, November 26:
The Senate defeated 57-35 a bill which would have eliminated the possibility of selling wheat to Russia. The bill, sponsored by Senator Karl E. Mundt (R., S. D.), would have prohibited the Export-Import Bank or any other federal agency from guaranteeing loans to finance trade with any Communist country. The defeat of this legislation, opposed by the late President Kennedy, was considered a vote of confidence for President Johnson.

Wednesday, November 27:
President Johnson spoke to a joint session of Congress, his first major speech as President. He emphasized early passage of the tax-cut bill and the civil rights bill and indicated that he would follow Kennedy's policies:

"On the 20th day of January, in 1961, John F. Kennedy told his countrymen that our national work would not be finished 'in the first thousand days, nor even perhaps in our lifetime on this planet.' But, he said, 'Let us begin.'

"Today in this moment of new resolve, I would say to all my fellow Americans, let us continue."

Thursday, November 28:
President Johnson delivered his Thanksgiving message to the nation, calling for an end to hatred and calling for national unity, promising "the best within me to work for a new American greatness, a new day when peace is more secure, when justice is more universal, when freedom is more strong in every home of all mankind."

Friday, November 29:
In the first test of Lyndon Johnson's popularity, the Harris Survey reports President Johnson leading all Republican contenders:

Johnson	53%	Johnson	59%	Johnson	55%
Nixon	40%	Goldwater	29%	Rockefeller	33%
Not sure	7%	Not sure	12%	Not sure	12%

An Executive Order issued by President Johnson officially established a commission to investigate the assassination of President Kennedy. The commission consisted of Chief Justice of the United States Supreme Court Earl Warren, Chairman, Senator Richard B. Russell, Senator John Sherman Cooper, Congressman Hale Boggs, Congressman Gerald R. Ford, the Honorable Allen W. Dulles, and the Honorable John J. McCloy.

WEEK OF DECEMBER 1-DECEMBER 7

Monday, December 2:
President Johnson presented the Fermi Award, the Atomic Energy Commission's top honor, to J. Robert Oppenheimer at the White House.

President Johnson began a highly publicized economy drive with an order to cut down on federal expenditures resulting from waste and from overstaffed offices.

Wednesday, December 4:
President Johnson announced that he planned to follow through on President Kennedy's plan for a "national assault on poverty." This announcement was made to the 1,500 delegates of the American Public Welfare Association.

President Johnson spoke with members of the Executive Council of the AFL-CIO, dedicating his administration to a tax-cut bill, a civil rights bill, and a poverty program which would aid the aged, the handicapped, the mentally retarded, the illiterates, the drop-outs, the unemployed and their dependent children, and the uneducated. First priority was given to more jobs:

"The goal of this administration is 75 million jobs in America."

The President also spoke with members of the Business Council, emphasizing the tax cut and asking for their cooperation. He promised thrift in Government: "We will get a dollar's value from every dollar we use."

Thursday, December 5:
The President held two closed meetings in which he indicated that his foreign policy would rest upon "strength" and "patience." This philosophy was presented in remarks to the

National Security Council and to a meeting of about 800 State Department officials.

Friday, December 6:
The President received a report dealing with a proposal for a multilateral nuclear force in his meeting with top military and diplomatic aides. Those present at the meeting were Secretary of State Dean Rusk, Secretary of Defense Robert S. McNamara, State Department Counselor Walt W. Rostow, the President's Special Assistant for National Security Affairs McGeorge Bundy, and Assistant Secretary of Defense for International Security Affairs William P. Bundy.

Saturday, December 7:
President Johnson presented 33 Medal of Freedom Awards at the first state occasion of the Johnson administration. The awards included the 31 awards picked by the late President John F. Kennedy plus two posthumous awards to Pope John XXIII and John F. Kennedy, added to the list of awards by President Johnson.

Bess Clements Abell, wife of Tyler Abell, was appointed as the new White House social secretary.

Elizabeth "Liz" Carpenter was appointed as Press Secretary and Staff Director for Mrs. Lyndon Johnson.

President Johnson met with reporters at his first press conference in the White House. He announced that he would speak at the United Nations on December 17.

WEEK OF DECEMBER 8-DECEMBER 14

Sunday, December 8:
President Johnson flew to New York for the funeral of Herbert H. Lehman, former Governor of and Senator from New York.

Monday, December 9:
President Johnson gave to Secretary of the Interior Stewart L. Udall the responsibility for certain oil policy decisions formerly lodged in the White House. This was done because of the President's past association with the oil industry.

Tuesday, December 10:
President Johnson met with a group of Congressional leaders to discuss the relative strength of the United States and the Soviet Union.

Wednesday, December 11:

An economy measure, announced by Secretary of Defense Robert McNamara, was the closing of 33 military installations. McNamara also announced plans to bring the civilian personnel in the Defense Department to the lowest number in 15 years.

President Johnson blocked a threatened strike against six airlines by the International Association of Machinists. He ordered the creation of an emergency board to investigate the differences between the Union and the airlines.

Thursday, December 12:

The House of Representatives approved a $527-million expansion of the manpower retraining program. This bill, in a slightly different form, was previously approved by the Senate. A $4.4-billion public works appropriation bill was approved by both Houses of Congress. This bill contained appropriations for river and harbor projects, the Atomic Energy Commission and for public works in depressed areas.

The Senate passed and sent for the President's signature a bill appropriating $102 million for the Peace Corps.

The House passed a bill for aid to education, appropriating $1.5 billion for vocational education, college student loans, and aid to impacted areas.

Saturday, December 14:

Thomas Mann, Ambassador to Mexico, was appointed Assistant Secretary of State for Latin American Affairs.

WEEK OF DECEMBER 15-DECEMBER 21

Monday, December 16:

The House passed a $2.8-billion foreign aid appropriation, $1.7 less than President Johnson had requested and $800 million less than Congress had authorized. An amendment to the bill which might eliminate the possibility of selling wheat to Russia was a provision forbidding the Export-Import Bank from guaranteeing credit for the Russian wheat deal as well as credit for trade with any other Communist countries. The entire bill was approved by a vote of 249-135; the amendment was approved by a 218-169 vote.

[258]

Tuesday, December 17:
President Johnson addressed the United Nations' General Assembly, pledging continuation of President Kennedy's policy and calling for an international "new deal" to build a better world.

Wednesday, December 18:
President Johnson held his second press conference, once again an informal affair. Most of his comments concerned the budget and economy. He made reference to a poverty plan but did not give any details.

At his press conference, President Johnson announced the appointment of Thomas C. Mann as a special assistant to the President. Mr. Mann, then Ambassador to Mexico, had recently been appointed Assistant Secretary of State for Latin American Affairs. He would, in his two new positions, coordinate all government activities concerning Latin America.

Friday, December 20:
In the Treaty Room of the Executive Mansion, President Johnson signed a treaty ending the Chamizal border dispute with Mexico. The treaty provided an exchange of some territory at El Paso, Texas.

WEEK OF DECEMBER 22-DECEMBER 28

Sunday, December 22:
A candlelight service marked the end of the period of mourning for John F. Kennedy. Religious leaders from the Protestant, Catholic and Jewish faiths lit the torch at his grave from the eternal flame burning near the grave. President Johnson lit his candle from this torch. Nearly 15,000 people heard Johnson's speech at the Lincoln Memorial:

"We buried Abraham Lincoln and John Kennedy, but we did not bury their dreams or their visions. They are our dreams and our visions today. . . ."

Monday, December 23:
About 200 members of the House and Senate attended a sudden-notice surprise reception given by President Johnson at the White House.

President Johnson escorted four women reporters on a spur-of-the-moment tour of the White House and revealed to them that

[259]

the military was seeking a $9-billion increase in the Defense budget next year.

President Johnson personally informed Miss Gerri Whittington of her appointment as one of his three personal secretaries. Miss Whittington, who joined the White House staff in 1961 as secretary to Ralph A. Dungan, Special Assistant to the President, is the only Negro secretary in the Executive offices.

Tuesday, December 24:
President and Mrs. Johnson attended the funeral of the late Representative William J. Green (D., Penn.) in Philadelphia. After the funeral, President and Mrs. Johnson flew to the LBJ Ranch for the Christmas holidays.

The House of Representatives passed (189-158) a bill giving the President discretionary authority to extend credit to Communist countries purchasing American goods. This vote completed House action on the foreign aid appropriations.

The Soviet Government newspaper *Izvestia* in Moscow published the complete text of President Johnson's address at the United Nations of December 17. Publication of the text of a speech by an American President is rare in Russia.

Wednesday, December 25:
Twenty-seven of President Johnson's relatives were his guests on the LBJ Ranch for Christmas dinner.

Friday, December 27:
President Johnson sent telegrams to Archbishop Makarios, President of Cyprus and leader of the Greek community in Cyprus, and to Vice-President Fazil Kutchuk, leader of the Turkish Cypriots, appealing to them to end the "terrible fraternal strife" in their country.

At a press conference held at his ranch, President Johnson announced that "federal civilian employment was reduced by more than 100 during November and stood nearly 3,500 lower than at the end of November last year." He also announced his invitation to President Adolfo Lopez Mateos of Mexico to meet with the President in Southern California on February 21-22, 1964, at which time both Presidents would receive honorary degrees from the University of California in Los Angeles.

Saturday, December 28:
West German Chancellor Dr. Ludwig Erhard arrived at the LBJ Ranch for a two-day business visit with President Johnson.

WEEK OF DECEMBER 29-JANUARY 4

Sunday, December 29:
President Johnson and Chancellor Erhard issued a joint communiqué pledging cooperation between Germany and the United States. They pledged support to such specifics as the reunification of Germany, the maintenance of the U. S. combat forces in Germany and effective aid to developing nations.

Monday, December 30:
The Senate, by a vote of 56-14, accepted the money items in the $3-billion foreign aid appropriations bill, and by a voice vote accepted the Soviet credit amendment adopted by the House of Representatives. This amendment gave President Johnson discretionary authority to extend credit to Communist nations buying American goods, and was an important milestone in giving the new President solid backing in his foreign policy.

Wednesday, January 1:
President Johnson sent a message to Soviet Premier Khrushchev and President Leonid I. Breshnev, in response to their New Year's greeting, which called for improved American-Soviet relations. Johnson's message emphasized a hope for peace, stating: "In our hands have been placed the fortunes of peace and the hope of millions; it is my fervent hope that we are good stewards of that trust."

President Johnson sent a message to the new government of Vietnam pledging full U. S. support against the Communist Viet Cong forces.

President Johnson announced the appointment of Edward M. Martin, former Assistant Secretary of State for Inter-American Affairs, as the new Ambassador to Argentina.

Thursday, January 2:
Esther Peterson, Assistant Secretary of Labor, was officially appointed to be President Johnson's Special Assistant for Consumer Affairs.

[261]

Saturday, January 4:
President Johnson began his "war on poverty" with a two-part program. First, the Selective Service was ordered to examine, as soon as possible, all registrants who were out of school, in order to identify those in need of physical or mental rehabilitation. Second, he ordered the Secretaries of Labor and of Health, Education and Welfare to initiate a manpower conservation program to meet the needs of those who fail to pass the Selective Service tests.

WEEK OF JANUARY 5-JANUARY 11

Tuesday, January 7:
President Johnson gave labor and business leaders a preview of his State of the Union address at a luncheon with union officials and a dinner with industrialists.

Wednesday, January 8:
President Johnson presented to Congress his State of the Union message. He called, at this time, for a $97.9-billion budget as compared with $98.4 billion in the current year. He declared "unconditional war on poverty in America." His requests included early passing of the tax-cut bill, passage of a civil rights bill and new legislation requiring higher overtime pay rates.

Thursday, January 9:
Attempts by Panamanian students to carry a Panama flag into the U. S.-controlled zone resulted in crowds of Panamanians seeking to storm into the United States Canal Zone.

President Johnson met with the Fine Arts Commission, indicating a desire to continue with the Kennedy administration's interest in the arts.

Friday, January 10:
President Roberto Chiari of Panama suspended relations with the United States early in the day. After hours of negotiation, however, the United States and Panama agreed to let the Inter-American Peace Committee attempt to settle their dispute. This decision succeeded a Panamanian request for action by the Organization of American States on the Panamanian accusation of American aggression.

Monday, January 13:
A military cooperation committee on which Panama and the United States would be represented was set up by the Organization of American States in order to prevent a recurrence of violence similar to that of January 9.

Tuesday, January 14:
The White House issued a statement that the United States would continue operating the Panama Canal and could not risk its security. In the meantime, Panama announced its intention to sever diplomatic relations with the United States completely and asked withdrawal of United States diplomats.

Italian President Antonio Segni arrived for a three-day visit. President and Mrs. Johnson gave their first state dinner at the White House in his honor.

Brooks Hays, a special assistant to the President, announced his resignation to become a professor at Rutgers University. He was the first Presidential assistant to resign since the President took office.

Wednesday, January 15:
President Johnson submitted to Congress a request for a $5.3-billion space budget for fiscal year 1965.

Theodore C. Sorensen resigned as Special Counsel to the President to write a book about the late President John F. Kennedy. His resignation was effective February 29.

Thursday, January 16:
President Johnson held a major bipartisan briefing session for Senators at a White House dinner. After the dinner, Mrs. Johnson took the Senators' wives on a tour of the White House while President Johnson gave the Senators a briefing in the White House projection room.

Saturday, January 18:
President Johnson, accompanied by Mrs. Johnson and Chief Justice and Mrs. Earl Warren, spoke at the ceremony dedicating the headquarters of the National Geographic Society in Washington, D. C.

[263]

Monday, January 20:
President Johnson lectured the Budget Bureau on economy and told them that he had found ways of saving money at the White House including cutting down the light bill. Budget Director Kermit Gordon, Deputy Director Elmer Staats and about 30 other officials arrived at the Cabinet Room in the White House to watch President Johnson sign his first budget message.

President Johnson's speech to a group of American Indians in the East Room of the White House indicated that the Indians would be among those to benefit from the administration's "unconditional war on poverty."

Tuesday, January 21:
President Johnson presented his Economic Message to Congress, asking for a budget of $97.9 billion which combined a cut in spending with a "war on poverty."

President Johnson's message to the Geneva Conference called for peace to be assured through an adequate and thorough nuclear disarmament program.

President and Mrs. Johnson welcomed Canadian Prime Minister and Mrs. Lester B. Pearson at ceremonies on the North Portico of the White House.

President Johnson announced the resignation of Edward R. Murrow as Director of the United States Information Agency and the appointment of Carl T. Rowan to succeed him. Mr. Rowan, formerly Ambassador to Finland, would be the first Negro to sit with the National Security Council and the Cabinet.

Thursday, January 23:
President Johnson signed a resolution renaming the National Cultural Center as the John F. Kennedy Center for the Performing Arts and authorizing federal financial aid for the project.

Friday, January 24:
Jerome B. Weisner, Special Assistant to the President on Science and Technology, resigned to return to a university career. His departure had been announced before President Kennedy's assassination.

Saturday, January 25:
President Johnson held his fourth press conference, again impromptu. He discussed the tax bill, the civil rights bill, the "medicare" bill, and the budget. In the absence of Press Secretary Pierre Salinger, who was vacationing in California, a long-time Johnson assistant, George Reedy, conducted the press briefing.

WEEK OF JANUARY 26-FEBRUARY 1

Sunday, January 26:
Queen Fredrika of Greece arrived in Washington from New York on a three-day, unofficial visit.

Monday, January 27:
President Johnson and his 114 guests honored Queen Fredrika and Princess Irene of Greece at a White House luncheon.

President Johnson delivered a housing program request to Congress, asking for legislation in the areas of housing for minorities, for low-income families, for the elderly, for the rural areas, and for military families. He also recommended an additional $1.4-billion appropriation for urban renewal over a 2-year period.

Tuesday, January 28:
Arthur Schlesinger, Jr., resigned as a special assistant to the President. Mr. Schlesinger, whose resignation was effective March 1, intends to write a book about his years with President Kennedy.

Wednesday, January 29:
Panama officially charged the United States with aggression before the Organization of American States. President Johnson conferred with Congressional leaders at the White House concerning the Panamanian problem several hours before the official announcement was made.

Thursday, January 30:
President and Mrs. Johnson were hosts at a dinner party for a group of Senators and their wives.

President Johnson appointed Dr. Herbert Frank York, Chancellor of the University of California at San Diego and La Jolla, to be a member of the President's Science Advisory Committee.

Friday, January 31:
President Johnson delivered his Agricultural message to Congress.

Saturday, February 1:
President Johnson held a news conference in which subjects included were foreign relations with Cyprus, Panama and Vietnam; the Bobby Baker case; medical care for the aged; and other topics.

President Johnson, at this news conference, announced the appointment of Sargent Shriver to direct the "war on poverty," while remaining Director of the Peace Corps.

Other appointments: William Attwood of Connecticut to be United States Ambassador to Kenya and James D. Bell of New Hampshire, a career Foreign Service officer, as Ambassador to Malaysia. Mr. Attwood recently served as Special Adviser to the U. S. Delegation to the United Nations' General Assembly.

WEEK OF FEBRUARY 2-FEBRUARY 8

Monday, February 3:
President Johnson announced that Dr. Eric F. Goldman, Rollins Professor of History at Princeton University, would coordinate the ideas of the nation's top scholars and specialists in a new unpaid position as an adviser to the President.

Tuesday, February 4:
President Johnson accepted the resignation of Timothy J. Reardon, Jr., from his position as Special Assistant to the President. Mr. Reardon's letter of resignation was written January 31, and his resignation effective as of March 1.

President Johnson witnessed the signing of the Twenty-fourth Amendment to the Constitution. The amendment, which eliminated the poll tax as a condition to voting, was signed by the administrator of the General Services Administration in the Cabinet Room of the White House. This was the first time a Constitutional amendment had been certified in the presence of the President of the United States.

Wednesday, February 5:
President Johnson spoke to a thousand civic and religious leaders at the annual Presidential Prayer Breakfast at the Mayflower Hotel. He emphasized the necessity of a separation of

[266]

church and state, but commented: "In these last seventy days, prayer has helped me to bear the burdens of this first office which are too great to be borne by anyone alone." He also suggested a Washington memorial to God.

In a special message to Congress, President Johnson asked for a campaign to protect consumer interests. He said that Mrs. Esther Peterson would lead the campaign, along with enlightened business interests, to protect the consumer from fraud and deception.

President Johnson attended the dinner for the Joseph P. Kennedy Foundation awards at the Americana Hotel in New York.

Thursday, February 6:
The President attended a publisher's luncheon at *The New York Times.* President Johnson was accompanied by Pierre Salinger and Jack Valenti. He was the first President to be a guest at a *Times* luncheon while in office.

Cuba cut off the supply of fresh water to the United States Naval Base at Guantanamo Bay.

President Johnson spoke at the 18th annual dinner of the Weizmann Institute of Science at the Waldorf Astoria Hotel in New York City. At this time he invited other nations to join the United States and Israel in research on using nuclear power to turn salt water into fresh water.

Friday, February 7:
President and Mrs. Johnson attended the funeral in Texas of Mrs. J. C. Kellam. Mr. J. C. Kellam, an old friend of the President's, was manager of the Johnson family television station in Austin.

The Senate passed the $11.6-billion tax-cut measure supported by the administration. The vote was 77 to 21.

President Johnson moved to guarantee the security of the American base at Guantanamo, Cuba, by making the base self-sufficient. The purpose was to be achieved by assuring the base control over its water supply and by reducing the number of Cuban employees.

Saturday, February 8:
Only three United States Representatives, out of the 26 Representatives and Senators invited, attended the Third Pan-Ameri-

can Interparliamentary Conference in Washington, D. C. The sixty delegates to the conference left feeling that they had been treated less than courteously by their host nation.

Week of February 9-February 15

Sunday, February 9:
Undersecretary of State George Ball flew to London for talks on the Cyprus issue. Mr. Ball then flew to Athens, Greece, for further talks. Between the times of Mr. Ball's arrival and departure from London, British Prime Minister Douglas-Home flew to Canada and then to Washington. Home's visit to the United States was arranged in 1963 after President Johnson took office.

Monday, February 10:
President Johnson delivered a Health message to Congress, strongly recommending hospital insurance for the aged based on social security payments. The President also introduced recommendations for a five-year program of federal mortgage insurance and loans for the building of new hospitals, nursing homes and nursing schools.

The House of Representatives passed the civil rights bill by a vote of 290-130. The bill was the most comprehensive civil rights bill in history. It forbids discrimination in employment, segregation in schools or in public facilities, strengthens laws protecting Negro voters and extends the Civil Rights Commission for four years. It also forbids discrimination in distribution of any federal aid in the form of grant, loan, or contract.

Tuesday, February 11:
President Johnson signed an act amending the Library Services Act and thereby increasing the amount of assistance under the Library Services Act and extending this assistance to nonrural areas.

President Johnson's speech to field officials of the Internal Revenue Service was mainly concerned with American foreign policy. At the close of his speech, he praised Secretary of the Treasury Douglas Dillon, stating, "Somebody once called him a Republican. I think that is about the worst thing I have ever heard said about him."

[268]

Wednesday, February 12:
   Sir Alec Douglas-Home, Prime Minister of Great Britain, accompanied by his wife and Foreign Secretary Richard A. Butler and his wife, were welcomed by President Johnson before an honor guard and representatives of the Diplomatic Corps at the North Portico of the White House.

   President Johnson accepted the resignation of August Heckscher, Special Consultant on the Arts. Mr. Heckscher began his work under President Kennedy.

   President Johnson spoke at the Lincoln Memorial in a ceremony observing the anniversary of President Lincoln's birthday. The President's speech was a plea for the civil rights bill, as he asked for an end to discrimination through law and leadership. The speech ended with these words: "Lincoln's words have become the common covenant of our public life. Let us now get on with his work."

Thursday, February 13:
   President Johnson issued an executive order prohibiting federal contractors and subcontractors from setting maximum age limits for most jobs. This order will tend to eliminate the widespread practice of not hiring anyone over forty-five years of age.

   President Johnson held a dinner party for Prime Minister Alec Douglas-Home in the State Dining Room. After the dinner, the President was host to a party with over 200 guests. At the party, the President demonstrated his excellent dancing ability by leading at least 50 women around the dance floor.

Friday, February 14:
   Over 100,000 residents of St. Louis, Missouri, greeted President Johnson as he attended the city's celebration of its 200th birthday.

   The President appointed Stan Musial, retired baseball player from the St. Louis Cardinal's team, as Director of the President's physical fitness program.

WEEK OF FEBRUARY 16-FEBRUARY 22

Monday, February 17:
   Roger L. Stevens, New York theatrical producer, was selected by President Johnson to be the new Director of the Johnson Administration's cultural program.

[269]

The United States Supreme Court, in a 6-3 decision, ruled that Congressional districts within each state are Constitutionally required to be substantially equal in population.

Tuesday, February 18:
President Johnson spoke to 70 members of the House of Representatives at a White House reception. Mrs. Johnson entertained the members' wives while the President spoke to the Congressmen.

The United States cut off military aid to Great Britain because Britain refused to join the boycott of Cuban goods. Military aid was cut to France and Yugoslavia for the same reason. A statement from Washington indicated that the aid was being cut by mutual agreement.

Wednesday, February 19:
Bobby Baker refused to turn over his records to the Senate Rules Committee as required by their subpoena issued to Baker by the committee on February 14. Mr. Baker invoked the First, Fifth and Sixth Amendments to the Constitution in his refusal, but relied mainly on the Fifth Amendment.

A joint committee of Congress agreed on an $11,545,000,000 tax reduction bill.

President Johnson chose Nicholas Johnson, lawyer and professor of administrative law, as Maritime Administrator, his appointment subject to the approval of the Senate.

Thursday, February 20:
Twenty-nine Cuban fishermen left for Cuba after being freed from a Florida court. The fishermen were arrested for poaching in state waters. Captains of the four fishing boats were found guilty and given a suspended sentence and fined $500. The charges against the members of the crews were dismissed.

Friday, February 21:
President Johnson began two-day talks with President Adolfo Lopez Mateos of Mexico in Los Angeles, Calif., where both men were given honorary degrees from the University of California at Los Angeles.

Saturday, February 22:
The conference between President Johnson and President Mateos ended with President Johnson's call to Latin America

to join in the "war on poverty" through the Alliance for Progress.

WEEK OF FEBRUARY 23-FEBRUARY 29

Tuesday, February 25:
The apparently sudden resignation of Roger Hilsman, Assistant Secretary of State for Far Eastern Affairs, was accepted. Mr. Hilsman was returning to an academic career.

President Johnson was again host to members of the House of Representatives. About 75 members attended the reception given at the White House. Secretary of State Dean Rusk spoke to the members in attendance at an hour-long briefing. Mrs. Johnson took the members' wives on a tour of the White House while their husbands were at the meeting.

Bobby Baker took the Fifth Amendment 120 times while being questioned by the Senate Rules Committee.

Wednesday, February 26:
President Johnson signed the bill creating an $11.5-billion tax cut. He promised a cut in the federal budget and stated his belief that the tax cut would strengthen the economy. The bill was approved by the Senate (74-19) earlier in the day.

Thursday, February 27:
President Johnson, accompanied by his wife and two daughters, made the first openly political trip of his administration. The President stopped at Palatka, Florida, to throw a switch setting off a ground-breaking explosion for the start of construction of a $146-million cross-Florida barge canal. He then flew to Miami Beach, Florida, to address a Democratic fund-raising dinner.

While the President was speaking in Miami Beach, a nearby train was dynamited in connection with a dispute between the Union and the Florida East Coast Railway Company. The President immediately asked Secretary of Labor Wirtz to confer with Florida Governor Farris Bryant and present recommendations for federal action in the strike.

Saturday, February 29:
President Johnson held his first live television news conference, marking the end of his first 100 days in office. The President, who seemed pleased with his first 100 days in office, made the major announcement of the "successful" development of the

A-11, an advanced experimental aircraft which has "a performance that exceeds that of any other aircraft in the world today."

President Johnson announced the nomination of Mr. William P. Bundy, currently Assistant Secretary of Defense for Internal Security Affairs, to the post of Assistant Secretary of State for Far Eastern Affairs. Mr. Bundy, brother of McGeorge Bundy, National Security Assistant, succeeded Roger Hilsman in the position.

The President announced the appointment of Mr. Daniel M. Luevano of California, a chief deputy director of the State Department of Finance in California under Governor Pat Brown, as Assistant Secretary of the Army.

The President also announced the appointment of Mrs. Frankie Muse Freeman, associate general counsel of St. Louis Housing and Land Clearance Authority, as a new member of the Civil Rights Commission. Mrs. Freeman, a Negro lawyer, had been active as a lawyer for the St. Louis Branch of the National Association for the Advancement of Colored People.

Acknowledgments

THE MATERIAL for this book had to be gathered in a short time because it was about events which were happening, and because the principal characters in the drama were changing even as the work was being done. Within the first month I thought I could detect changes in how a man looked at his work and how he remembered a particular event. Many of my personal impressions, of course, seemed too speculative to set down in this book, but they were strong enough to urge me on to seek all the early records available as swiftly as possible. Today was the day to find out today's reactions to the transition.

This book also had to be written in a short time, for since this is a Presidential election year it seemed only reasonable to try for early publication at a time when most citizens would be most interested in this story.

This speed of research and writing meant that this writer, more than most writers, is indebted to the many persons who helped gather material and edit the manuscript. We all worked on a tight schedule. We all struggled with the sometimes panicky problems of trying to write history—and make a reasonable attempt at objectivity—while the history makers and history writers alike were revolving at high rates of speed. My editor, Peter Israel, and his assistant, Carol Sturm, were particularly patient with a manuscript arriving in patches.

The material for this book came from many sources. There were official statements, press briefings and press conferences, and eventually we had a coordinated file, by subject, of clippings of news and comment from all kinds of newspapers, magazines and journals.

Another principal source of information was interviews with White House staff people. Notes on these were always recorded immediately. All these interviews were on a not-for-attribution basis, but many of them were tape-recorded. So in addition to this book our work produced a unique resource—some of this history as recorded in the words of the persons who lived it. In due course the author will deposit these files with the person already at work on the Lyndon B. Johnson library, Mrs. Dorothy Territo.

I worked without any full-time secretary or assistant, but I had need of quite a few part-time helpers. This writer counts himself quite lucky that he found such a resourceful crew.

Each person named below has worked many times after midnight or through long weekends to scan publications, to index tape recordings, or to double-check names and dates, or type and retype the basic material.

So the author is grateful to a number of persons, including Miss Sally Womack, and her mother, Mrs. Mona Womack; Mrs. Zelda Segal; Mrs. Harriet Chadayammury; Mrs. Jeanne Loosbrock; Miss Vicki Dailey; Miss Cathy Friedman; Miss Nancy Goodlin; my patient wife, Renee, who never forgot to put a date on a clipping, and her father, Mr. Harry Rosen, who read for us through business magazines and newspapers.

Among official sources, it seems best not to name them all, but to thank all the old and new White House persons, and Cabinet officials, who courteously submitted to dozens of interviews and phone calls. The writer is particularly indebted to Pierre Salinger, who on the 14th day after the assassination took time to consider this project and thought it worthwhile. Nothing here should be construed as implying "the White House cooperated" in the writing of this book, other than to state the Press Office made its facilities available, temporary "clearance" was given to enable me to attend press briefings, and to permit me to interview key people if they had time to be interviewed. At one time a White House official originated the proposition that I should have an interview with the President, but that was never arranged. So the author had the disadvantages and the advantages of not having been in direct communication with the main subject.

This writer naturally feels gratitude for many astute writings in the daily press, particularly for reporting in the New York and Washington papers, and most particularly for the writings of Walter Lippmann, Richard L. Strout, I. F. Stone, and James Reston.

Among the books always at hand were those written about the Presidency by Clinton Rossiter, Sydney Hyman, Douglass Cater, Helen Fuller, Eric F. Goldman, Richard Neustadt and Theodore C. Sorensen.

Index

Bundy, McGeorge, 25-28, 30, 37, 40, 50-51, 70, 78, 97-99, 163, 185, 208, 253, 257, 272
Bundy, William P., 257, 272
Bureau of the Budget, 26-27, 30fn., 35, 44-45, 58, 66-67, 112-115, 264
Busby, Horace, 31, 49-50, 59, 66, 86, 97-98, 182, 235
Busby, Mrs. Horace, 31fn.
Butler, Richard A., 269
Byrd, Harry Flood, 122

Cabinet, 25, 29, 36, 38, 41-44, 59, 66, 70, 88, 94, 97ff., 129, 141, 155, 157, 187ff., 194, 238, 241, 264
Cahn, Robert, 196fn.
Canada, 155, 268
Caplin, Mortimer, 210fn.
Carey, William D., 26-27, 110-111
Carpenter, Elizabeth, 18, 22-23, 28, 31, 186, 202, 210, 252, 257
Carpenter, Les, 207
Carter, Clifton C., 18-20, 31-33, 59, 70, 85-86, 195, 252
Casals, Pablo, 226
Case, Clifford P., 146
Castro, Fidel, 114
Cater, Douglass, 127-128, 179-180, 193-194
Catledge, Turner, 134
CBS, 21
Central America, 152
Central Intelligence Agency, 32, 37, 50, 97, 253
Chase, Salmon P., 146
Chiari, Roberto, 160, 262
Christian Science Monitor, 178-179
Chronicle, San Francisco, 182
Churchill, Sir Winston, 73, 166, 168
CIA. See Central Intelligence Agency
Civil rights, 40, 44, 47, 53, 60, 62, 89, 97, 111, 119-121, 157, 163, 220, 223-225
Civil rights bill, 119-122, 124, 130, 143, 239, 255, 256, 262, 265, 268, 269
Civil Rights Commission, 268
Clay, Henry, 74, 82
Cleveland, Harland, 153-154
Clifford, Clark, 66, 88, 96, 145
Clifton, Theodore, 21
Coffin, Frank M., 35
Cohen, Benjamin, 88
Cold war, 169, 173, 245

Columbia University, 57fn., 62
Communism, 54fn., 62, 118-119, 156, 160-161, 170-171, 255, 258, 260, 261
Compromise of 1850, 63
Congress, 30, 35, 39, 41, 44-45, 50, 52, 58ff., 68, 81, 84, 89, 109, 119-126, 128-131, 145, 146, 157ff., 168, 181-183, 187-188, 191, 194, 199, 202, 210, 214, 219ff., 229, 235, 238-239, 255ff., 262-268, 270
Congress for Racial Equality, 120
Connally, John B. Jr., 16, 19, 22, 40, 42, 221, 251
Connally, Mrs. John B. Jr. (Nellie), 16, 22, 25, 40, 251
Consolidated Edison Co., 133
Constitution, 24, 242, 252, 266, 270
Cooke, Jay, 146
Coolidge, Calvin, 10, 24fn., 47, 57-58fn.
Cooper, John Sherman, 140, 256
Corcoran, Thomas, 88
CORE. See Congress for Racial Equality
Courier-Journal, Louisville, 191, 198
Crawford, Kenneth, 184-185
Crosby, Bing, 73
Cuba, 29, 38, 114, 134-135, 151, 161, 164ff., 170ff., 208, 267, 270
Curry, Jesse E., 252
Curtis, Carl, 140
Cushing, Richard Cardinal, 254
Cyprus, 151, 158ff., 260, 266, 268

Daily News, Chicago, 198
Daily News, N.Y., 63
Daley, Richard, 53
Dallas, Texas, 9-10, 13-21, 23, 28, 34, 38, 42, 46, 51, 134, 137, 152, 216, 221, 227, 230, 236, 239, 244, 251ff.
Daniel, Clifton, 134-135
Daniel, Price, 220
Davidson, Roy, 249
De Gaulle, Charles, 153-155, 160, 161, 172, 202, 231
Democratic campaign (1964), 56, 63, 148, 214, 220, 246
Democratic National Committee, 85
Democratic National Convention, 1960, 216-223
Democratic Party, 54fn., 55-56, 62, 68, 84-85, 89, 98, 113, 117-118, 122, 130, 145, 220-221, 224, 231, 237, 271
Dept. of Agriculture, 114, 129

[276]

[277]

Goldberg, Arthur J., 30, 40, 220, 225, 253
Goldfine, Bernard, 145
Goldman, Eric F., 88, 91-93, 186, 266
Goldwater, Barry, 47, 63, 145-146, 212, 255
Goodwin, Richard, 97
Gordon, Kermit, 26-27, 44-45, 66, 110ff., 264
Graff, Henry F., 57fn., 62-63
Graham, Philip, 218, 221
Grant, Ulysses S., 30ff.
Great Britain, 101, 152fn., 161-162, 270
Greece, 155, 158, 265, 268
Green, William J., 260
Greenwald, Lillian. *See* Mrs. George Reedy
Griffin, Gerald, 207
Guantánamo, Cuba, 135, 267

Hagerty, James, 185fn.
Haile Selassie, 46, 153
Halleck, Charles A., 122, 188
Hamilton, Alexander, 73, 211
Harding, Warren G., 57fn., 167, 215
Harkness, Richard, 196-197
Harriman, William Averell, 30, 253
Harris, Rev. Frederick Brown, 11
Harris (Louis) polls, 117-118, 255
Harvard Business School, 72, 89
Harvard University, 72, 74fn., 89, 101
Harwood, Richard, 191
Hatcher, Andrew T., 139, 185, 202
Hauft, Milton L., 210fn.
Hayden, Carl, 14fn., 61, 123
Hays, Brooks, 263
Heckscher, August, 269
Heller, Walter W., 40-43, 97, 127-128
Hemingway, Ernest, 73
Herald, Boston, 182
Herald Tribune, N.Y., 47, 68, 141, 146-147, 162, 182, 187, 230
Hickam Field, Honolulu, 41-42
Higgins, Marguerite, 198
Hill, Lister, 89
Hilsman, Roger, 104, 271, 272
Hitler, Adolf, 153
Hodges, Luther H., 41, 69-70
Holborn, Fred, 186
Holland, Cecil, 113, 191
Holmes, Oliver Wendell, 74, 89
Honolulu, Hawaii, 41-43

Hopkins, Harry, 71, 75fn., 78, 96
Hopkins, William, 67
Hornig, Donald, 66
Horwitz, Solis, 90
House of Representatives, 31, 81, 97, 122ff., 130, 239, 253, 258, 259, 260, 261, 267-268, 270, 271
Housing, 229, 265
Houston, Texas, 71-72, 74
Houston Symphony Orchestra, 204
Howe, Louis, 75fn.
Hughes, Sarah T., 23-24, 195fn., 252
Humble Oil Co., 72
Humphrey, Hubert, 27, 28, 39, 54-55, 58-59, 63, 89, 123-124, 128, 217, 222
Hurst, Dr. Willis, 31fn.
Hyannis Port, Mass., 30, 32
Hyman, Sidney, 97, 179

Ickes, Harold L., 99
Ikeda, Hayato, 155
India, 59, 180, 197, 226
Indonesia, 161-162
Inquirer, Philadelphia, 82
Inter-American Peace Committee, 262
Internal Revenue Service (Dept. of the Treasury), 110, 114-115, 166-167, 268
International Asso. of Machinists, 258
International News Service, 86
Iran, 155
Irene, Princess (Greece), 265
Iron Curtain, 54fn., 153
IRS. *See* Internal Revenue Service
Israel, 155, 267
Izvestia, 260

Jacks, Hurchel D., 251
Jackson, Andrew, 73, 211
Jackson, Henry, 218-219
Jamaica, 155
Japan, 45, 155, 226
Jefferson, Thomas, 154-155
Jenkins, Walter, 26, 31, 36, 64-65, 68-70, 78-81, 84, 86, 96-98, 123, 137, 140ff.
John Birch Society, 62
John XXIII, Pope, 257
Johns, Lem, 18
Johnson, Andrew, 57fn., 184, 215
Johnson, Lady Bird, 10, 13-14, 16-19, 22ff., 28, 31, 38, 51-52, 59, 83, 97, 115-116, 122, 144ff., 154, 175ff., 186, 195, 201, 202, 205, 207ff., 218ff., 228, 251-

[280]